Dedication

This book is dedicated to the man who I've moved with for 32 years, my supportive and loving husband, Gary, and to our daughter Michelle and son Adam, who—whether they wanted to, or not—moved right along with us until they were in college. They all supported me unconditionally in this project. I also want to dedicate this to our extended family, and to the wonderful friends we've met along the way. They've played an important part in shaping who we are today.

In Memoriam

To Diane Yankelevitz, my oldest sister, who inspired my first cross-country move, and continued to encourage me to complete this project. I am forever changed by your ideas about living, and about life after life, and I miss you.

Table of Contents

Introduction

I watched my husband's face closely, as he told me about his job inter-
view. I'd seen that look of hope and excitement on his face before and
knew I didn't want to do anything to dampen it. I rolled my eyes, but I
was determined to keep an open mind. I ran upstairs for our atlas, as I
always have at times like this, so that I could see where we would move
if this worked out, and what cities we would be near. How far would
we need to drive to visit family & friends? Were there getaway spots
close enough to drive to for a long weekend? Was the city large enough
for me to find the amenities I'd grown used to and liked?

In the 32 years my husband and I have been together,
we've made seven interstate moves and one local one. All
but two of these were corporate moves, for which my husband's company paid our relocation expenses. We've lived
in upstate New York, Atlanta (twice), Southern California, St.
Louis, Chicago (twice) and Nashville. We moved our children with us most of these times (we're empty nesters now),
and also moved them to college dorms and apartments
multiple times. Prior to our marriage, after graduating high
school in the suburbs of Baltimore, I lived in 14 various dorm
rooms, apartments, and houses in 3 states. In addition to
these moves, I coordinated relocations for my husband's
parents from a condo in Florida to a smaller unit in Atlanta,
and then into three different units in assisted living facilities.

Although at times I may not have initially been excited
about the idea of moving, once into the process I have always found it to be an exciting adventure—a new chance
to find a "nearly-perfect home", reinvent myself, make new
friends, learn new things, and discover new areas of our
country. Being a tourist is one thing, but actually living in
an area really expands your knowledge, not only of that
part of the country, but of different ways of thinking about
things and doing things. Our daughter, who often was *not*

happy with us for moving her, said at age 26, "It might have seemed unfair at the time, but now that I'm an adult, I can appreciate how those experiences provided me with a broader perspective and helped me to be less hesitant about taking risks and exploring the world."

We now have dear friends in many parts of the country. They are friends with whom we keep in touch by phone and e-mail, whom we travel to see sometimes, and welcome into our own home or even meet for a short vacation elsewhere at other times. We treasure them all and have grown considerably by knowing each one of them. We can't imagine their not being a part of our lives.

Moving is a project. It takes time and organization and work. I can't deny that. In the chapters which follow, I'll help you through this process. There are often glitches in a move, but with a "can do" attitude you can deal with them and move on. My goal is for you to make your move a positive experience, and an adventure. Your world is about to e-x-p-a-n-d in exciting ways!

Chapter 1

Making The Decision

"During this time, everything seems turned-upside-down. Your mind is constantly thinking about this possible move and all of its ramifications. So many decisions need to be delayed until you determine whether or not the move will actually take place. You may be resistant to the move, and not at all sure that you want to leave your current home. Then, if it turns out that it's not going to happen, you find yourself being relieved and disappointed all at once."

This chapter will suggest the questions you should consider, and then help you gather and evaluate the information you'll need to answer these questions. The answers will help you to determine if this is a move you'll choose to make. Also included are tips to help you to stay organized. A move can be overwhelming on several different levels, so it's essential to keep your move-related information where you can easily find it.

Things to Consider

Whether the move you're contemplating is one to a new state, or the other side of the metropolitan area you're living in, there are many things for you to consider. Some of them may not apply to your situation, and some of them overlap, but they basically boil down to:

- <u>Is the job a good fit?</u>
  If you're moving for a job, is it a good one for you (or your spouse)? Is it one you're excited about?

Does it offer the stability you require? Does it offer the opportunity to learn new skills as well as the possibility of advancement? What are the time commitments? (Is overtime required? If so, is it compensated, or will your salary be enough to make it worthwhile? Are evening and weekend hours part of the deal? Is travel required? If so, how much?) What is the compensation package, including salary, bonus and extras (such as a company car)? What percentage of medical insurance will be paid by the company, and how much choice is there in medical plans? How much vacation time, personal leave, and sick time will you get? What is the relocation package? (Will the company cover the real estate commission, packing and moving, temporary living expenses, moving your cars, and so on?) Only you and your partner can evaluate whether this position is a good one for you and your family at this time.

- Will your quality of life be good in that location? Considering the things which are important to you and your children, will your lifestyle be a good one?

  Make a list of things which are important in your life. Does your child play ice hockey, so that ice rinks and local programs are important? Are your children talented in art, drama, or music? If so, what kinds of programs do you want or need for them, and how important is this? You may want to explore religious organizations in the area, for worship and/or recreational possibilities. It's a good idea to locate whatever services or facilities are important to you and your family, both to add to the equation of whether to make the move, and also to help you narrow down the areas in which you'll want to live, if you do decide to move. This, in turn, will help you determine what housing you can afford, which will help you decide if the move will work financially.

- <u>Will it work financially?</u>
  - ⌐ Will your company purchase your house when they relocate you? In unsettled real estate markets, it could take a LONG time to sell property and if they want to relocate employees, they may need to make that guarantee.
  - ⌐ How much do you anticipate netting after selling your house and paying off the mortgage? The best way to arrive at this figure is by getting a Comparative Market Analysis (CMA) from several Real Estate agents. This is discussed later in this chapter, and in the beginning of Chapter 3. During a volatile real estate market, pay the most attention to prices of homes which have sold in the last few months. Often, companies moving an employee will pay the real estate commission for the relocation, so you may not need to consider that fee. Be conservative—use a realistic figure, not the high end of what you might get for your house if a miracle happens.
  - ⌐ Using that net figure as a down payment, and considering current interest rates, what kind of house and neighborhood could you expect to afford in the new location? Will that kind of house and neighborhood be acceptable to you?
  - ⌐ Remember to consider start-up costs in a new home, possibly including window treatments, decorating, utilities and phone/cable set-up fees.
  - ⌐ If you're moving to a more expensive city, will your salary be increased enough to allow you to live as you'd like to in your new surroundings? Housing costs can vary dramatically between cities, even between similar-size cities, such as Atlanta and San Diego. Perhaps you're moving to a less expensive, smaller town, and looking forward to simplifying your needs and your life.

In that case, you may not need as much income as you've been making. It's your decision. Just consider all the factors.

- Other considerations
  If you and your partner both work, will there be ample job opportunities for the other partner? Will the company help the spouse find a new job? Will you still be able to visit close family members and friends periodically (by flying or driving), if this is important to you? If someone in your family has particular health needs, are there physicians and medical facilities available to meet those needs?

Things To Do

You'll need to gather information in order to properly evaluate the pros and cons, and make an intelligent decision. Here are some ways to gather information:

- Contact at least one real estate agent or agency in the new city.
  While this may seem premature, it's definitely one of the first steps to take in making your decision. You can either get a recommendation from someone you know in the area, find a real estate agency online, or your company may be able to recommend several real estate salespeople to consider. It doesn't hurt to talk with several realtors, to decide who you're most comfortable dealing with. Asking a realtor to send information does not obligate you to work with them. Seeing how they deal with you on the phone, what information they send you, and how they communicate can be instrumental in determining who you want to work with. See the guidelines in "Working with a Real Estate Agent" in Chapter 7. Most of the major real estate firms are easy to locate online. You can be up-front with them and tell them you're

considering a move to their area and would like information.

You'll need to give each of the Real Estate agents an idea about your requirements—price, number of bedrooms & baths, whatever is most important to you. Other important information is where the job is located, and how long a commute is acceptable. The agent should be able to tell you which areas would be the best for you to consider. In addition to current real estate listings, agents can send you information about the area, including school systems, cultural events, tourist spots, and a map.

When you get the listings, you probably won't be able to know what kind of areas the listings are in, but you'll still get a feel for the town and what kind of housing is available at what price. It's a start, and will give you an initial feeling of how much you'll need to spend to get an appropriate house in the new city.

- Search online ads. This can be a little tricky if you don't know what areas to look in yet, but it can still be helpful. You can find more information on this in Chapter 7.

- Contact the local Chamber of Commerce and request information about the area from them. Once you've narrowed your possible areas down to several school districts, you might also want to request information from the school districts themselves. School districts are important for resale, even if you don't have school age children. A lot of this research can now be done online, but it doesn't hurt to request that the materials be sent to you. I believe you'll be able to evaluate them more clearly if you have them all spread out in front of you, rather than trying to remember what was where (from your internet research).

- <u>Check out the city online</u>. There are a number of websites which list information about various cities. You can search for just the city, or the city and any particular interests you have. Or you can go to one of the following websites to get detailed information:

  - ⌐ **www.RealEstateJournal.com** – Provided by the Wall Street Journal. In "Tool Kit" (towards the bottom of the page, just above "Buying and Selling" and "Home and Garden"), enter the zip code under "Neighborhood Data" and check out all the information it provides.
  - ⌐ **www.city-data.com** – Maps, statistics about residents, cost of living, weather, and much more, organized by city, county or zip code.
  - ⌐ **www.moving.com** – Select "Learn and Explore", then "City Profiles". Provides demographics, climate, crime statistics, and more, organized by zip code. Select "Compare to Another City" to see information side-by-side. *Be aware that the information is just for the zip code you select, which in most cases is not a whole city.*
  - ⌐ **profiles.nationalrelocation.com** - Demographics, statistics, hospitals, colleges, universities and more. It is not clear how current this information is.

- <u>Familiarize yourself with the new location</u> by reading local newspapers and/or reading local news online.

- <u>Review your Credit Reports</u> from all 3 credit reporting agencies, since you *may* be applying for a home loan before long. Phone 1-877-322-8228 or go to www.annualcreditreport.com to order Credit Reports from Equifax, Experian and Trans Union. If you order online, you'll be able to view the reports immediately; if you order by phone, it will be weeks before you see it. You are entitled to a free Credit Report annually from each of the three agencies. If you've already gotten one in the last 12 months, you'll probably have to pay for it this time, but it will be worth it. Viewing the reports will give you an opportunity to dispute any negative items and hopefully get them corrected before they negatively affect your borrowing options. It often is a slow process, sometimes taking months, so do act on this right away.

You'll also want to get your FICO Credit Score, as this will affect what loans you can get and on what terms. You can access your FICO Score from the Fair Isaac Corporation at myfico.com, but you will need to pay a fee for this.

Be aware that at least one of these credit reporting agencies may require a credit card for your free report, and if you read closely, you'll see that they'll "automatically" enroll you in a credit watch, and will bill your account for a monthly fee. If you encounter this, I suggest you order the report, print it, and then immediately CANCEL that membership before you forget about it. Be sure to get a cancellation number, or employee name and ID number before you hang up the phone, just in case they put through a charge anyway.

- <u>Keep your finances in good shape</u>. Make sure you pay your bills on time (even if it's just the minimum due) and try to avoid moving large sums of money around (or at least keep track of the details). If possible, don't take on any large loans at this time. Follow these suggestions from now until you have completed the purchase of your new home.

- <u>Go on a look-see trip</u>. In many cases, a prospective employer will pay for the two of you to visit the city where you would be living, and explore housing as well as the area in general. This is a great opportunity, and the best way to gather the information you'll need in order to judge what your quality of life would be. You should take advantage of this if at all possible. Find someone to stay at home with the kids, if you can. By planning ahead, you can get a great deal accomplished in 2-3 days. If things go very well, both in job negotiations and with your visit to the new city, you just might return home with a contract to purchase your new home! We've done that several times ourselves. (But don't let that scare you—most people take longer.)

When you go for your visit in the new city, not only should you look at homes to see what you can get in your price range, in the areas in which you might want to live, but you may want to visit places which are extremely important to you. If place of worship is a very big part of your life, you may want to plan on visiting several in the area and perhaps meeting with their clergy. Alternately, you might want to visit the local JCC or YMCA/YWCA, schools, ice rink or whatever. Don't expect to find exactly what you're leaving, but if you are comfortable that these facilities/services will serve your needs, then move on to the other considerations, and try to look for a home within a reasonable distance from these facilities which are important to you.

- Get a Comparative Marketing Analysis on your current home.
  Some real estate agents use other terminology, but basically a market analysis is a suggested listing price for your home, considering many factors. Agents will also give you suggestions of how to prepare the house for listing, and will explain how they would plan to market your home. This is a job interview for them. They will understand that you haven't made your decision yet and will appreciate the

opportunity to be considered as the listing agent if you do decide to move. Getting an idea of how much your house should sell for is often one of the major factors involved in making the moving decision, and it's perfectly acceptable to have several agents come to give you that information, as well as show you their marketing plan.

A prepared listing agent should arrive in your home complete with a market analysis, including the listing price, selling price, and days on the market of comparable homes in your area. You won't necessarily select the agent who suggests the highest listing price. You want someone who can back up her recommendation with facts, and who will suggest a realistic listing price.

See Chapter 3 for how to select Real Estate Agents to interview, what information to gather before you call them, and relationships with Real Estate Agents.

• <u>Find out who pays for what</u>. If an employer is moving you, find out what expenses they will be paying. Will they pay to have movers pack you? (Many do.) Will they pay for temporary living expenses (housing, food and transportation) between the time you move out of the house and when you're unpacked enough to live in the new house (usually the day after your things have been delivered)? Sometimes, companies will pay for housing & food for one spouse, while the other remains in the old house with the children, and keeping it spruced up while waiting for it to sell. There is always a time limit on these relo (relocation) expenses; and sometimes there is a set amount that the company will let you use how you see fit. KEEP RECEIPTS for all moving expenses, because what the employer won't cover may be tax deductible.

You may want to consult your accountant to find out which items are deductible.

Stay Organized

As soon as you begin considering a move, get yourself some file folders in which to keep information, so that you stay organized throughout the whole process. Keep these folders in one location, preferably in a file cabinet, plastic file box, or in a desk. I like a plastic file box without a lid, because it's portable and easy to access.

- <u>Label one folder with the name of the new city</u>. This folder will include area maps and information which you'll receive from real estate salespeople, the Chamber of Commerce, school districts, and—once you are settled—Welcome Wagon, Newcomers, or other outreach organizations.

- <u>A second folder will be for Selling the house</u>, and will include information from real estate agents you interview and a list of items which should be done prior to listing the house. Later on, you'll add your listing contract, Offers to Purchase, and associated documents. When you select a real estate agent, staple his/her business card to the folder for easy access.

- <u>The third folder will be labeled **Moving**</u>. When you get moving estimates, they should be placed into this folder. After the mover loads your belongings onto the van, place the inventory sheets and contact numbers for the moving company and the driver into this folder and take it with you. If you plan to do some of the move yourself, information about van or truck rental and moving supplies can also be included in this folder.

- <u>Your fourth folder should be for **Buying** your new home</u>. This will include information about real estate salespeople in the new city, listings of interest, your Offer To Purchase, Physical Inspection Report, and so on.

- Once you've made the decision to move, <u>create a fifth folder for **Address Changes**</u>. Start collecting pertinent information (magazine mailing labels and where to send address changes, for instance) in the folder so that you'll have it handy when you have your new address and effective date. When you start giving out your new address, keep a record in this folder (or on your computer) of who you notified, when and how (mail, phone, online). This will save you from duplicating notifications and you'll be able to talk intelligently (providing date and method of notification) if you need to fuss with anyone about not updating their records. If your credit card company charges you a late fee because they continued to mail your statement to your old address after 2 months, you'll have a good case for them to remove the fee and any record of a late payment, if you can provide this information.

Evaluating the Pros and Cons

Now it's time to make a simple chart. Assuming you have a choice between 2 jobs in 2 cities, your chart will have 3 columns and as many rows as you need. Below is an example, just to get you started.

	Los Angeles	St. Louis
Salary	90,000	70,000
Financial	Less discretionary income (due to housing price & cost of living)	More discretionary income
Job	Similar to current job and very impressed with the company, so feel this job is a good fit. Might need to change companies to advance, but lots of jobs in this field are in the area.	It will stretch current skills; a little scary but exciting. Opportunity for advancement within the company, but not many other companies locally in this field.
Recreation	Great but long drive time	Not as good but very convenient
Traffic	Awful	Much better
Affordable Housing	Small & older	Newer & larger (especially in suburbs)
Location	Near family	Aunt Adele 1 hour away
Schools	Might need to choose private schools	Public schools are excellent in suburban area we'd be in

Obviously, your chart will have different, or at least additional, items in the left hand column, and some of these items will tell you that you need to gather additional information in order to evaluate the answers. However, once you've made a chart and filled it in with all the pros and cons which are floating around in your mind, I believe the answer to "Should we make this move?" will become obvious to you. If you're still not sure, talk about it with some good friends—ones who will listen, rather than tell you what to do. Sometimes when you talk about things, you realize how you feel about them. It can be an emotional decision, but if you gather all of the facts, and consider all of the aspects, you'll make the sensible decision.

And if that decision involves a relocation......*READ ON!*

Chapter 2

Preparing Your House

"There are so many things to think about, I don't even know where to begin. How do we figure out what to do with our house to get it ready to go on the market?"

It has been said that "Selling a house is nothing more than a price war and a beauty contest." The purpose of preparing your house is to make it more appealing to potential buyers, which should *decrease* the time in which it sells, *increase* the amount of money you get for your house, or both. This chapter will help you do the things you can do fairly quickly in order to achieve those goals.

You may also want to enlist the help of a professional stager, after you've done most of the things suggested in this chapter. In fact, many real estate agents currently include this service when you list with them. Learn more about that in Chapter 3, under reviewing the Real Estate Agent's Marketing Plan.

Many Buyers have a difficult time *imagining* ...imagining what the house would look like if it weren't so cluttered.... imagining what the house would look like if it were clean... imagining what it would look like if their furnishings wouldn't clash with the red paint in the living room or rest on worn-looking carpeting in the dining room. You don't need to redecorate the whole house, but it IS to your advantage to eliminate some of the things which make people have a difficult time seeing themselves and their belongings in your home. You'll get more for your home if you do, and you'll most likely sell it more quickly, too. Here are some guidelines to help your house look its best.

Make a "To Do" List

Grab a clipboard and a legal pad. Go through the whole house with your partner and/or an honest friend, and make a list of what needs to be done in each room. Look critically, and try to see things through the eyes of a prospective Buyer. Don't be overwhelmed—you can (hopefully) get help from your family for some of what needs to be done, and if you need to hire a cleaning crew, handyman or tradesman for some of the rest, it will be money well-spent. Here are some things which might go on your list:

- Clean windows and light fixtures, and wipe down woodwork and doors throughout.

- Applying a new coat of paint will definitely make the house look cleaner and fresher, but even washing it here and touching it up there—if it's done properly— can make a big difference. If you need to have an entire room repainted, consider using a neutral color (off-white, white, beige or putty) instead of something a Buyer may need to change. Be sure to repair any cracks or holes before repainting.

  Hint: To cover up a few marks on the wall, if you have paint which is a perfect match, dip a sponge into a small amount of paint & squeeze the sponge nearly dry. Dab it lightly over the marks, so that there's not a clean line where the paint begins and ends. Apply a 2ⁿᵈ coat after it dries, if necessary. You may want to do this in an inconspicuous place first, to make sure the match is good enough for the repair to be invisible when dry. Paint often fades over time, especially when exposed to sunlight. However, if the paint colors match, it's amazing how well this technique can work, and it can certainly save time and money, if done properly.

- Wallpaper, especially if it's outdated, can be perceived as something which will need to be changed or eliminated. Although trends will undoubtedly change over time, current designs rarely include wallpaper. If you have the resources, strip it and repaint the walls in a neutral color.

- Burned-out light bulbs should be replaced.

- Bathroom & kitchen caulk should be replaced if it doesn't look great. Repair faucets, if leaky.

- Closets (including linen closets), bathroom and kitchen cabinets, pantry, and any other built-in's need to be clean and tidy. Remove enough things to make them look spacious. Give prospective Buyers the impression that there is room for all of their belongings. (I usually find, while doing this, that I have a lot of things I don't really use and it's a relief to have them out of the way.)

- Toilet seats which are in bad shape should be replaced.

- Chips in white enamel sinks or bathtubs can be touched up with a bottle of appliance paint, available at most hardware stores.

- Make sure the entryway, traffic paths and stairways are clear of clutter and hazards.

- Ovens, microwaves and cooktops should be clean. If your stovetop drip pans aren't clean and shiny, replace them.

- Wipe down your dishwasher, and try to keep it odor-free.

- Even if you plan to take your washer, dryer, and refrigerator with you when you move, buyers may want to include them in the offer, and may decide to look in them before they do. It's fine for these appliances to look like they're used, but if they look very unkempt it may present an impression that you don't take fastidious care of other things in your home, either. <u>You want to remove any reason you can for people to eliminate your home.</u>

- Anything that needs repair should be repaired, preferably before the house is shown. <u>It's much better for buyers to not even see a problem, than for them to imagine the cost and aggravation of getting it repaired themselves.</u>

- Get your carpets cleaned if they're soiled or matted down. If they're in really bad shape, consider replacing them with new carpet in a neutral color. You don't need to purchase extremely expensive carpeting, especially since the Buyers may want to replace it anyway, but if they know it looks presentable so they don't have to do it right away, it will certainly help. Again, your Real Estate salesperson may be a good person to consult about this.

- If the kitchen countertop or cabinets are very dated or in bad condition, replacing or refacing them may make the difference between Buyers purchasing your home or another. IF BUYERS ARE COMPARING 2 FAIRLY SIMILAR HOUSES WITH SIMILAR PRICES, they will often select the house which needs the least work in order to make it "livable" to them. That said, <u>if you're considering a costly replacement</u>, do discuss this with your real estate agent. They should be able to guide you as to whether you should make the improvement and whether you are selecting an appropriate material (countertop, kitchen flooring, etc.) for the project, according to what is typically used in similar homes which are selling in your area.

- Eliminate any material which mold or mildew has permeated (such as carpeting in your basement) and use a dehumidifier to eliminate any dampness (which causes mold and mildew to grow in the first place).

Now, take your clipboard outside...

- <u>A good first impression is important.</u> Grass should be cut, shrubs trimmed, porches de-cluttered. Leaves should be raked, hoses coiled or put away, snow shoveled, pine straw or bark chips refreshed...whatever it takes to make the home look like it's well cared-for. Obviously, this needs to be kept up while the house is on the market. You may even want to put some potted flowers in front of the house—just avoid placing them by the front door, if they will attract bees.

- The front door may need cleaning or repainting, and the doorbell should be in good working order. If you have a personalized door knocker, replace it with a new one, making sure not to leave any old holes visible.

- If the exterior of the house needs painting, repair, or power washing for mold or mildew, get it done.

- Consider whether the roof, sidewalk, or concrete driveway would look a lot cleaner and fresher if they were power-washed. If their appearance detracts from the overall impression of the exterior, it may be worth the investment and may not cost as much as you anticipate.

...and into the garage. The garage should be clean and look tidy.

- Collect balls and toys lying around and place in a plastic bin or a box.

- Items which are not used frequently should be neatly placed in garage cabinets, the basement or shed, if available.

- Bicycles can be hung up or put in the tool shed or basement, if they make the garage look like there's not enough room—but if they're used regularly, I'm not telling you to put them where the kids can't get to them. Your children need to work off their energy somehow.

- Vacuum the garage. Sounds obsessive, I know, but it's a great way to get rid of all those yucky spider webs and (hopefully dead) insects, not to mention the dirt, and it will really make your garage look a whole lot more appealing. Why, I even do this occasionally when I'm NOT moving. Of course, I discard the vacuum cleaner bag right after doing this, so I don't have any tiny little spiders crawling around inside it. Another plus to doing this is that you won't be moving these spiders and their webs to your new home.

Exclusions

While you're examining each room in your house, note any items you'd like to take with you, such as a dining room chandelier, shelf or window coverings. Generally, anything "attached" to the house is considered part of the sale unless you specifically exclude it, and your real estate agent will be able to guide you if you have questions about this. If you don't want to part with an item, other than window coverings, you would be wise to place the item out of sight and replace it with another which is suitable for the room. If you remove a shelf, make sure you replace it with another or leave the wall in such good condition, that others will not know a shelf was ever there. If you want to keep your chandelier, I strongly suggest that you get another one and have it installed NOW so that Buyers don't even see it. Then you have eliminated a possible point of contention.

Appliances (washer, dryer, and refrigerator) are common items to exclude from the sale of a house....although Buyers may draw up a contract including them in the sale. At that point, you would have to decide whether it's worth dickering over (and possibly losing the contract). If you have a contract that is very pleasing in every other way, you may not want to take the chance that the Buyer won't accept or resubmit the offer. She may decide not to continue with the process, in which case you've lost the sale over these items. Still, it's often best to exclude these from the listing so that you're not "giving them away", since Buyers probably won't offer any more for the house with the appliances than they would without.

You may be an avid gardener, and want to take some of the plants from the garden. This is fine, as long as you put this in the Listing, and the Buyers agree to it. The main concern will be that it doesn't LOOK like things have been removed, so the Buyers will want to be assured that the property will still look attractive. If you want to take trimmings or clippings before the Buyers see the house, that's no problem as long as you've left things looking nice.

Delegate The Work

Once you have your To Do List, decide who will do which things, and what items you will want to get outside help to do. If you don't know what professionals to call on, ask neighbors, friends or co-workers who have had work done.

In some cities, there are local directories (printed and/or online) of home service providers, compiled using feedback from local homeowners. These may be a good source for a company you can count on. Home Reports (www. HomeReports.com) and Angie's List (www.AngiesList.com) are two examples of these types of directories. Do be aware, however, that some of these require the business to pay a fee in order to be included in the directory, so there are obviously other good service providers out there who aren't included because they couldn't or wouldn't pay the fee.

Paring Down

To show your house at its best, you'll want as little clutter around as possible and the appearance of having plenty of space for everything. This should provide great motivation for finally letting go of those clothes you haven't worn in 5 years and the toys your children have outgrown, and even furniture that you don't need or want anymore. Even if you're renting and don't need to sell a house before you move, it's still appropriate to go through your things before relocating. It doesn't make sense to move things you aren't using or won't be using in your new home—you will just have to pay the movers more money, deal with where to put the things, and live with more stuff in your new home than you need. LESS IS MORE and life will be much less complicated and more peaceful if you don't have to deal with things you don't love or use. SO...go through your belongings, large and small, to determine what makes sense to keep, what should be thrown away, and what should be moved on to someone who can make use of it. If you're not going to use it and you don't love it—get rid of it. This is a big project, no doubt about that, but one that will pay off for you (and others).

- First: get yourself some large trash bags, and a few boxes.

- Next: Go through each room of the house and sort things to
  - ⊶ give away
  - ⊶ offer to family/friends
  - ⊶ remove temporarily (like clothing, knickknacks, or kitchen utensils you can live without for a few months)
  - ⊶ throw away
  - ⊶ sell

Use the large trash bags to collect the trash. Use the boxes for items you'll want to store in the garage or basement, since they'll look neater in boxes stacked against a wall. Use either bags or boxes for giveaways, but make sure to make a list of those items you're donating to a non-profit organization, so you can deduct them on your taxes. *See Charitable Donations later in this chapter.*

Note: When disposing of medications, the FDA urges us not to flush them down the toilet—unless the patient information specifically directs us to— or throw them into the trash. Instead, remove them from their container, and mix them with used coffee grounds or kitty litter in a sealable plastic bag or other container, and then place in the trash. This procedure will help protect our water supply and environment.

- For giveaways:

  - ⊶ find a Goodwill, Salvation Army or other charitable thrift store location where you can drop things off and/or arrange for an organization to come pick things up.
  - ⊶ Libraries often welcome donations of books.
  - ⊶ Home improvement goods, such as furniture, home accessories, building materials and appliances, may be donated to Habitat for Humanity ReStores, which will sell them to the general

public at a fraction of the retail price. To locate your closest store, and to find out what materials they accept, phone 1-800-422-4828 or visit www. habitat.org/env/restores.

- For things you'd like to sell:

  - See if there's a consignment shop in your area which will take furniture or some of your nicer items. Ask consignment shops how they work. Do they set the price or do you? What percentage of the sales price you get? Do they mark things down (and how much) after a given time? Is there a time limit for how long items may remain in their store? If things are not sold within a given amount of time, do you have the option of having them give it away and you getting a receipt for the donation? If it is difficult for you to transport the items, are they able to pick them up?

  - Consider selling furniture or other pricier items using Craig's List. This is a vehicle for placing local classified ads online, and is available in many cities inside the US and in 50+ countries. Most ads are free and photos are encouraged. Usually, purchasers pick these items up, so you won't need to pack and ship. You get to keep all the proceeds. Craig's List even has a "free" area, and people have been known to pick up stained rugs and other bulky items, which will save you the trouble of disposing of them (plus, you know you're not sending stuff which someone might want to use to a landfill). Go to www.craigslist. org for more information. And do take appropriate safety precautions when a stranger comes to your home.

  - Consider selling shippable items on eBay. Place online classified ads, usually with photos, for a fee. Purchasers may be in the US or in other countries. Usually you need to ship merchandise to the purchaser, either by taking it to a shipper/ packager (such as UPS Store, Pak Mail, and some office supply stores) or doing it on your own. You should estimate the packing & shipping charges prior to placing the ad (although shipping costs may vary depending on where you need to ship it). Go to ebay.com for more information, and select your location along the right side of the screen.

☛ Consider letting a business sell it online. They do all the work—figuring out what it's worth, taking the photos, placing the ad, negotiating the sales price, packing and shipping the merchandise— in return for a percentage of the selling price. There are many of these businesses around, such as 877isoldit.com (phone 877-isoldit) and Snappy Auctions (www.snappyauctions.com). Check out the particular location you would use with the Better Business Bureau, before taking in your things.

If you're having a difficult time letting go of your possessions, think about it this way: you are fortunate enough to have all this STUFF, way more than you need. Wouldn't it be a thoughtful and generous thing, if you were able to send some of the clothing you really aren't wearing anymore, or items you really don't need, to someone who has very little and could be wearing that clothing and using those items? You probably wouldn't even miss them, once they're gone, but they could be so appreciated elsewhere. This is the mindset which helps me when I know I really need to get going. And then I try to get the things out of my house as quickly as possible so I won't change my mind. I'm not saying give away things you're using, just the things you think you *might* use but never do. I've said it before, and I'll say it again: if you don't use it or really love it, let it go.

Charitable donations: It is important to itemize whatever you give to a charity, assign a value to it, and get a receipt for it. Staple your list and the receipt together, and file where you'll find it when doing your taxes. There are special rules if the donation is valued above a certain amount ($250 at this writing), and the organization can advise you of this. If you want help determining the value of common items, including clothing, there are some guides available online. Two such guides are at www.SalvationArmySouth.org/valueguide.htm and charity.LoveToKnow.com/Goodwill_donations_value).

How to De-clutter—the Big Stuff and the Small Stuff

Eliminate clutter throughout the house. Believe me, I know this is not easy, but it is *very* important. And now that you've pared down your possessions, it should be a lot easier.

- **Minimize** the number of things that are sitting on dressers, tables, desks and shelves. Reduce the number of personal photographs you have around, especially those on the refrigerator, and propped up on various surfaces. In fact, I usually clear the refrigerator of all my magnets, children's artwork, and notes when selling my house, so that things will look as neat and clean as possible, and less of a distraction. A candle here, a plant or sculpture there will look much "cleaner" and allow people's eyes to focus on the rooms instead of your collections. Think about what a model home looks like. That should be your goal. A house with a "lived in" look may be fine for other times, but when your house is on the market, you want Buyers to be able to picture themselves living in your home. The more it looks like a model home, and less like someone else's personal space, the easier it will be for them to do this.

- **Decide** which pieces of furniture should not be moved to the new house. Plan how and when to dispose of those pieces. You can give them to friends/neighbors/family, donate them to charity, or try to sell them using consignment shops, newspaper ads, ebay, Craig's List, garage sales, or by posting ads on the bulletin boards of local grocery stores. If the furniture is a vital piece, like the dining room table or the living room sofa, you'll probably want to keep it in the house until the house is sold. However, if you're planning to get rid of a chair from the family room, and the room would appear more spacious and comfortable without it, then it would be a good idea to dispose of it as soon as possible.

- **Store** small items you're removing, and which you want to keep, in your dresser drawers (where buyers won't be looking) or box them up and place the boxes neatly in your basement, attic, or crawl space. But fair warning: DON'T place them in a built-in unit or in cabinets, as prospective buyers WILL look there.

  If you have nowhere to store the extra pieces of furniture, clothing, and boxes which you want to get out of the way but plan to keep, consider renting a storage unit, or imposing on a family or friend's basement, while your house is on the market. However, if there is room to neatly stack some boxes in the basement or crawl space, while still leaving the appearance of there being enough room in the house, go for it.

While you're tossing unneeded items, hang onto some of your old address labels. They'll come in handy when sending out Change of Address notifications. The BEST thing to use for change of address requests is the label used on the magazine or mailing you're trying to change, but if you don't have it, using your address label on the change of address form or letter will save you a little time and probably be more legible for the receiver.

Any Other Suggestions?

After you have attended to the items on your "To Do" list, pared down, and de-cluttered, your house is almost ready to show. During this time, you'll also be interviewing Real Estate agents. They may have some additional suggestions about how to make your house more appealing. Take advantage of these interviews, and ask for each one's suggestions. Their answers may not be identical, but are always worth considering.

Congratulations! You've accomplished a lot. Now that your house looks its best, it's time to decide—if you haven't already—how you're going to try to sell the house (By Owner or using the services of a Realtor), select your Salesperson or By Owner method, and learn some hints for the best way to show your house.

Chapter 3

Selling The House

"There are so many choices about how to sell a house now....how do I decide what's the best way for me? And what's important to keep in mind when people want to look at the house?"

In this chapter, you'll learn how to determine a good asking price for your home, select the way in which you will go about selling it (and how to find the right person and/or company to help you do that), and how best to show your home to potential Buyers. If you decide to "list" your house with a real estate agent you will sign a "listing contract" (more on that in this chapter); then you and your agent will create a "listing", which describes your property to agents and potential buyers. Information and suggestions about listings are included in Chapter 4.

Before you begin...

Make a List of Recent Improvements which have been made to the house, such as when it got a new roof, windows, water heater or furnace. This will add to the value of your house, because potential buyers won't worry about needing to invest in these major items if they know they have a lot of life left. Keep this list available when you meet with real estate agents to get your market analysis, so they can use it when comparing your house to like properties, in order to come up with the best price at which to list your house. Some of these notes may be added to your real estate listing, if there's room, and almost certainly they will be included in the handout which will be available for those who tour your home. A pile of these handouts—usually made by real estate agents—are generally placed on the kitchen counter or foyer table, along with a dish or bowl where Buyers' Agents can leave their business cards.

While you're at it, gather additional information about these improvements—the name and contact information for the company which put on your roof, for instance, the date the improvement was done, and any warranty which covers it. When you're closing the sale of the property, it would be nice to pass on these documents to the new owners.

Gather other helpful documents you may have available, such as the survey which was done when you purchased the property, the layout of the house (you're especially likely to have this if you purchased it directly from the builder), and any previous listing of the house. If you do have a previous listing, I suggest that you put it aside to review *after* the new listing has been drafted, to encourage creativity but make sure you don't miss anything.

Get a Market Analysis & Interview Real Estate Agents

A **Market Analysis** (a.k.a. Market Evaluation or Comparative Market Analysis) evaluates all of the factors regarding the current local real estate market, the condition and location of your house, the listing price of similar homes on the market in your area, and the price similar homes have actually sold for in the recent past. It will give you an idea of approximately how long it may take you to sell your home, and suggest a price range in which to list it.

- Contact several potential real estate agents, and make appointments for each of them to come to your home individually to provide a Market Analysis. You'll probably want to list your house with a real estate company, but **even if you ultimately decide to try selling it yourself** or use one of the alternate methods listed later in this chapter, I still strongly recommend meeting with agents first. You will learn a lot and you will be better prepared to make an informed decision about which route to go. You'll also save interviewing time later on, if the alternate method you selected isn't working for you, and you decide you do want to list with a real estate agent. During the appointments, you'll establish a rapport with each agent (or eliminate them because you can't), review their market analysis and pricing suggestions, learn how they plan to market your home, find out how successful they've been in selling houses, and get their suggestions on showing your home. Some agents are now scheduling two appointments for this purpose, supposedly to better compare homes on the market and those recently sold with yours, after viewing your home during the first visit.

Expect to answer some basic questions when you set up the appointment with an agent, so that they can come properly prepared. They'll probably want to know the number of bedrooms and bathrooms, whether you have a finished basement, recent improvements such as a new roof or furnace, whether the exterior of your home is brick or siding, and so on. They'll use your answers to select similar homes for their market analysis, so be patient with their questions. Collect the materials each agent brings, your notes on what they recommend you do to the house before listing it and your impressions of the agent, and place these into your "Selling" folder. *See "Stay Organized" in Chapter 1.*

After all three interviews, you can decide who you feel is going to work the best for you (or if you're going to try selling the house using a different method). Just tell the agent at the end of each

interview that you have additional interviews scheduled, and that you'll get back to them when you've
made your decision. This is pretty standard, and they
should not pressure you to list with them before you
have a chance to meet with other agents. If they're
good, they know there's a good chance you'll be
using them. If you're comfortable with the communication between you and an agent, respect their
opinions regarding the sale of your house, and feel
that he or she will do the best job at selling your home,
then you know who to choose as your listing agent.

- How do you find good potential Selling Agents (a.k.a.
  Listing Agents)?
  Ask friends/neighbors for Selling Agent recommendations, and also keep an eye out for "For Sale" signs in
  your area, to see which companies and agents are
  active. You'll especially want to note which agent has
  a lot of "SOLD" signs. When you ask friends/neighbors
  for recommendations, you're not asking if they have
  a friend or relative who is a real estate agent. You're
  looking for an agent who has sold a lot of homes in
  your area and has a good reputation. This is a business decision and you need the agent who will do
  the best job for you. The right agent can minimize the
  time it takes to sell your house, the stress you endure
  in the process, and can save you tens of thousands
  of dollars (or more) in the long run. Look in the newspaper real estate ads, and in local magazines. If an
  agent has achieved a certain level of sales or status
  in their field, it will be in their ad. Select the best three
  agents you've heard or read about, and schedule
  appointments with them.

- Sharing information
  Before you share private information with an agent
  about your motivation for selling, time constraints, or
  financial needs, consider whether that information

could compromise your negotiating position, if a prospective buyer were made aware of it. If so, you'll want to be sure the agent you open up to will only be representing you and your best interests, and will not later represent a Buyer for your house and possibly share that information with him. In lieu of discussing your confidential information, what you can do, until you select an agent to list with, is to request a 30-day sale price, a 60-day sale price or a 90-day sale price (presumably the highest, which is why it will take longer to sell at that price). Then you can select the price which fits your sense of urgency. *The only way to be sure an agent is representing only YOUR interests is to sign a listing agreement which specifies that.*

* <u>A note about disclosures...</u>
State laws vary, but in most cases Sellers are required to tell prospective Buyers about things which could affect the sale of the property. This may include whether appliances, heating and air conditioning systems, sprinkler systems, and so on, are in working order, whether additions or major repairs have been completed without obtaining the required permits, and whether significant defects exist in the structure of the house. Additional disclosures might include Home Owners Association dues, neighborhood nuisances, or known sex offenders in your area. There also are laws in some states which require the disclosure of known radon gas issues or the existence of lead-based paint on the property, and others. None of the laws we're aware of require you to do professional testing to determine the answer—they just require you to disclose what you DO know about. In some states, a form needs to be completed in writing; in others it may be verbal, and in still others it may be voluntary. There are some exceptions to disclosure laws, which include foreclosure properties and certain types of property transfers. The real estate

salespeople you interview can tell you about the laws which apply to you, and in many cases may help you to determine the best way to eliminate a problem, so that it becomes a non-issue.

- <u>What price should you ask for your house?</u>
Like anything else, a house is worth what someone will pay for it. In a slow market, with many properties available, a property will sell for less than it will in a hot market, when properties are being scooped up almost as soon as they're put up for sale. In some places, like Southern California, it's not unusual to hear about bidding wars, in which a Buyer may offer significantly *more* than the list price in order to be awarded the sale. (We should be so lucky as to be the Sellers in *that* situation!) Fluctuations in the market (such as a major downturn of housing sales) can make pricing even trickier than normal.

In order to do a Market Analysis, a good sales agent will come prepared with a list of "comparables". Comparables are homes similar to yours, which are currently on the market or which have recently been sold in your neighborhood, or a similar neighborhood, in your area. This requires some knowledge of the area, because many characteristics will make a difference in how much a house is worth, including school district, lot size & features, location with respect to busy streets, amenities in the home, condition of the house and condition of the neighborhood.

You'll show the agent your house, including any special features it has, go over your list of recent improvements, and other characteristics of your house (lot size, cul-de-sac location, nearby high tension wires or location on a busy street, for instance) which might make it more or less valuable than similar homes in your area. All of this information, as well as how quickly you need to sell your home, will help the agent establish a reasonable price range at which to list your house.

If you are entertaining the idea of moving to a larger home in the area but are in no great hurry, you might want to list it at a slightly higher price and be willing to wait for the right buyer. If, on the other hand, you already have a contract to purchase another home contingent on the sale of your current home, you might want to price it more aggressively, so that it hopefully will sell more quickly.

Ultimately, YOU make the decision of what the listing price will be. Considering the opinion of several real estate agents, as well as your personal situation, the decision should be fairly clear to you. The advice, and reasoning behind it, is one way in which to evaluate which agent you feel will do the best job for you. You should NOT select an agent just because she suggests the highest listing price for your home.

An interesting tool on the internet is Zillow. Located at Zillow.com, it lists the price homes have recently sold for, and current homes on the market. However, in some cases the information is incomplete or not up-to-date, and it does not include details about condition or upgrades. It's helpful to use as a tool to find what homes in your area should be looked at as "comparables" when a real estate salesperson does a market analysis on your home, and to give you a rough idea of home values in an area in which you're interested. Realize, however, that this tool doesn't give you the full picture.

You may hear the term "Buyer's Market" or "Seller's Market". When there are a lot of properties for sale at a given time, and they're not selling very quickly, Buyers have a lot to choose from, and may be able to buy the property at a lower price than they would otherwise. This is called a "Buyer's Market". If, on the other hand, properties are selling briskly and very close to, or even above, the asking price, this is called a "Seller's Market". Obviously, you'd like to be a Buyer in a Buyer's Market and a Seller in a Seller's Market. Unfortunately, when you're relocating you don't always have the luxury of waiting until the market is perfect for you to buy or sell property—you just do the best you can, according to your circumstances.

In a slow market, you may want to leave the door open for a lease purchase, where people rent with the option-to-buy, or consider owner financing. I don't necessarily recommend any of these, but they are things to explore if you might otherwise endure the hardship of not being able to move when you want to, or carrying two mortgages for longer than you're comfortable doing so. Be very careful if you provide financing for your Buyers, especially if these funds represent a large portion of your assets. If you do want to pursue Seller Financing (a.k.a. Owner Financing or Carry-back Loan), consider using a company such as Circle Lending (circlelending.com) to set up and manage the loan. If the market is really bad, and you're fairly certain that it will bounce back in a year or 2, you might want to consider renting the house and putting it on the market when conditions are more favorable for selling.

There are several reasons for not pricing your house *too* high. Agents and Buyers are most excited when a house is first listed. Those first few weeks are obviously the best time for a house to sell. If you've set the price way too high, you may have to lower it in order to get showings and offers. When a house stays on the market for an extended amount of time, potential Buyers start thinking something is wrong with it, or that the Sellers are probably desperate, and then they may offer an even lower price for the house. Also, even if you do get an offer at the inflated price, when the Buyers apply for a mortgage, an appraisal will be ordered. If the appraisal doesn't stand up to the price you agreed on, the deal may fall through. There's nothing wrong with listing your house a little higher than the comparables show, especially if the market is right. However, keep these cautions in mind before deciding on a price which is much higher than you might realistically expect to get.

Once you have the general price range for listing your house in mind, consider this: agents working with Buyers select listings to show to them by specifying, among other things, a price bracket (such as $300-350,000) when they do their MLS search. So you wouldn't want to list a house for $351,000, for instance, because a search might eliminate many of the people who should be looking at it. Since you're so close to a break point, you'd be better off listing it at $349,900. It sounds like a lot less, and will come up on a search of homes under or up to $350,000.

- <u>What is the Agent's Marketing Plan?</u>
  Most agents will come to the interview with examples of ads they place, and a complete marketing plan. Some hints on marketing:

- Don't list with anyone who doesn't use the MLS (*See "Benefits" under "Listing with a Traditional Full Service Real Estate Agent: Things You Should Know" in this chapter*) or at the very least offer an online listing on a <u>very</u> well publicized website. One of the main jobs your listing agent has is to make other agents aware of your house, so that they will bring prospective Buyers to your property. The MLS is one of the most effective ways of doing this.

- Lots of ads are good. Ads in the paper generally include one photograph. How often will they place ads, and in which publications?

- Online listings have become extremely important. An online listing usually includes multiple photos of your home—inside and out—and can be a great tool, especially for buyers who need to screen potential purchases from their home, either due to medical problems or their geographical location. More and more, folks are looking at online listings just because they *can*, and they go in person to see the ones which look like the best fit. Because online listings are so important now, the wording is very important and good photos are essential.

- There are photographers who specialize in creating virtual tours of homes for sale, as well as photos for the brochure (see below). Find out whether your agent will have a professional do this task, or whether the agent plans to take the photos himself. *For more information about online photos, see "Showing the Home" in this chapter.*

- Brochures are created to showcase your home. These will be placed in the house (in the entry area or kitchen, usually) so that potential Buyers will take one with them. The brochure should include a number of color photos, both inside the house and out. It should also include a listing of the great features that your home, and your neighborhood, have to offer.

- Lockboxes are good because they make it easier for agents to show your house. A lockbox is something an agent can place on your front door. Inside the lockbox is a key to your house. Agents will still phone for appointments, but if no one is home, they can obtain access to the house without having to run to your real estate office to pick up the key and then run back to drop it off after the showing. This will make it more convenient for folks to view your home, so many more *will*. Also, an electronic lock box will record who opens the box, which is helpful since not every agent will leave his/her business card in your home, as is customary. This record will allow your Listing Agent to follow up with the agent who showed your home, to get feedback about their client's reaction to your property.

- Open houses for real estate agents—with the proper bait, such as a good lunch buffet provided by your agent—are a great tool. Once the agents do come and view your home, they're more likely to suggest the house to their prospective buyers. Real estate agent open houses are generally held on a weekday morning, or into the lunch hour. Agents from your Listing Agent's office may "caravan" from listing to listing, so don't be surprised by a sudden onslaught of agents who walk quickly through your home and then are gone as suddenly as they came. Hopefully, they'll come back soon with their Buyers. Your agent should give you plenty of notice about when the caravan will come.

- A new phenomenon is blossoming to take the place of the traditional caravan in some areas: virtual caravans. In this case, agents view virtual tours of the homes on a computer, rather than driving around to view the actual houses. Although it's not the same as seeing the house in person, it does save a great deal of time and fuel, and anyone who is interested can certainly then schedule a viewing.

- The Selling Agent should regularly check with agents who show your home to find out if their clients are interested, and if not, why. That may help you to fix problems others see or perceive, or adjust the price to the right level.

- Open houses for the public are often better at letting your neighbors view your home, and getting clients for the salesperson to sell other houses to, than in selling your house. However, if your house doesn't sell quickly, or is in an area where people often move to a different house within their local area, then it may be helpful. An exception to this is in a very hot market, such as that which has often been seen in southern California, where an Open House may be held right after the property goes on the market, and all offers received by that evening will be reviewed at once. This is the type of environment in which Buyers often bid higher than the Listing Price, when the market is up.

- Fliers can be distributed to homes in your area and/or to real estate agents in the area. The more often real estate agents are reminded about your home, the more likely they'll take Buyers to view it.

- Ask how often the agent will be in touch with you, and during what hours you may contact them. Do they offer a cell phone number or e-mail address for you to use? If they suggest e-mail, ask how often they check for messages and tend to respond. A good answer is at least several times a day.

- An increasingly popular technique to show a house at its best is called "staging". Often, a listing agent will pay for someone to come to your home and make suggestions as to how it will show the best. The stager may bring accent pieces to your home, or use what you have, but either way, they will often move furniture and accessories around, and may suggest that you remove some things. Because so many other

Sellers will be using this technique, and their houses are your competition, I strongly suggest you take advantage of this service and try to keep an open mind about the stager's suggestions.

- Show Us Your Stats. Ask agents you're interviewing about the homes they've listed and sold over the last several years. What percentage of their listings sold? How long were they on the market? Approximately how close to the original listing price did they sell for? The answers to these questions will give you clues as to how good the agent is at marketing a house, "reading the current market" and pricing a house properly. Ideally, buyers get a good price for their home, but the house doesn't stay on the market too long and have to be reduced in price—both of which are negatives to prospective buyers. A lot of factors influence how quickly a house sells, including some controlled by the buyer, but overall you'll get a good idea of how successful this agent has been. Most active agents will have this information available and many will have included it in the materials they've prepared for you.

- Other things you may want to ask an agent is how long they have been active in real estate, and what awards or designations they have received. (A good salesperson will tell you about awards or designations without your asking for them.)

- It's important to use an agent who has a great record of selling homes in your area, as they will have a better handle on how to best promote a home in your neighborhood and will probably have a better relationship with other agents who are representing Buyers in your area. We've tried using someone who was a friend and, in another case, someone who was nice and had helped us look for a house to buy, but was not great at listing and marketing homes. In both cases, our house didn't sell during the listing period, even though it was a good time of year and it was priced fairly well. We then listed with the RIGHT agent and it was sold within 2-3 weeks. Big difference.

- How can we make the house show better?
  As you interview each agent, ask what they would suggest you do to ready your home for showings. They'll have personalized suggestions for your house, as well as a number of general ones. Don't take the agent's suggestions personally—they are experienced and objective, and are tuned in to what may turn potential Buyers off. A little extra painting or moving some furniture around or replacing the kitchen floor (don't panic—it doesn't have to be super expensive) may make a big difference in how quickly you get an offer, and how nice that offer might be. Remember, if you do any redecorating, choose NEUTRAL colors. *See the end of this chapter for a full list of general hints for showing your home.*

Listing with a Traditional "Full Service" Real Estate Agent: Things You Should Know

- Benefits
  One of the benefits of listing with a real estate agent is that your property will be listed in the MLS (Multiple Listing Service). This is the standard tool which all agents, no matter which company they're with or city they're in, use to access what's on the market. There are some alternate methods listed later in this chapter, which will also allow your house to be on the MLS—for a price (*see "Should we sell it ourselves" later in this chapter*). If it's not in the MLS, there's a good chance real estate agents won't tell their clients about it and Buyers won't find it on their

own. According to the 2008 National Association of REALTORS® Profile of Home Buyers and Sellers, 84% of Sellers were assisted by a Real Estate agent when selling their home, and 81% of Buyers purchased a home through a real estate agent or broker. The figures are probably closer to 100% of executives being transferred by their companies. That's a large group of possible buyers who might never know about your home if it isn't listed on the MLS.

When you list your property with a traditional, or "full service", real estate agent, you are signing up to receive all of the benefits the agent and his/her broker can offer. Included are brochures of your property, a sign outside your house, a listing on the MLS, marketing of your property (which may consist of ads, open houses, mailings, etc), and the benefit of their experience in guiding you through the whole process. They facilitate the showing of your property and field any questions Buyers and their agents have. If you need a referral for painters or real estate legal services or whatever, they often keep a list of reputable choices. Selling agents will follow up with agents who have shown your home, evaluate any feedback they get from these contacts, present Offers to Purchase and help you evaluate their worth, and assist in the negotiation of contracts. They've even been known to agree to spruce the house up between showings when you're out of town and/or help in other ways as circumstances arise. You don't have to worry about the safety issue of letting strangers into your home without a chaperone and other such things. They can make the whole process easier for you by relieving you of the burden of dealing with things outside your area of expertise.

If you decide to list the house, you can sign the contract before you've prepared the house. Just let the agent know what date you will be ready for it to be shown. Preferably, this should be within a week or so after signing. Agents and Buyers will get excited when a listing is new, and that's when the most demand usually is for showing the property. You don't want to dampen their enthusiasm by making them wait too long. If it's convenient for you both to sign the contract on a Wednesday night but you'll need the weekend to finish preparing the house, you certainly can tell the agent the first date it will be available to be shown is on Monday. That said, the weekends are the most important times for showing a house, so if you'd like to sell quickly, try to make it ready to be shown at the beginning of a weekend.

- <u>Types of relationships</u> a real estate agent can have with you:

  - A **Selling Agent** (also known as a **Listing Agent**) is a real estate agent with whom Sellers have signed a contract to market their home. The agent agrees to represent only the Seller, and not disclose confidential information (such as how low a price they would accept). They <u>are</u>, however, required to disclose physical defects about the home which are known or readily apparent.
  - A **Buying Agent** is a real estate agent who helps prospective home buyers find and purchase a home. This agent usually places the interests of the Buyer first. However, in some states agents are required to advise you that they must represent you <u>and</u> the seller (even if they're not the Listing Agent). In those cases, you should not share information with them which might affect a sales negotiation, as they may be required to share this information with the Seller or the Seller's Agent.
  - In some states, an agent listing your home may ask you to sign a **Dual Agent** agreement. This

means that the Listing Agent has your permission to also function as a Buyer's Agent on your home. The good part about that is that she can show the house to any of her potential Buyers. Also, since she would be earning a larger percentage of the commission if she were both Selling and Buying agent, the agent might be willing to give up some of her commission to help bridge the gap between what you want to get for the house and what the Buyers are willing to pay. The negative aspect of the relationship is that since the Agent should not reveal proprietary information to either party, such as how low a price the Sellers would accept or how high a price the Buyers are willing and able to pay, the amount of guidance they can give their clients during the contract negotiation is limited.

Most real estate agents wear both hats, although many specialize in one aspect or the other. An agent who works well with people who are looking for a home, is not necessarily an expert on marketing a home. It takes a lot of effort and networking and experience to be a great Selling Agent, and a different set of skills to be a successful Buyer's Agent, so don't automatically assume you will use the same person for both types of transactions.

- A **Transaction Broker** or **Facilitator** is someone who helps the Buyer and Seller reach an agreement and process the transaction, but does not represent either the Buyer or Seller. Do not share information with this person if you don't want the other party to know it. We have never even considered using someone in this capacity, but wanted you to know that the role exists. You can locate one by searching online for "transaction broker" and your city and state.

- <u>Types of Listing Contracts</u>
  There are 4 different types of listing contracts, described below. The length of time the listing is for and, sometimes, the percent of commission are somewhat negotiable. Remember that this is a legal contract—you are not required to accept an Offer to Purchase which meets all of your stated requirements, but you may be obligated to pay the real estate commission if such an offer is presented, even if you don't accept the offer.

  ### ☛ Exclusive Right to Sell
  This is the most common type of listing contract. No matter who finds the Buyer—even if it's *you*—the Listing Agent earns a commission. If another agent finds the Buyer, the Listing Agent shares the commission with that agent. Being assured of earning a commission when the property sells is the reason why the Listing Agent is willing to put the time, effort, and financial investment into marketing your home to other agents and to the public. *In this book, when I refer to "listing with a real estate agent", I'm referring to this type of listing contract.*

  Exclusions: If you already have some people who may be interested in purchasing your property, it is possible to sign an Exclusive Right to Sell Listing, allowing you to sell to those specific people within a certain time frame without paying the real estate commission. You would need to name the specific people, and generally the time frame is for 30 days or less. Naturally, although they will begin trying to sell your home as soon as you sign the listing, the real estate folks will want to invest minimal funds in marketing your home until that exclusion has been removed or the time frame expires.

➻ Open Listing

This is generally used by folks who are trying to sell by owner. It's an agreement that if a real estate agent finds a buyer for your home, you will pay them a sales commission (about half what you would normally pay, since you won't owe the part that would go to the Listing Agent). You can sign an Open Listing with as many agents as you want, however do not expect them to do any marketing (ads, fliers, etc.) for your home, place it on the MLS, or assist you in any other way. If you sell your home yourself, you will not owe them a commission, so it would be a poor investment on their part to make those efforts.

➻ Exclusive Agency Listing

With this type of listing, your agent will earn a commission only if the house is sold through a real estate agent or broker. If you sell it yourself, they don't earn any commission. Because this is so risky for the agent, he/she is not likely to invest much time, effort or money in marketing your home since there's a good chance they won't earn the commission to repay their investment. They'll probably just place it in the MLS and show it if they happen to have a Buyer who is interested.

➻ One-Time Show a.k.a. Showing Listing

This is usually used by an agent showing an FSBO (For Sale By Owner) to a potential buyer. The listing includes the name of their client and guarantees that the Selling Agent will receive a commission if that party purchases the house. It is meant to prevent the Buyer and Seller from negotiating on their own and not paying the salesperson their commission. The agent will not be marketing your home and will not place a listing on the MLS.

- <u>Length of Listing</u>
Listing Contracts vary in length, generally from 60 days to 120 days, although 30-day listings are not unheard of. We prefer a 60-day listing, but agents will often explain that they can't spend major funds marketing a home with such a "short" listing, so we often agree to 90 days. DON'T sign one for longer. And make sure you can cancel the listing contract after 30 days if you're unhappy with how it's being marketed—and that there's little or no charge to do so. You and the agent may choose to put in writing exactly what you expect them to do, based on their marketing plan, so that conditions allowing an early cancellation are clearly defined and would come as no surprise. This is a fair thing to agree to, because if the agent doesn't do what he/she promised to, they aren't earning their commission, and you should have a right to find another agent who will. Even if they follow their marketing plan and have been actively trying to sell your house, if the listing expires before the house is sold, you may decide to list with someone else who you feel may have more success. It's up to you to decide at that point who you feel has the best chance to market your house successfully—it is a business decision and shouldn't be based on your reluctance to hurt someone's feelings.

- <u>Commission</u>
Commissions across the country vary from 4-7% of the sales price, but most are 6%. The commission is paid by the Seller, from the proceeds of the sale, at closing, and is shared among the Listing Agent, Selling Agent, and both of their Real Estate Brokers. If your listing agreement is for a lower-than-average commission, you may experience fewer showings since some of the Buying Agents would rather show their clients homes which will earn them more profit if the showing results in a sale. Still, it doesn't hurt to

discuss this with a prospective agent. If they normally charge 7%, it's not impossible that they will agree to 6%, especially if they think your home will sell fairly quickly without a large marketing investment on their part. With the growing popularity of Sellers using For Sale by Owner methods, some Realtors are lowering their sales commissions to compete more attractively with these FSBO companies. It will be interesting to watch how things change in this industry over the coming years.

Should We List With a Traditional Real Estate Agent, Try To Sell It Ourselves, Or Use an Alternative Method?

Now that you've gotten a market analysis from several real estate agents, it's time to decide whether it's worth trying to sell your house without using a real estate agent.

- List With a Real Estate Agent
  If you're being moved by a company which will pay the real estate commission, it's pretty much a no-brainer: use a traditional real estate company. You will get professional advice throughout the process, be safer when the house is shown, probably sell the house faster, and will endure much less stress during the whole process.

  The methods of marketing property have been expanding quite a bit recently. Some full-service companies are charging slightly (approximately 1%) less commission than others, in order to gain a greater number of listings and sales. Naturally, other full-service companies want the commissions to remain at the same, higher, level. In some states there is litigation pending, to deal with this dispute. I advise you to find out what the story is in your state, so that you can make an informed decision as to how much commission you're willing to pay. But keep in mind that, in most cases, "You get what you pay for".

- Selling it yourself

  If you're not being moved by a company which will pay the real estate commission, and you're lucky enough (or were wise enough when you bought the house) that homes similar to yours in your area are very much in demand, you may decide to try selling it yourself, at least for a short time.

  You'll want to involve an attorney who comes recommended by people you trust, and who is very experienced with real estate transactions—but make sure she will agree not to represent other clients in the purchase of your home. It's important for your attorney to only have your best interests as her goal. You might want to ask her for references, and ask the references if they would use the same attorney again for future real estate transactions. That will probably get you an honest assessment of their feelings. The attorney will review any Offers to Purchase you would like to accept, make suggestions, and facilitate completing the transaction. Many attorneys charge a flat fee for assisting in the sale of a home.

  Right away, utilize word-of-mouth. Tell everyone in your area, especially your neighbors, that you're putting your house on the market, in case they know of anyone who might be interested. We purchased one home this way, after telling every acquaintance we knew in a particular subdivision exactly what we were looking for. We found out the house was going to be sold when the owner told her neighbor—my friend—that they had just made the decision to purchase a larger home, in order to accommodate an ill parent. We viewed the house the next day (they insisted on taking a day to tidy up) and negotiated the terms the following day. The next-door-neighbors later told us they may have considered upgrading to that house, if only they'd known it was going to be sold before we signed the contract. It was sweet for the Sellers, too, because they didn't have to do any work on the house to prepare it for listing, didn't have to deal with showing the house to lots of prospective buyers, and didn't have to pay a commission.

If word-of-mouth doesn't work fairly quickly (and in most cases, it won't), you can place an online ad using the major newspaper in your area. Some of these newspapers are listed in Chapter 7, under "Newspaper Classified Ads". You may want to include the phrase "Agents protected", which means you're willing to pay a commission (approximately 3%) to a real estate agent bringing a Buyer who purchases your home. If you do, you'll probably be asked to sign a One-Time Show or Showing Listing before the agent will show the property, in order to assure him that he'll earn a commission if that particular person buys your home. Obviously, this would increase the number of potential buyers who visit your home, but it's up to you whether you're willing to go this route.

Marketing a home properly takes a lot of time and energy, and you also have to keep in mind the potential risks (to you, your family, and your belongings) of showing the property yourself. For most people, I would not recommend you try to sell by yourself for long, unless you really don't care whether your property sells or not. I realize that sometimes people just want to see if they can get a really good price, and would rather not sell it otherwise. Unless you fall into that category, if your home hasn't sold in a relatively short amount of time, I would suggest you list with an agent or move on to one of the other methods of selling your house.

- <u>Alternative methods to market your property</u>
  There are a growing number of companies which provide a variety of services designed to help you sell your home, without paying a standard, or in some cases even sub-standard, real estate commission. Many have a flat fee program, with additional charges for optional services. Others charge a small commission, and offer limited services. Some will charge a fee for an electronic lockbox, advertising in their real estate magazine, providing a yard sign, radio or TV exposure, taking photos of your house, listing your home on the MLS, and so on. Others will include some of these items in their basic service. With some companies, the basic fee is only paid when your house sells, but be sure to read the fine print and make sure you understand all of the conditions. Do the research you need to, in order to determine what method you're most comfortable with.

  Some examples of these types of companies—and please understand that I am not recommending them, only making you aware of their existence—are:

  Assist2Sell at **www.assist2sell.com**
  Broker Direct at **www.brokerdirectmls.com**
  Buy Owner at **www.buyowner.com**
  By Owner at 1-800-ByOwner or **www.ByOwner.com**
  For Sale By Owner at **www.forsalebyowner.com**
  Homes By Owner at **www.HomesByOwner.com**
  Sale By Owner Realty at **www.salebyownerrealty.com**
  Zip Realty at **www.ziprealty.com**

  Additional sites are located in Chapter 17, under "For Sale By Owner (FSBO) Assistance Companies" I'm sure there are many more, but these will help you get started.

When considering alternative methods, remember that since the percentage of Buyers using the internet for their home search is very high, it's extremely important that you use one of the companies which advertises online. Online listings and the MLS are the two most important ways to reach potential Buyers. Actually, many of these alternate real estate companies will refer to listing properties on MLS—but in many cases, it's not <u>the</u> Multiple Listing Service which traditional Real Estate Agents use.

Another word of caution—try to compare apples-to-apples *before* letting a representative from one of these companies come visit you in your home. Select the top two or three companies which offer the services *you* want and which you feel the best about, before making appointments with them. Salespeople can be very persuasive, and it makes sense to be very informed before being in the position where you might be tempted to sign on the dotted line. I strongly recommend you visit with several companies before deciding which one you feel best about working with.

These alternative methods of selling might save you a fair amount of money in commissions, but could also use up valuable time (especially unwise if your house is going on the market at a critical time, such as a month or 2 before school starts). It could also be a real hassle, or worse, to (a) be available to show the house on short notice, (b)have to supervise your children while accompanying buyers around the house and (c) accept the security issues of inviting strangers into your home without a real estate professional present. Plus, by not listing with a traditional real estate agency, you may limit your property's exposure to many buyers, who only work with real estate agents. Even if you work with an organization such as Sale By Owner Realty (sale-byownerrealty.com), which lists the property on the MLS, many agents will choose not to show your property because their commission will be so much lower than it would be otherwise. You'll have to explore the alternatives, and carefully weigh what each one will do for you and at what price.

You may decide that it's worth the extra money to have a professional full-service real estate company handle, and advise you on, the many aspects of selling your home, so that you can focus on what alone can be time-consuming and stressful enough—preparing your home to be shown and keeping it looking its best while it's on the market, as well as dealing with the many details and preparations involved in your upcoming move. This is a very important business decision, and should be decided by your comfort level with the options and common sense—not a sense of loyalty to a friend or acquaintance.

Home Owner's Warranty

No matter how you plan to market your home, a fairly inexpensive feature you can add to your listing is your willingness to purchase a Home Owner's Warranty for your house. This type of policy will typically pay to repair or replace the home's heating, air conditioning, plumbing, and electrical systems, as well as some built-in appliances, should they fail due to normal wear and tear, within one year of the sale. There may be a service call fee when a technician makes a service call, and naturally it will be in the insurance company's best interest to repair something, or replace it with a very basic unit (rather than an upgraded one, which the Buyer might prefer to have). However, it does provide some peace of mind to a new owner, since it provides protection against unexpected costly repairs for a period of time. Currently, these policies generally cost about $300-500, although the price may be more for homes larger than 5,000 square feet.

Showing the home

I won't kid you. Doing this right takes work. But it pays off big time, so do the best you can.

- ONLINE PHOTOS
  It's safe to say that more people will look at photos of your house online than will ever walk through your door. So when the photographer is coming to take those photos, make your house look *extra* special— like a model home. Remove soap dispensers and sponges from the kitchen sink, and appliances from the kitchen counters. Set the table and put a vase with flowers in the center. Put fresh flowers in the bedrooms and bathrooms. The flowers don't need to be expensive.....one bunch of mums and some greens can be cut up to fill a number of small vases. Turn every light on and adjust towels so they look their best. Walk through your house with a critical eye, thinking of how things will look in a photograph, and then put things away or adjust their position to make your house look its very best.

- AVAILABILITY
  Make it easy for Buyers to see your home. Ideally, real estate agents will call you at least several hours ahead of the time they would like to show your house. But sometimes, they will be driving by with their clients, on the way to another house, when they spot yours and want to see it and the agent will call from in front of your house, using her cell phone. You can refuse, but I don't recommend it. You can ask for 5 minutes or so, to tidy up and leave, which in most cases will work out fine. Remember, the easier you make it for agents to show your home, the faster you will get an

offer. If Buyers can't get into your house at their convenience, they're not likely to purchase it.

During one weekend house hunting trip in Chicago, we were very interested in a house we had seen early in the weekend. After viewing many other homes in a day and a half, we felt this house was the one we wanted to buy, but we wanted to view it one more time before making an offer on it. The female owner of the house was a nurse working night shift and her husband absolutely would not permit us to view the house during the day on Sunday, even knowing that we had to leave town later that day. We offered to be very quiet, and to avoid the Master Bedroom, but he would not permit it. We needed to find a new home during that trip, so looked at other alternatives and purchased another house instead.

Lockboxes: Described earlier in this chapter, under "What is the Agent's Marketing Plan?". It not only helps your home to be accessible, it allows you to be away from home when the house is shown. A prospective Buyer can look at the house more objectively if you're not there, imagining it as *his* house, rather than yours. Newer electronic lockboxes record which Real Estate salesperson accessed the box, which makes it easier to follow up with potential Buyers. The vast majority of homes listed by real estate agents do use lockboxes.

- SMELLS
  Eliminate sources of bad smells, such as last night's fish dinner or pet odors or garbage or mildew, rather than trying to cover them up. Avoid using anything with strong odors, such as incense or curry. Air the house out, empty the garbage, clean that kitty litter, and try to avoid cooking foods with not-so-great odors, like liver or fish, when you know the house is going to be shown, or on weekends, when the house

is more likely to be shown on short notice. I think this is a great excuse to avoid cooking a lot of nights.

Then **add** something to make the home smell appealing and cozy. Incense will turn some people off. *Mildly* scented candles are OK, but for safety's sake extinguish them before you leave the house and be sure hot wax is out of reach in case small children come along. Baking smells are always good (unless you burn the cookies—which I did once, right before the house was to be shown). You can buy cookie dough now which can be broken apart to bake a few cookies at a time. This is a perfect way to get a yummy smell with fairly short notice.

- SOUNDS
  Turn off the TV and stereo, or at least turn the volume down. If you want to leave music playing, be sure it's mellow and soft. Avoid crying, barking, loud talking, and so on, as much as possible.

- LIGHTS
  Turn on all the lights in the house when you know the house will be shown, even during the day. It will make your house look cheerful and bright. I don't like wasting electricity, either, but in this case it's worth it.

- SIGHTS
  The more your house looks like a model home, the better. Keep counters in the kitchen and bathroom, and mirrors throughout the house clean, tidy, and free of excess "stuff". Keep the floors swept and vacuumed. Be sure to clean up strands of hair on the bathroom sink, on the floor, and in the tub and shower. Put out clean towels, new soap, a nice tablecloth and fresh flowers. Make sure curtains and blinds are hanging evenly, and open them during the daylight hours, unless the view is awful. If you have dirty clothes in

a laundry basket, just place a towel neatly on top, and tuck it down the sides—it'll look fine. Keep your garage door closed as much as possible while your house is on the market—your home will look much better from the outside that way.

Keep the house picked-up, even when you think no one's coming. I understand that the kids need to play. Let them! But don't let it get so messy that it can't be picked up in 10 minutes, and ALWAYS try to leave it in great shape before you leave the house. One time when we had a house on the market, we went out at 7pm for a 1-hour errand, and came back to find cars in our driveway. The agent must have phoned while we were gone. As I said before, you just never know when agents and their clients might drive by your house on the way to another one, and decide they'd like to view yours. The agent picks up her cell phone, makes a call or 2, and Bingo. They're ready to knock at the door. You can make things difficult by saying agents need to make appointments with a given amount of notice, but those clients in the car outside your house may be the ones who wind up buying your house IF they can get inside to see it. The more available the house is, the better the chance it will sell quickly.

- PETS
  Make sure your listing includes information about your pets, for several reasons. One, you wouldn't want an agent to open your front door without knowing he should keep your cat inside, or open the gate to your backyard and have your dog escape. Second, you don't want to put potential Buyers and their agent at risk if your dog perceives them as a threat. Third, if people are concerned about, or distracted by, your pets, they may not give your house the consideration it deserves. For these reasons, take dogs and cats

with you, if possible, when you leave the house, or at least keep them in a crate or out of the way. Put up a warning sign on the basement, garage, or bedroom door if your pet is inside, although it would be preferable to allow free access to all parts of your house.

- <u>TRY TO BE AWAY</u>
  As a Buyer, I MUCH prefer when the Seller is not at home. I understand when there are special circumstances which require an exception to this. However, I feel much more at ease to explore the property, discuss the pros & cons out loud (without worrying about hurting anyone's feelings), and picture living there with my family and possessions, when the homeowner or tenant is not in the house.

  That said, if the baby's sleeping, you don't have to wake him up and leave. They *will* understand, and you can ask that they skip the baby's room if that's important. There may be other times when it's inconvenient, and you'll have to make a choice. If you do stay, be polite and briefly answer any questions you may be asked; but otherwise, let the salesperson do the talking and you just hang out with your family in one room, if possible.

Now that you have gotten a Market Analysis, decided on an asking price, and determined how you plan to go about marketing your home, read on for inside information about Listings.

Chapter 4

Creating And Interpreting Real Estate Listings

"What do all those abbreviations in real estate ads mean? And what can I include in a listing to make potential Buyers eager to come look at my house?"

The purpose of the listing is to give prospective Buyers basic information about your property, and get them to come see your house. Once they're there, they will presumably fall in love with it and present you with an offer. So you want the house to sound extremely appealing, but without misleading potential Buyers about anything. If your ad is misleading, Buyers may feel you aren't trustworthy and may be concerned that there will be problems with the house or with the sales transaction. So paint the property in a positive light, but definitely be truthful.

Type or Style of House

One of the first pieces of information to state is the type of house, such as 2-story Traditional. Some of these descriptions are:
    Colonial
    Contemporary
    Traditional
    Ranch or Split Ranch
    2-story
    Split level

Tri-level
Townhome
Duplex

General Information

The listing includes general information, such as the number of bedrooms and baths, lot size or dimensions, year the house was built and so on. There is also space provided for comments and this is where to highlight what makes your house really special. You'll have a limited amount of space for these features in your listing, so select the ones which would most make prospective buyers want to see YOUR house before others.

Features

Here are some features which often attract prospective buyers. Note that some features, such as hardwood floors, may not be as popular in 10 years as they are now. You'll need to pay attention to current trends. Also, these features may be less available in lower priced houses and other, more extravagant, features may be sought after in higher-priced properties. That said, these are some features which are currently coveted in "executive" homes;

2nd floor laundry
2-story family room
2-story foyer
3-car garage
All brick or 3 sides brick (or even "brick front")
Architectural beauty
Basement stubbed for full bath [3]
Bay windows or bayed breakfast area (or Master Bedroom or wherever)
Bonus room (this is a room off the master bedroom, often used as a sitting room, office, storage, sewing room, etc)
Built-in bookshelves (name the room they're in)

Ceiling fans throughout
9' Ceilings
Cherry cabinets
Close to (schools, shopping, restaurants)
Convenient to (schools, shopping, restaurants)
Convenient to—or 'Easy access' to—[insert major highway] or "1 minute to I-85"
Crown molding
Cul-de-sac lot
Daylight basement (meaning it has windows and possibly doors)
Deck (large, huge, and/or private)
Double ovens
Double vanity (in bathroom)
Eat-in kitchen
End unit (for townhomes)
Fenced backyard
Exercise room
Fireplace (indicate quantity if more than one)
Flat backyard
Flat driveway (often preferred for basketball and children playing)
Formal dining room (rather than a combination living/dining room or eating area)
Formal living room (rather than combined open areas)
Former model home
French doors in [name location]
Front and rear stairs
Full finished basement
Garden tub/ separate shower
Gated community
Golf community
Gourmet kitchen
Granite countertops
Great in-town location
Great schools and community
Guest suite (bedroom attached to bathroom)
Hardwood floors

High ceilings (sometimes specified 9' or 10' ceilings)
His and her walk-in closets
Home theater (or media room)
Huge deck
Huge island kitchen
Huge windows
Imported tile countertops
In ground pool
Irrigation or sprinkler system
Jetted tub
Jack and Jill bathroom [2]
Kitchen overlooks family room
Kitchen with breakfast nook
Kitchen with breakfast bar
Lakefront
Large walk-in closet
Leaded glass cabinet doors
Level lot
Lot (large, or can say approx. acreage)
Lots of storage (or 'abundant storage') space
Lush landscaping
Many upgrades
Marble fireplace
Maple cabinets
Master on main (rather than on the 2nd story)
Master suite (or Master BR) on main level
Master suite with sitting area
Master Suite with trey ceiling
Master Suite with vaulted ceiling
Media center
Motivated sellers (if you're very willing to negotiate)
Move-in condition
A Must-See Home
Neutral décor
Oceanfront
Open areas
Open floor plan

Oversized 2-car garage
Oversized master
Owner financing (see Chapter 3, under "What Price Should You Ask for Your House")
Pantry or walk-in pantry
Partially finished basement
Perfect location
2" Plantation blinds
Pool (sometimes considered an "attractive nuisance" since often people will not want to accept the responsibilities and potential risks which come with a pool)
Priced to sell (if you've set a very competitive price)
Private backyard
Professionally landscaped
Public sewers (only worth saying if this is an important selling point in the area—in most large metropolitan areas, it's standard)
Quiet neighborhood
Rear-entry garage
Screened-in or wraparound or covered porch
Security system
Separate in-law suite
Separate laundry room
Separate shower (as in "whirlpool tub with sep shower")
Serene setting
Shows like a model
Side-entry garage
Split Ranch floor plan[1]
Stainless steel appliances (refers to refrigerator, oven, range and dishwasher)
Stepless ranch
Stone fireplace
Sunroom
Swim/tennis community
Tree-lined community
Updated (kitchen or bath)
Upstairs loft

Vaulted family room (or family room with vaulted ceiling)
Walk-in closets
Walk-out basement (meaning it has a door leading outside)
Waterfront
Well-maintained neighborhood
Wet bar
Whirlpool tub
Wine cellar
Wooded lot, large lot, acre+ lot

[1]A "split ranch" is one in which the master bedroom is off of one side of the kitchen/living area, and other bedrooms are off of the other side of that area.

[2]A "Jack and Jill bathroom" is a bathroom located between 2 bedrooms. Each bedroom has a door into the bathroom, and often the tub/toilet area is separated from the vanity/sink area for ease of sharing the facility.

[3]"stubbed for bath" means the pipes are in place so that putting a bathroom into the basement will be much less expensive a project than it would otherwise be. It may be stubbed for a powder room—just a sink & toilet—or for a "full bath", which would include a bath/shower.

You may also want to indicate proximity to hospitals, if they are very close. This may attract hospital employees as well as those with chronic conditions requiring hospital visits.

Descriptive Terms

Here are some descriptive words to make your home's features sound extra-appealing. Use with an appropriate feature, some of which are suggested below.

Awesome
Beautiful
Breathtaking
Desirable
Dramatic (2-story foyer, entry)
Dynamite
Elegant
Exquisite
Fantastic
Freshly painted
Great (location, etc)
Gorgeous
Huge
Immaculate
Incredible
Lavish
Like new
Lovely
Luxurious (bath)
Nestled (on a private
wooded lot)

Outstanding
Perfect (location)
Pristine
Private (fenced backyard or
deck)
Secluded (could be viewed
as a positive or not)
Serene (setting)
Spacious
Spectacular
Spotless
Striking
Stunning
Superior
Updated
Upgraded
Very clean
Well-maintained
You will fall in love with...

Abbreviations in Listings

Since space in listings is limited, and long ads are expensive, abbreviations are widely used. Here are some abbreviations typically found in listings, and what they mean:

Ac (as in 12 ac.) = acre(s)
AC or a/c = air conditioning
Appls = appliances
Approx = approximately
BA = bathroom
½ BA = powder room (toilet and sink—no shower or tub)
2 c gar or 2 car gar = 2 car garage
5 BR/3.5 BA = 5 bedrooms, 3½ baths
2-sty = 2 story house
BR = bedroom

B'ful = beautiful
Bkyd = backyard
Bldr = builder
Blt-in = built-in (as in bookshelves)
Blt in = built in (as in 1990)
Brkfst area = breakfast area
Bsmt = basement
Crpt = carpet
Ceil fan = ceiling fan
Cntr tops = counter tops
Comm = community
Contemp = contemporary
Custom cab = custom cabinets
Cvd = covered (as in covered deck)
Down = downpayment
DR = dining room
Dbl garage = double garage
Exc cond or Ex cond or EC = excellent condition
Fin bsmt = finished basement
Flr plan = floor plan (as in 'open floor plan')
Flrs = floors
Fncd (or fen) yard = fenced yard
Fnt = front
Fplc or FP = fireplace
FR = family room
Frml LR = formal living room
Gar tub = garden tub
GR = great room (combination living room & family room)
Grt rm = great room
Great schls = great schools
Hdwd flrs = hardwood floors
Hm thter = home theater
HVAC = heating & air conditioning
Inspect. = inspection (often meaning "open house")
Isl kitchen = kitchen with an island
K (as in 3K sq ft) = thousand
Kit = kitchen

Kit w/brkfst bar = kitchen with breakfast bar
Lg = large
LR = living room
Lkview = lake view
Mi = miles
Mstr = master
N'hood = neighborhood
Owner fin = owner financing
Prof lndscpd = professionally landscaped
Prvt bkyd = private backyard
Pts = points (part of mortgage charge –see Chapter 6 for explanation)
Remod kit = remodeled kitchen
Renov = renovated
Schls = schools
SD = subdivision
Sep DR = separate dining room (as opposed to a LR/DR combination)
Sep in-law ste = separate in-law suite
Sf = square feet
S/T comm. = swim/tennis community
Sq ft = square feet
Sty = story
Sunrm = sunroom
Swim/tenn = pool/tennis courts in neighborhood
Terr = terrace
Trad = traditional
Vltd = vaulted
w/ = with
war = warranty
yd = yard

Interpreting Listing Terms

Here are what listings often *really* mean when they say:

- **"Handyman Special"** or **"fixer upper"** means there's a lot of work to do on the house.

- **"Cozy"** and **"charming"** usually means the house is relatively small.
- **"Agents protected"** means that although the house is not listed with a realtor, the owner will pay a commission to a real estate agent who sells the house—usually ½ the commission they would pay if they listed the house, since there's no commission for a listing agent.
- **"Great for first time buyer"** means it's a very modest property—don't expect anything big or fancy.

Now that you understand the terms and abbreviations typically used in real estate listings, you can use these to create or enhance your own listing, and understand other listings when you're looking for a new home to purchase.

Chapter 5

Evaluating Purchase
Offers And Negotiating The Sale

*It is said that "A bird in the hand is worth two in the bush". When you
get an offer on your home, you would be wise to seriously consider it,
because you never know how long it may be before the next offer will
come along.*

It's exciting to receive an offer to purchase your property, but it's vital to evaluate all of the details, as well as
how solid the offer is, before you decide how to respond.
In this chapter, we'll guide you through factors to consider
as you evaluate the offer. Also included are a few words on
negotiating, and what each party is responsible for, after an
agreement has been reached.

Purchase Offers

A written **Offer to Purchase** is usually completed by the
Buyer's Real Estate Agent or attorney. You will have a specified amount of time to evaluate the contract and respond
to it, often 48 to 72 hours. Obviously, a very important part
of the purchase offer is the price, but there are other very
important factors, too—some of which may make one offer
more attractive than another, regardless of which has the
higher price. The other elements are: the amount of earnest
money, contingencies (financing, physical inspection, sale
of another property, etc.), closing and possession dates,
and what is included in the sale. How urgent it is for you to

sell the house quickly, and whether, under current market conditions, you are likely to get another offer in the near future, should also be considered.

There are 3 ways you can respond to the Offer to Purchase:
1. Accept the contract "as is".
2. Respond with a counter-offer, including any changes which are important to you and which you hope the Buyers will accept.
3. Refuse the offer.

It's important to realize that once an offer is accepted and signed by all parties, it is a valid contract and legally binding on both the Buyer and the Seller. So be sure you understand the contract and everything that it says before you sign on the dotted line.

Here are some of the things you'll want to consider:

• <u>Price</u>: Are you pleased with the price the Buyer is offering?

You've already had a real estate agent do a CMA (Comparative Market Analysis) on your house to help determine a fair price for the property. Obviously, you'd like to get as much for the property as you can, but be aware that when the Buyer applies for the mortgage, the lender will require an appraisal. If the appraised value of the house is much lower than the amount the Buyer is trying to borrow, the lender will most likely refuse to approve the mortgage. At the other extreme, Agents are required to present an offer no matter how low it is. You can always counter at a higher price, so do take the time to consider the rest of the offer.

One caveat: If the offer is for the Listing Price or higher, and all other terms are as specified in your Listing, you may be obligated to pay the full Real Estate Commission, even if you choose to turn down the offer. The Real Estate Salespeople will have done their job and you signed a Listing Contract agreeing to pay them for doing it.

- <u>Earnest Money (Deposit)</u>: Are the Buyers putting down enough?

  The amount of earnest money attached to the offer indicates how committed the Buyer is to completing the transaction, since the funds would be forfeited if the Buyer backs out for a reason not provided for in the contract. In the event of an issue related to the contingencies—such as the physical inspection revealing major problems with the property that the Buyer is unwilling to accept—the earnest money would be returned. Discuss with your Real Estate Agent what an appropriate amount is for the earnest money, and under what conditions might it be returned. Earnest money is kept in an escrow/trust account and is applied toward the purchase price at the time of closing.

- <u>Inclusions</u>: Are you okay with any that have been added?

  There are things which are almost always included in the sale—if they're present in the house—such as the dishwasher, oven/range/stove, garbage disposal, tacked down carpeting, smoke detector, built-in shelving, garage door opener, sump pump(s), central air conditioning, central humidifier, ceiling fans, existing storm and screen (windows and doors), window blinds and shutters and everything else physically attached to the house.

  Items which vary sale-to-sale and are frequently negotiated include clothes washer and dryer, refrigerator,

TV antenna or satellite dish, and curtains, valances and draperies.

A Buyer may elect to include some furniture which is "made for the space", such as book cases, bar-stools, or even a patio set, in the offer, especially if the offer is close to the asking price. If the listing shows that the Seller is not including the washer, dryer and refrigerator, these items are almost always open for negotiation. If anything extra is included in the offer, the Seller can always counter, excluding those items. And the Buyer can always counter-offer including them again, if he's willing to take the risk of losing the deal. You just have to decide what's important to you, and whether you're willing to risk losing the contract by not accepting the terms that the Buyer is offering.

- <u>Closing & Possession Dates</u>: Are they acceptable to you?

    There's no right or wrong answer to this—it depends on the Buyer's and Seller's situations. It can make a big difference to either one if the other is flexible—so if the date is really important to you, have your real estate agent communicate that to the inter-ested Buyer's Agent. Generally, the Buyer's Agent will contact the Seller's Agent to let them know they are preparing an Offer to Purchase, so this will give your Agent an opportunity to relay this information.

    If an Offer to Purchase is presented with a date which is not of your choosing, then you have the option of being flexible (since it may be very important to the Buyers), countering with an alternate Closing Date, or modifying the Possession Date. This is an issue which can be discussed between the Real Estate Agents, to help you determine how to respond in writing.

Generally, possession takes place immediately after closing, but in some states, or if you specifically negotiate an alternate arrangement, the closing and possession dates can differ.

In some cases, the Buyer agrees to let the Seller pay rent to remain in the home for a given period of time. I don't generally recommend this due to the risks for the Buyer—although these risks can be minimized by keeping some of the Seller's funds in an escrow account, to be returned when he has moved out and the property proves to be free of damages unseen in the walk-thru or occurring after closing. Whether a family is trying to time their move to the beginning or end of the school year, waiting for their new home to be completed, or anxious to move out-of-town so the family can be reunited with the spouse who's already begun his new job there—closing and possession dates can be very important to both Buyers and Sellers.

- Home Owner's Warranty
  (*in some states these are called "Home Service Agreements" or "Home Protection Insurance"*)
  Even if you haven't already offered one, a Buyer may include a stipulation stating that the Seller is to provide a one-year Home Owner's Warranty Policy (provided by American Home Shield, or a number of other companies) including HVAC, and not to exceed $(*insert an appropriate top figure for what this should cost*). This is a policy which the Seller purchases (or the price can be shared between the Buyer and Seller), and which covers the Buyer for the first year of home ownership. It typically covers major systems (furnace, air conditioner, plumbing) and major appliances, and is not an unusual thing at all to ask for.

To check out what it should cost, go to American Home Shield (www.ahswarranty.com/), or the websites of other companies offering this coverage, and select "get a quote". You'll need to provide the zip code, whether square footage is less than 5,000 square feet or more, the year the home was built, and dwelling type—single family house, condominium, etc. To find other companies offering this type of coverage, search under "Home Owner Warranty". Purchasing the policy will make the Buyers less fearful that they'll have any sudden major expenses related to the house, and will make Sellers more confident that the Buyers won't come back to them if the furnace, for instance, suddenly stops working a week after closing.

- <u>Seller's Responsibilities</u>
  A good sales contract will include Seller's responsibilities, such as maintaining the property in its present condition, conveying good and marketable title to the property, providing a valid property disclosure (if required in the property's state) and a Termite letter in some states (see below).

- <u>Mortgage Contingency</u>: Is the Buyer planning to pay cash for the property?
  If the sale is contingent on obtaining a mortgage, is the Buyer pre-approved, or at least pre-qualified, for an appropriate size mortgage? Are the terms of the mortgage they're looking for (term and interest rate) realistic?

  It's very common for an Offer to Purchase to be contingent on the Buyer obtaining an unconditional written Mortgage Commitment for a certain amount of money, within a given amount of time, at an interest rate not to exceed a certain amount, at a term not to exceed a given number of years. It also specifies the size of the Buyers' down payment. Many of the newer sales contracts are much more specific about the type of loan one intends to apply for, also including whether the rate is fixed, adjustable or interest only. The Buyers are required to diligently pursue approval of this loan in good faith. If they are turned down, they need to immediately notify you (through your Real Estate Agent), and provide you with a letter from the lender denying the loan and detailing all of the reasons for the denial. This is to help prevent Buyers from using this contingency as a way out, if they get cold feet about proceeding with the transaction.

If a Buyer has been pre-approved, the chances of this contingency being satisfied are excellent; however it's not a done deal until the Buyer applies for THIS mortgage for THIS property, and gets approved. If you have a choice between two otherwise identical contracts, it would be a no-brainer to accept the one where the Buyers are paying cash (in which case, there would be no Mortgage Contingency), or lacking that, one in which the Buyers have been pre-approved for a mortgage. Of course, you would stipulate that a Buyer paying cash would provide proof within a short time frame that he has the required funds.

- Attorney Review
  Often, an Offer to Purchase will state that the respective parties have five days in which their attorneys may review the contract, and approve, disapprove, or make modifications to the contract, other than the purchase price. If an agreement is not made within a given period, say ten days after signing of the contract, then the Offer is null and void and earnest money is refunded.

- Home Inspection
  A Buyer may include in the Offer to Purchase that within a specified time (often five days) they may have

a professional Home Inspector examine the property in depth. They then have the right to request that you (the Seller) repair any defects in the property noted by the Inspector. There are a lot of important things which may be revealed in this inspection, such as mildew in the attic from a leaky roof, stucco which is about to separate from the exterior walls, foundation problems, improvements not built to code, electrical connections which were done incorrectly (probably by a non-professional), and other things which may not be obvious to most of us. The Inspector will also undoubtedly find items which are minor, but helpful for the Buyer to know as they become the owners of the home.

Following an Inspection, if there is anything of significance found (translation: anything important enough for the Buyers to request that the Sellers fix, or anything which makes them feel that they should no longer purchase the property), the Buyers then provide the Seller with a copy of the Inspection Report within the amount of days stated in the contract. The Buyers and Sellers, usually through their Real Estate agents, then negotiate the resolution of any issues which arise through this inspection—which ones the Sellers will fix within a given amount of time or compensate the Buyers so they can fix it after closing, and which the Buyers agree to live with. If the parties aren't able to agree, or if issues are revealed which make the property unacceptable to the Buyers, then the contract is null & void, and earnest money is refunded. A slightly longer time period may be allowed for certain testing (such as lead or radon). Be sure to read the fine print. **This is not a way for Buyers to get out of a contract when they've just changed their mind**. There have to be significant problems in major components of the property.

If the Offer to Purchase doesn't include a limitation on how much you might be required to spend on these repairs, you might want to counter with a limitation, such as $500 or $1,000. This may or may not be typical in your state, but it's something to consider.

Reasonably-timed visits to the house are usually also included, so Buyers can bring in a decorator to order window coverings, for instance, or measure room sizes to verify whether furniture will fit in given places. There shouldn't be many of these, and they should be arranged at everyone's convenience. Being considerate not only makes everyone's lives easier, but if issues arise (as they often do, in a home sale transaction), they will be resolved much more easily and equitably if you haven't already alienated the other party.

An inspection (usually called a "walk-through") is also done by the Buyers immediately prior to closing. This is mainly done to assure Buyers that the property has not been altered since the Offer to Purchase was accepted, and that there is no damage which was previously hidden.

- Appraisal
  Especially if the Buyer is going to be applying for a loan, the sale should be contingent on the property appraising at a price greater than, or equal to, the purchase price of the offer. If it appraises for less, then a loan may be difficult to obtain.

- Termite Inspection
  In areas where termites are an issue, the Sellers will usually be required to provide proof of inspection by a licensed pest control operator, showing no termite infestation. If infestation does exist, or has in the

past, the treatment needs to be documented and any damage to the property needs to be repaired and disclosed to the Buyer. There are time limits for all of these actions to take place. If a recent inspection has already been performed, the report can be provided when the contract is accepted.

- **"Contingent on the Sale Of"**
  It is very common for an Offer to Purchase to state that the offer is "Contingent on the Sale of" the Buyers' current home.

  If the offer is contingent on the sale of another property (usually their current house), there are many things to consider.
  - Is there already a sales contract on the property? (If so, it's appropriate to inquire about the details in order to determine how solid that contract is.)
  - If not, is their house on the market now?
  - If their house isn't on the market, when do they realistically expect to list it? (hopefully within a week or so)
  - If it is on the market, how long has it been listed for sale? (very long is not encouraging)
  - Is it listed at a reasonable price considering its location, style and condition?
  - Is the market good right now for the type of house at that location?

  If you're listed with a good real estate salesperson, she will consider the answers to these questions, as well as your current selling market, and help you determine whether this offer is worth tying up your property. If you do make a counter-offer on a contract with a contingency on the sale of another property, I strongly suggest you include a **3-Day Release Clause**, often referred to as a "Kick-out" clause. (see below)

- <u>Timing of Contingency Clause Removals</u>
  Does the contract require the Buyer to act on any contingencies within a reasonable amount of time? This is often 10 days to apply for a loan, and 10 days in which to provide a copy of any inspection reports, along with any requests for repair or replacement. If the time periods are much longer than this, you risk your property being tied up for too long, while waiting to see if the contract is a solid one.

Additional Response Options

- <u>3-Day Release Clause</u>: an important item to add to a Counter-Offer

  If you receive an Offer to Purchase containing a "Contingency on the Sale of" the Buyer's current property, you'll want to consider the factors above, regarding how solid an offer it is. If you're not sure another Buyer will be waiting in the wings, and you feel there is a good chance the prospective Buyer's property will sell in a reasonable amount of time, a more conservative approach than just accepting the contract, would be to counter with a "3-Day Release Clause". With this clause in your amended contract, if you receive another offer which doesn't contain a "Contingency on the Sale of", you advise Buyer #1, who now has 72 hours (basically 3 days) in which to remove her contingency. If she does remove it, she proceeds with the purchase at the agreed-upon terms and price in the original contract, even if this price is lower than that offered by Buyer #2. If Buyer #1 sends the Seller notice that they will not be proceeding, Seller is free to proceed with the sale to Buyer #2.

  Here's why it's risky to accept a contract without including the 3-Day Release Clause: When you have a signed contract on a property, regardless of what contingencies it contains, your property will be classified as "under contract". Agents can tell whether a 3-Day Release Clause exists, and usually don't mind showing properties under these conditions. Without it, although technically the property may be shown to other prospective Buyers, generally it isn't, because real estate agents would rather their clients find a house which is available to purchase, and which can likely proceed to closing without a lengthy delay. (That's how Real Estate agents make their money, after all.) Buyers who need to buy in a given time frame will also want to focus on houses which are available. If they made an offer on a house with a contract already existing, without a kick-out clause, they might have to wait until the time limit on any contingency expires (30 days? 60?) before they would have a chance.

Without a back-up contract, if the time limit on the contingency expires and the Buyers have not sold their property, your listing is back on the active market. This is not a great thing because the longer your house is on the market, the more difficult it is to sell and the lower a price you're likely to get for it. So, the safe thing—if you feel that the offer is otherwise good—is to accept a contract Contingent on the Sale of another property, including the 3-Day Release clause.

- If you are in a "hot" market, and know that lots of buyers will be competing for your property, you may want to counter the offer *removing* any contingencies you don't want to live with, and altering the sales price or any other terms to which you object. Your prospective buyer may, or may not, be in a position where she is able to purchase your home while still owning another one or be willing to accept your changes. But she can always counter the counter-offer, putting the conditions back in. Often, verbal negotiations between the two agents, each communicating with their client for responses, will result in an agreement and then the final contract is prepared and signed by all parties. Be aware, though, that once you have formally countered an offer, it doesn't necessarily mean that the prospective Buyer will continue negotiations. They may decide that they no longer want the house, for any reason, and just walk away. You have to be willing to take that chance if you choose to counter an offer rather than accept it as written.

Negotiating

There are whole books devoted to negotiating, and I wouldn't presume to cover the topic in a few paragraphs here. The purpose of this chapter is to make you aware of some aspects which pertain particularly to buying and selling houses and condominiums.

One thing which can be helpful is learning what is motivating the other party. Have the Buyers been transferred from out-of-state and are they anxious to get settled into a new home before school starts? If so, the closing date may be more important to them than getting a better price. Would this be their first home and it would really help them financially if the refrigerator, washer, and dryer were included in the sale, so the cost of the appliances would be included in the mortgage and they would have less "out of pocket" expenses? It doesn't hurt to gently explore what is important to people you're negotiating with, without giving away your bottom line. A great sale is when both parties feel they have gotten what is important to them.

It is also said that, in negotiations, "He who cares least wins". If a Buyer indicates that she's in love with this house and absolutely has to have it, you have a strong hint that she's not likely to hold out for the best deal she can get, because she won't want to take the chance of losing the property. Whatever your negotiating style, consider what is important to you and think through each response (within a reasonable time frame) to make sure you're comfortable with all of the contract terms.

After a Contract Has Been Signed by all Parties

First, breathe a sigh of relief that you're well on your way to completing the sale of your home.

Here's what's next:

- Sellers' Obligations
  What you need to do now depends upon the terms of your contract. Some things you might be required to do are:

  1. Obtain a termite letter or report. Call your pest control company (or select one, if you don't currently have a termite policy) and set up a termite inspection. Let them know you are selling the house. They will be familiar with what is required and should be able to set up the inspection soon. Hopefully they will find no active infestations and no damage, and will provide you with the proper document attesting to that. If they do find a problem, you will need to have the infestation treated and have any damage repaired. You will need to disclose this information to any potential Buyers, and your real estate salesperson can help you do this appropriately.

  2. Cooperate with the Buyers as they make appointments to have the Home Inspection performed, and make any other necessary visits to the property.

3. <u>Continue to keep up the property</u> by mowing the lawn, repairing anything which breaks, and generally taking good care of things.

4. <u>Move forward with your search for a new home</u>, if you haven't already found one.

5. <u>Clear up any liens or other encumbrances</u> on the title to the property prior to closing. Some of these you may not know about until the title search is performed.

6. <u>Purchase a Home Owner's Warranty for the Buyers</u>, if the contract calls for you to provide one. You can initiate this once the Buyer's financing has been approved and you know when the closing date will be. The closing date will become the effective date of the policy.

• <u>Buyers' Obligations</u>
These are some of the things the Buyers will need to do in order to fulfill possible requirements of the contract:

1. Set up a Home Inspection, if included in contract terms.

2. Apply for a mortgage (unless they're paying cash).

3. Obtain a Homeowner's Insurance policy (required if they're getting a mortgage; certainly advisable even if they're not).

Chapter 6

Mortgages

"When you look for a mortgage, it's not just the monthly payment you need to look at. The type of mortgage, interest rate, closing costs, and dealing with a reputable company are just as important."

In this chapter, we will discuss sensible borrowing, types of mortgages, how to shop for the best terms, rate locks, and what information you'll need to gather for the mortgage application. At the end of the chapter is a glossary of some common mortgage terms, entitled *Financial Terms You'll Want to Know*.

You may think it odd that this chapter is placed *before* the chapter entitled "Finding a New Home", but there is a good reason for this. First, you will have a better idea of how much you will want to spend on a new home after you've read this chapter and thought about it. Second, you'll be at a distinct advantage if you begin your house hunting with a Pre-Approved Loan. Hopefully, you have already viewed your credit reports and done your homework to improve your credit score, if needed. *See "Things To Do" in Chapter 1.* Your credit score may affect the interest rate and terms available to you, and this is the time for you to find out how that pertains to you and your potential mortgage loan.

How Much Should You Borrow?

You need to decide for yourself what size mortgage you can afford and are willing to take on. Members of the housing and mortgage industry will sometimes be happy to have you borrow significantly more than you really should. It's not fun being "house poor"—spending so much on your mortgage payments that you have little left for discretionary spending (such as decorating, vacations, clothing, recreation, eating out and entertainment) and savings. Remember that when you own a home there are additional expenses, such as homeowner's insurance, property taxes, home maintenance and, in some cases, Homeowner's Association (HOA) dues. Make sure that you will be able to afford the monthly payments easily enough, so that you will have the additional funds with which to pay for expected and unexpected expenses (medical, auto and home repairs, appliance repair/replacement), and especially so that you don't risk losing the house or compromising your quality of life too severely.

Sometimes people think it makes good financial sense to take a large mortgage in order to get the deduction on their taxes for the interest they'll pay. Here's an example which will make it clear that this is not a good reason to buy more house than you need:

You have a monthly mortgage payment of $1000, approximately $950 of which is interest in the beginning years of a loan. If you are in a 30% tax bracket (state and federal combined), your annual picture looks like this:

You spend on interest: 12 (months) x $950 = $11,400
You get a tax deduction of .3 x $11,400 = $3,420
Therefore you have spent $7,980 in after tax income ($11,400 - $3,420) to save $3,420 in taxes.

If this is getting you the house that you want, need, and can afford, that's great. However, if you are stretching for more house because it seems like a good idea to have a bigger tax deduction, you are kidding yourself, because it is costing you money big time. Better you should spend your extra funds on furniture, landscaping, improvements—and especially saving for retirement and your children's education.

How to Shop for a Mortgage

Explore getting a home loan from multiple sources, so that you get the best available loan which is appropriate for you. This may vary according to your credit score, financial circumstances, needs and goals. There's more to compare than just the interest rate, and you certainly don't want to shop for a mortgage or a house by "monthly payment" alone. Know what to look at. *See "Comparing Loans" below.*

The sources you can consult include:
- Direct lenders (such as your bank or credit union, or a mortgage banker)
- Mortgage brokers (who have many lenders from which to choose).
- Sellers (sometimes the owner of the house you're purchasing may be willing to offer financing to you, in order to sell the property sooner.)

Internet mortgage providers often charge the least for their services, but you'll need to be cautious. *See "If You Are Applying for a Mortgage Online" below.*

Very important! <u>Anytime you apply for a loan, the company you apply to will look at your credit report.</u> Multiple credit checks alone can impact your credit rating, so <u>be very selective when you authorize a credit check</u>. Also, be aware that credit bureaus have been known to sell your information to mortgage companies as soon as a credit check is run on you for a mortgage. Do not assume the companies which contact you at this time are all good ones.

Mortgage Brokers usually act as independent contractors, bringing borrowers and lenders together in order to originate a loan. They typically work with the borrower to determine what type of loan is most appropriate. Then they consider a wide range of products and recommend the one or ones they feel will work best. They take the loan application, process the loan, act as liaison between the Borrower and Lender, and guide the Borrower through the process. Because Mortgage Brokers provide services for both parties, they are often paid for the appropriate service by each party. It is not uncommon, however, for the lender to pay all of the Mortgage Broker's fee. If the Borrower does need to pay it, the Mortgage Broker's fee is paid at closing as part of the Closing Costs. If you work directly with a lender, they may charge you a similar amount and call it an Origination Fee or Discount Point. It usually costs about the same amount to obtain a loan using a Mortgage Broker, direct lender, or other loan originator. What's important is to work with an individual or company you trust, select the right type of loan for you, and to compare the terms of the loans that you're considering.

How do you know if a Mortgage Broker is a good one to work with? An excellent way is to be referred by past customers whom you know and respect. Another is to find out if he's a member of The National Association of Mortgage Brokers (NAMB). Members must be licensed mortgage brokers, and must adhere to NAMB's Code of Ethics and Best Business practices. NAMB also has an education certification department and 3 levels of certifications. Check out their website www.namb.org for more information.

Investigate to make sure mortgage companies and mortgage brokers are licensed to do business in your state by contacting the proper authority in your state. In most cases, it's the state banking authority. You can get this information online at www.consumeraction.gov/state.shtml or www. consumeraction.gov/banking.shtml OR you can search online for (_enter your state_) "state banking department". In California, for instance, enter "California State Banking Department". You may find additional helpful information on these websites, besides being able to do a licensing search. However, be aware that in some cases, it is not the state banking department which supervises mortgage companies and mortgage brokers. You might also want to check the Better Business Bureau (www.bbb.org) for reports on specific mortgage brokers, financial institutions or other loan originators.

If you are applying for a mortgage online it is _especially_ important to make sure who you're dealing with _before_ providing your personal information. According to Marc Savitt, a Mortgage Broker and Past President of the NAMB Board of Directors, there are two concerns:

1. It may not be a legitimate company, but just a shell, planning to steal your identification.
2. It may be a legitimate company but not give the proper level of service. For instance, if you apply for a mortgage but they don't do the necessary follow-up, the time allotment to get mortgage approval may expire before a mortgage is granted. Now you have no mortgage, and you could lose your sales contract unless you can convince the Seller to grant an extension and you're able to secure another mortgage within the new time frame.

So if you are considering applying for a mortgage online, be sure to first check on the company as indicated above. Also, it's best if the company is headquartered in your state or a state near to you. Those farther away may be more likely to be problematic.

There are some very good banks, mortgage companies and other organizations online, which make the application process convenient and efficient. In some cases, the first time you'll need to see the mortgage broker is at the closing, having dealt with some issues over the phone and by signing the necessary paperwork via a delivery service. Whether you work with someone online or in person, make sure you are dealing with a trustworthy company.

Types of Loans

- Fixed rate mortgage: The interest rate remains the same for the life of the loan (usually 30 or 15 years). Although a fixed rate 15-year mortgage will have monthly payments higher than that of a 30-year mortgage, it will have a lower interest rate, and will cost you a LOT less interest over the life of the loan. For instance, a $200,000 loan paid at 5.999% over 30 years will cost approximately $231,631 for interest (not counting the principal you also pay); the same loan amount and interest rate over 15 years would include "only" $103,768 in interest payments. Note also that rates are almost always lower if the loan term is shorter.

- Adjustable rate mortgage (ARM): after an initial fixed-rate period (of 1 month to 10 years), the interest rate can fluctuate at various intervals over the life of the loan. A 5/1 ARM, for instance, has a fixed rate for 5 years and the rate is adjusted annually after that. In other words, the interest rate—and thus, your monthly payment—can go up or down, depending on a specified index, such as Treasury Bills or the Cost of Funds Index. Information about the indexes is available at www.infotrak.com. The initial rates for ARM's are almost always lower than the rates for fixed rate loans, but over time they may become much more expensive.

To compare various ARMs, look at:
- What Financial Index the rate is based on (and how much margin is added to it when they compute your new interest rate)
- How often the rates are adjusted

    ☛ What are the rate caps (how much can the rate go up each time, and what is the highest it can be during the entire loan period)?

    ☛ Is it possible to convert to a fixed loan? (if so, when and what are the details?)

- Balloons: Usually 5-Year or 7-Year Balloons, a.k.a. 5/25 or 7/23 Balloons, these are amortized over 30 years, so are similar to 30-year-fixed rate mortgages, as far as the monthly payments are concerned. The difference is that after 5 or 7 years, assuming you still own the home, the entire loan balance is due OR there may be an option to convert to a fixed rate for the remainder of the 30 years. This would be at a slightly higher interest rate than the current 30-year fixed rate, and would only be available if this were still your primary residence. If that option is not available or attractive, then you would need to refinance at whatever interest rates are available at the time. Since interest rates for a balloon mortgage will be slightly lower than that for a 30-year fixed rate, it can be a good choice for those who plan to sell the home before the balloon is due. It is a poor choice for those who may still be in the house and might have trouble qualifying for a new loan at that time, unless the option to convert is assured. Also, if interest rates are higher when the loan is converted, your monthly payments will go up, as will the cost of the loan.

- Interest Only Loans: None of the monthly payment goes towards the principal—it only pays interest on the loan—so unless property values increase, you're not building equity in the home or paying off the loan. And if property values go down, you will owe more than your house is worth. This happened to a lot of homeowners in recent times, and is commonly referred to as being "upside down". There may be specific situations in which this type of loan makes sense, but for most borrowers: think twice. If this is the only type of loan you can afford, perhaps you need to wait awhile until you've been able to save up for a down payment. Then, hopefully, you will also be able to manage a monthly payment which will include some amount towards the principal.

The interest rate for a fixed rate mortgage will always be higher than the interest rate for an adjustable rate mortgage. If interest rates go up, the financial institution holding the mortgage can raise the rate on an ARM, but they're stuck with the rate of the fixed rate mortgage. If you're planning to stay in the house long-term, it's probably advantageous to get a fixed-rate mortgage. Assuming your credit is good, if interest rates decline significantly, you can probably refinance your mortgage to take advantage of the lower rates. In the meantime, you're protected from rising monthly payments (and possibly much higher costs over the life of the loan) in case interest rates go up.

Government Mortgages

You may be eligible for a mortgage loan that is insured or guaranteed by a federal government agency, such as the FHA (Federal Housing Administration), VA (U.S. Department of Veterans Affairs) or the Rural Development Housing program. Fannie Mae (the Federal National Mortgage Association) may also be helpful in securing your loan. These loans may be advantageous by requiring little or no down payment, more lenient qualification requirements, and/or no PMI (private mortgage insurance) included in your monthly payments. If you believe you may be eligible for one of these programs, by all means check it out so you know all of your choices. Websites are listed at the end of this chapter, under *Financial Terms You'll Want To Know*.

Conventional loans

Mortgages which are not government mortgages (see paragraph above).

Comparing Loans

See **Financial Terms You'll Want to Know** at the end of this chapter, for more information about words, phrases and abbreviations included in this section.

- Rates and fees can change daily, so compare terms which are available on the same day.

- Decide what type of loan is most appropriate for you, and then look at interest rates and APRs, points (if any), and an estimate of closing costs for that type of loan with a variety of lenders.

- If comparing ARMS, look at the margin each lender will add to the index in order to determine your future interest rates.

- Don't select a loan based solely on the monthly payments you'll make when you first get the loan. Consider the long-term cost and increasing payments.

- Even a small difference in mortgage rate can mean a huge savings over the life of a loan.

- Make sure there is no Prepayment Penalty!

- Verify that you're looking at a loan from a reputable mortgage company.

- Review the "Good Faith Estimate of Closing Costs" which your potential lender can supply, and question anything you don't understand or think you shouldn't be paying. Some items which may be negotiable are:

title insurance (especially if the Seller has owned the home for less than 10 years), the originator's fee (if any), and the amount you pay each month into an escrow account for taxes and insurance (if required).

A great resource is available at www.hud.gov. Select "Buy a Home", "Shop for a Loan" and "Looking for the Best Mortgage". You'll be able to view a brochure which contains a lot of helpful information, and also a Mortgage Shopping Worksheet.

Rate Locks

Interest rates are set when the mortgage is finalized (generally at closing) unless the rate is locked in prior to that day. You can choose to "lock in" the interest rate when you apply for the mortgage, or if you decide to let it "float" (not lock it in), you may be allowed to lock it in at any time before closing. Your decision should be based on whether you think interest rates are going up or down over the coming weeks. Obviously, all other things being equal, the lower the interest rate you get, the less the loan will cost you. Some lenders charge a fee to lock in a rate, but check around to see if that is common practice. If another lending institution offers a similar loan package without charging extra to lock in a rate, you may decide to use them instead.

Mortgage brokers cannot commit to lock in a rate—it must be locked in by a lender. Also, there is often a lag of several days before the lock request is granted, during which time wholesale prices can go up or down.

If you do decide to lock in a rate:
(a) get it in writing, signed and dated.
(b) make sure it's locked in for a long enough period for your loan to close.

If you only get a lock for 30 days but closing doesn't take place until 60 days later, the rate lock was meaningless.

What You'll Need For the Loan Application

This has changed quite a bit over the last few years. Previously, you'd expect to meet in person to complete a loan application, and you'd be required to bring cancelled checks (for the last 12 months' rent or mortgage payments), multiple pay stubs, as well as a slew of additional paperwork. Credit Reports and electronic information have altered things dramatically. At this point, you may choose to apply in person, but by far the majority of mortgage applications are taken over the phone or via the internet. Applications made over the internet are often followed up by a few additional questions over the phone.

Some of the items you may need to provide are:

- Payment for the application fee, appraisal and credit report
- Driver's license (or other government-issued photo ID)
- Your social security number
- W-2's for the last 2 years
- Pay stubs for the last month
- Bank statements (all pages) for the last 2 months, for all of your accounts (to verify your assets)
- Sales Contract for the property you're purchasing
- Property address of home you're selling, if any (and sales contract, if you already have one)
- Employment information for the past 2 years (name, address, phone of employer) for you and co-borrower
- Liabilities, including credit cards, car loans, home equity loans, etc. (Account numbers, addresses, and current balances)
- A list of other assets, including rental income, stocks, bonds, real estate and automobiles owned, and so on
- Phone numbers for your attorney and realtor
- Proof of last 12 months rent or mortgage payments
- Business tax returns, if you own your own business

- Divorce decrees and separation agreement, if applicable
- Bankruptcy papers, including discharge papers, if applicable

Among other things, you will be asked how you plan to hold title. There are quite a few ways, and they differ from state to state. Some of the possible ways to hold title are: Tenancy in Common, Joint Tenancy, Tenants By the Entirety, Title in Trust, and in states which have community property laws, there are Community Property and Community Property with the Right of Survivorship. You may want to consult with your attorney to determine which option is the best for your situation in the state where the property is located.

If you aren't totally comfortable with any loan document, when you get them, have a Real Estate attorney look it over <u>before</u> you sign the papers. **Never sign blank forms.** Ask questions until you understand everything. You should get and keep copies of everything you sign. Request that you receive the Closing Statement 24 hours before Closing so that you have time to review it thoroughly and minimize any last-minute surprises.

Financial Terms You'll Want to Know

Adjustable Rate Mortgage (ARM): the interest rate—and thus, your monthly payment—can go up or down, depending on a specified index, such as Treasury Bills or the Cost of Funds Index.

Amortization Schedule: A timetable for paying off a mortgage loan. It shows the amount of each payment, the amounts which are applied to principal and to interest, and the remaining balance after each payment is made. There are many amortization calculators online; just search for "amortization calculator" or "amortization schedule".

Annual Percentage Rate (APR): Interest rate which shows the cost of the mortgage as an effective yearly rate. This may be higher than the stated or advertised interest rate, because it takes into account the costs of the mortgage, including points, origination fees, and certain other charges paid at closing. When comparing APR's, make sure the APR for each loan includes the same items and keep in mind that some of these charges are paid up front rather than spread over the life of the loan.

Bridge Loan (a.k.a. "Swing Loan"): A short-term loan often secured by the Seller's current home, used to close on the property the Seller is buying, before the sale of the current home. Sometimes employers relocating employees will provide a bridge loan to facilitate the move prior to the sale of the old home.

Buydown: A lowering of the interest rate for several years at the beginning of the loan, for an additional charge. When that time period is up, the interest rate reverts to a higher rate.

Clear Title: Ownership that is free of liens, defects, or other legal encumbrances.

Closing: This is when the mortgage documents are signed, funds are disbursed, and the property is transferred to the Buyer. Also called **escrow** or **settlement** in some areas of the country. In some states, the Buyer and Seller do not sit down together to accomplish this.

Closing costs: A Good Faith Estimate must be provided to potential borrowers. More and more companies are guaranteeing the maximum amount of closing costs in writing. Closing costs include the application fee, survey fee, recording fees, credit report fees, appraisal fee, title insurance, state and local taxes, and more. If you compare closing costs from different lenders, be sure they've included the exact same items (and not neglected, for instance, city taxes). Also important to compare is Line 901, the Daily Interest figure. This figure can vary by thousands of dollars, depending on what day during the month they assume closing will take place. If you close in the beginning of the month, you'll pay 30 days of interest; on the last day of the month, you'll pay the least amount. Ultimately, you'll be paying the same amount of interest; so you only need to be aware of this when you're comparing closing costs, so that you're comparing apples to apples.

Escrow: (see Closing)

Escrow Account: There are 2 kinds of Escrow Accounts associated with home ownership. (1)Money held by a neutral 3rd party (often a real estate broker) prior to closing. An example is the Earnest Money you put down when you agree to purchase a home. (2)A lender may require that your monthly payments include an extra amount to be set aside in an account for you and the money is used to pay your property tax and homeowner's insurance bills when they come due.

Equity: The value of a property minus any loans (including a mortgage) or liens against it. For example, if your house is worth $200,000 but you have a $120,000 mortgage on it, the equity you have in the house is $80,000.

Fannie Mae & **Freddie Mac:** These are two companies which don't lend money directly, but work with lenders to help ensure that money is available and affordable for low, moderate, and middle-income families. Fannie Mae is a nickname for the Federal National Mortgage Association; Freddie Mac is the Federal Home Mortgage Corporation. They are owned and operated by shareholders, but financially protected by the U.S. Government. For more information, see www.fanniemae.com or www. freddiemac.com.

FHA (Federal Housing Administration): The part of the U.S. Department of Housing and Urban Development (HUD) which insures mortgages and loans made by private lenders to Americans with lower incomes purchasing modestly priced homes. For more information, see www.hud.gov.

Financial Index: Most Adjustable Rate Mortgage rates are computed according to one of these major indexes:
(1) One-year Treasury Bill
(2) 11th District Cost of Funds Index (COFI), or
(3) London Interbank Offered Rate (LIBOR).

First Mortgage: A mortgage that is the primary lien against a property (as opposed to a Second Mortgage, such as a Home Equity Loan).

Interest: The fee charged for borrowing money.

Interest rate: The amount you pay for the use of the lender's money. When quoted as an APR (annual percentage rate), it describes the interest rate for the whole year (annualized), including any fees.

Lien: When a contractor (such as a roofer or a company putting an addition onto your house) invests in a job, they may put a lien on your house until they have been paid in full. It's important to make sure contractors remove any liens once the job has been completed and they have been paid in full. Liens may also be placed on property due to unpaid taxes, unpaid Home Owners Association fees; unpaid child support (in some states), unpaid debts, or for a divorced spouse's financial interest in the property. Liens will show up during a title search and may interrupt the sale of the property.

Lease-Option (a.k.a. lease-with-an-option-to-buy): Sellers rent a property for a certain amount of time, giving the renter the option to purchase the home for an agreed option price, within a specified period of time. Usually, part of each rental payment goes towards their future down payment and, possibly, closing costs.

Lease-Purchase: The same as a Lease-Option, but in this case the Renters are obligated to purchase the home under the agreed-upon terms.

Loan Origination Fee: A fee to cover some of the costs of processing a loan, such as taking the loan application, processing and underwriting the application, and closing the loan. It is often expressed in points. One point = 1% of the loan amount.

Margin: The amount a lender adds to an index, when determining the interest rate for an adjustable mortgage.

Mortgage Banker: A company, individual, or institution that recommends the best loan they can obtain for a borrower. They then originate, underwrite, and close the loan. They may retain and service the loan, but usually they sell the servicing rights to another financial institution.

Mortgage Broker: An individual who shops around for the best loan for a borrower, and brings the borrower and lender together. The mortgage broker originates and closes the loan, but does not underwrite or service it.

Mortgage Insurance: Protects the lender against a loss if the borrower defaults on the loan. This is usually required when the down payment on a house is less than 20%. You may be allowed to discontinue it when your loan balance is reduced to approximately 80% of the value of the house. *Do not confuse this with Mortgage Life Insurance, which pays off a mortgage in the event of a borrower's death.*

Originator: Anyone in the mortgage industry who takes your mortgage application.

Points (a.k.a. Discount Points): A fee paid by the borrower to the lender to reduce the interest rate on the loan. One point = 1% of the loan amount. This fee is usually paid in cash at closing. It's important to factor in this up-front fee in, when comparing loans, since the fee is not spread over the life of the loan.

Power of Attorney: A legal document which allows one person to act on behalf of another. It can grant complete authority (such as when an elderly parent can no longer take care of her own financial affairs) or can be limited to a certain task (such as completing a real estate transaction) or period of time.

Prepayment Penalty: A special fee or penalty if you pay off the loan early (such as when you sell your house or want to refinance before the life of the loan is completed). I know of no reason why you should need to accept a Prepayment Penalty clause in your mortgage loan, and we have never done it.

Private Mortgage Insurance (PMI): See *Mortgage Insurance*

Rate Lock: Locking in a specific interest rate (and points, if appropriate) for 30, 45, or 60 days so that the interest rate doesn't fluctuate with the market until closing. A rate lock is binding on the lender and the borrower, but make sure it's in writing and that it's for a long enough period of time so that you can close on the home sale before it expires.

Rural Development Housing (a.k.a. Rural Housing Service): A service of the US Department of Agriculture, which provides mortgages for eligible moderate to very low income rural homebuyers. For more information, go to www.rurdev. usda.gov/rhs/ and select "Single Family Housing".

Second Mortgage: A loan which is taken after a first mortgage, using the same property as collateral. Usually it has a higher interest rate than the first mortgage, and is often taken out for home improvements, debt consolidation, or emergencies.

Settlement: (see *Closing*)

Title: A legal document, which is evidence of a right of ownership to property.

Title Insurance: Protection against loss from any title disputes which may arise, and any liens which might affect the property's ownership. The insurance protects the lender against claims plus any legal fees which arise from these problems. The premium is a one-time fee, which is paid at closing. All mortgage lenders require that you purchase this in the amount of the loan. To protect yourself, you would need an Owner's Title Policy in the full amount of the property's value.

Title Search: Research of public records to verify that the Seller is the legal owner of the property and has the right to sell it, and to determine if there are any liens or claims against the property.

Underwriting: In real estate transactions, this is the process of evaluating a borrower's credit history, ability to repay the loan, and value of the property involved.

VA Loans: A mortgage loan guaranteed by the U.S. Department of Veterans Affairs. For more information, or to find out if you qualify for a V.A. loan, go to www.homeloans. va.gov or phone 1-888-244-6711. VA loans require low or no down payments.

Chapter 7

Finding A New Home

"How do we determine what neighborhoods to look in for a new home? Should we rent first, to get a 'feel' for the area? The new area may have different housing prices than what we're used to, so how do we figure out what price range we should we be looking at? Are there special things to look for, or to avoid, in a home?"

In this chapter, you'll learn the pros and cons of renting vs. buying when you move to a new area. We'll walk through determining your price range, what to look for in your new home, and some things to avoid. You'll find hints on how to remember the "good ones" after a whole day of viewing houses and, in the Appendix, you'll find a form to help you do it.

Should We Rent in the New Area First?

Some people think it's a good idea to rent an apartment or a house for awhile, as you get to know the area. Then you can begin to search for a home after you have a better idea of where you'll want to live. This may work for you, but we have chosen not to do that for a number of reasons.

1. If the place you rent is smaller than the one you're leaving, chances are you'll have to put some of your things into storage temporarily. While I'm sure there are a number of wonderful and dry storage facilities around, and it's a great solution for certain situations, we have certainly heard stories of people whose

possessions have been damaged (usually due to water) while stored, or lost—either in the process of moving from their old home into storage or from storage into their new home. Problems are more likely to happen when you move some of your things into one place and some into another, because it's easy to lose track of what arrived and what didn't. (Use stickers of 2 very different colors on items you're moving, to indicate which place they're going to, and hopefully you'll avoid this problem.) Also, if your possessions don't fill up the van, the moving company may put one or more other shipments onto the same van and despite their best efforts, it's possible for them to deliver a few of one person's items to another person. If you're not reviewing the items going into storage on that end, you're less likely to realize something is missing. So if you can possibly manage it, I suggest you move directly from one home into another permanent home.

Also, be aware that when items are placed in storage, you are responsible for storage charges, warehouse valuation coverage and additional delivery charges when your things are moved from the storage facility into your new home. Some of these charges vary, depending on whether the shipment is considered temporary "storage-in-transit" or permanent "long term storage".

2. If you have school-age children, they will most likely be attending school while you're in temporary quarters. If you're building a house, and would be renting temporarily, you can most likely start them in the school they'll attend when you move into your new home. Then, the transition will be a lot easier when you're finally settled. However, if you're planning to take some time to get to know the area before deciding where to buy a home, that means your children may be starting in one school now and will have to switch

to another one a few months or a year or two down the road. It may be very difficult for them to adjust to a new school district, new home, new neighbors and new friends so soon after the last move. It will lengthen the amount of time their lives are disrupted and will be almost like a whole new move. Even if you're only planning to move 20 minutes away, although they may get together a few times with their "old" new friends over the first few months, it would be unusual for them to maintain the relationships long-term if their friends attend different schools and after-school activities. We have always chosen to avoid making our own children do it twice in such a short time span. We just make the best decision we can, in selecting the area in which we want to live, and have found a house in that area.

3. If you count on having the tax deduction a mortgage provides, obviously you would miss out on that during the time you're renting. You may want to discuss this with your accountant to assess the impact this would make.

If you still feel that renting a home would be best for you and your mate or family, you may still want to do a short version of looking at houses to determine what area you think you'll be most comfortable living in. Then you can look for a rental in your desired area and begin building a relationship with that community. A good real estate salesperson will understand that this time would be well-spent with you, because if you work well together, you're likely to use her when you decide you're ready to purchase a home there.

Before You Begin Househunting

Consider what you're looking for in a new home. Sit down and make a list of what you NEED in a home and what you WANT.

What do you need to have in a home? Obviously you don't NEED a 2-story colonial with a side-entry garage, 5 bedrooms, 5 baths and a finished walk-out basement. But for this exercise, the question is: "Considering the financial situation you're in, what are the essential things you're looking for in your new home?" How many bedrooms and baths must be in an affordable home before you would accept this move? Is a basement essential? Must you have a first-floor master and/or guest bedroom? Is Central Air Conditioning vital? (In some homes it may not be possible to install it, or it may be very costly to do so.) Is it important to be in a subdivision...or to NOT be in a subdivision? Must you have a family room *and* a formal living room? Is it important for you to have a gas stove (versus electric) in the kitchen? (If a house is all-electric it may be extremely expensive or impossible to bring in gas.) Does a family member have special needs, which require wide doorways for a wheelchair, or a stepless entry to his/her room? The fewer things which are on this list, the more properties you will be able to consider. But if you would really not make an offer to purchase a home which has less than a 2-car garage, for instance, this is the time to write it down.

Next, you get to dream. What would you *like* to have in your new home? If you can get by with 3 bedrooms, would you really like 4? Would you be happiest with an old home you can restore, a fairly new one which has already been improved (with extra towel racks and beautiful landscaping, etc), or a brand new one where you can bond with all the other new neighbors and select the light fixtures and countertops? Would you most like to be on a cul-de-sac, in a neighborhood with a lot of children? Or an older home with a lot of acreage? Do you really want walk-in closets in the Master Bedroom, and a tub in the Master Bath? How about a laundry room on the main level or upstairs near the bedrooms? What are you enjoying in your current home that you'd like to have again? What are you lacking and wish you had? Are these things important enough to make the list? *Thinking and talking about this should be a fun experience, so relax and enjoy the process.*

Now, a reality check: Chances are, you're not going to find a new home which meets all of your desires, unless your funds are unlimited. However, once you've given the topic some thought, it should become apparent to you which things are more important to you than others, and if you communicate these to your real estate agent it will help both of you to use your time most effectively to find the homes in which you can live most comfortably.

Obviously, different parts of the country have varying housing costs and styles of homes which are built. If you're moving from Atlanta to L.A. or Chicago, you're in for Sticker Shock, as well as the reality that they just don't build homes the same way in different parts of the country. For instance, you may have always lived in a house with a basement, and thought you always would. But if you're moving to southern California, you'll quickly discover that you're not going to find a basement—at least not the type of basement you're used to seeing. Building materials vary in different locations, and building trends (such as size and style of master suites) take awhile to move around the country. You may simply have to "adjust" to the way things are done where you're moving.

Once you've started looking at what your dollars can buy, you may realize you need to compromise. If you really want a larger house you may decide you don't need to live by the ocean. Or you may decide that living near the beach is more important than a den, that 4th bedroom, *and* the extra bath. You won't know until you start looking, what exactly you're going to find, so try to keep your mind open and consider all the possibilities.

You've already explored, in the chapter on Making the Decision, what is important for you to have in the new area—perhaps being near a hospital, facilities for the arts, an ice rink, or religious institutions. Whatever things are important to YOU to be near, plus being within a certain distance from work, will hopefully narrow down what area of town you would most like to live in. If you're not familiar with the town you're moving to, your real estate agent will certainly be able to use these factors to determine which areas you should plan to look in first. Communication of your needs and desires are an essential part of working with a Real Estate Agent to find your new home. Even if you decide to look for a house on your own, it's still important to clarify what's important to you, before you start the search. As Bloody Mary sang in *South Pacific* , "You've got to have a dream; if you don't have a dream, how you gonna have a dream come true?"

Determining Your Price Range & Getting Loan Pre-Approval

Pre-Approval for a Mortgage
This will not only set your mind at ease, but will also give you an advantage when you make an offer on a property. As Leslie McDonnell, a top ReMax Agent in Lake County, Illinois, says, *"The contract is by definition a more solid one, since the Sellers won't worry about whether you can obtain a mortgage, and they may be more likely to accept your offer."* An experienced real estate agent can suggest a good mortgage broker or you can ask around for a recommendation. *See Chapter 6 for more about selecting a mortgage.*

Once you've completed a loan application, hopefully you will be pre-approved for a loan up to a given amount. This, of course, is subject to the particular property you select being appraised for an amount higher than what you're planning to borrow. It also is contingent on your financial status not changing negatively—so be sure not to make any major purchases prior to closing without discussing it with the lender who has pre-approved your loan.

Determining Your Price Range

Obviously, figuring out what price range you should look in is important.

Consider...

- How much you should borrow. *See this topic at the beginning of Chapter 6.*

- Not "stretching up".
  In the past, it was a common practice to "stretch" to buy a home which one expected to be able to more comfortably afford in the future, after career advancements took place. In today's job market, these things are less certain than they were in the past, and it's more important to have the "wiggle room" to put aside savings to cover family expenses in case one has to spend months searching for a new job after being laid off.

- The lifestyle you want to have in the future.
  If your mortgage application included 2 people's incomes, think about whether you might like the option to put one of those incomes into savings. That may allow one of you stop working at some point, such as when children come along. Perhaps saving more towards retirement is more important than having a more luxurious house. You might want the option to retire earlier, have more money to spend during your retirement, or have less stressful golden years with your mortgage paid off before retirement.

- What property values are in the area. You may be able to get what you want *without* spending as much as you can afford. It doesn't hurt to look in lower price ranges to see if you find something that works for you and leaves you with more money to do other things.

- <u>The Listing Price is just that.</u> Since Sellers almost always will accept less than that amount—sometimes significantly less—it makes sense to consider homes listed up to a somewhat higher price than you would be willing to pay.

Now that you've examined what is really important to you, what other things you would like in a home, and what your price range is, you're ready to begin looking for homes.

Working with a Real Estate Agent

Selecting an agent

The best way to locate an agent to help you find a new home is to get a good reference from people who have worked with an agent to purchase their home. If you are relocating to an area where you don't know anyone, you will probably need to rely on your new co-workers or your company's relocation company, if they use one. You want someone who is experienced and successful, and someone who knows the area well. A person may be a great agent in Skokie, Illinois, but if you are looking in Libertyville, you'd be much better off finding someone who is an expert in Libertyville and Vernon Hills. It is best to get several names and contact all of them, especially those who come recommended by more than one person.

Tell the agent what you're looking for in a home and neighborhood, and ask them to send you a packet with information about the city and some sample listings for you to look at. Select one agent to begin with, based on your phone conversation and evaluation of the packet they sent you, and make an appointment to look at homes when you're in town. If you don't "click" with this agent, try the next one on the list. A good agent will make himself available when you are in town, or will find a very capable associate to work with you if he is unable. If you give an agent fair notice that you'll be in town and wanting to shop for a home all day Saturday and Sunday, and the agent takes you out for 2 hours and then back to your hotel (when there are many more homes appropriate for you to see)— you should seriously consider finding a different agent.

You'll be relying on this person not only to alert you to potential problems they see with a particular property, but also to guide you in where to look for a home, how much is appropriate to pay for the property (although, of course, only you can decide how much you want to offer), and through the rest of the purchasing process. It's important to work with someone you feel is experienced and capable, who shows integrity, and is someone with whom you feel comfortable. An agent can save you all kinds of time and trouble during the process, and they don't earn a cent unless and until you purchase a property through them. And then, the Seller pays their commission.

Buyer Broker Agreement

Real Estate agents earn their living through commissions. They can invest an enormous amount of time, energy, and fuel as they identify potential homes and drive Buyers around to dozens of them. However, unless a Buyer purchases a home through them, they don't earn a cent. It is not unreasonable, then, for an agent to ask you to sign an Exclusive Right to Represent Agreement. This protects them against a potential Buyer deciding to negotiate the purchase of a house directly with a Seller, even though the agent has shown them the property. If you're considering purchasing directly from an owner, or from a builder who won't pay a commission, you may need to look at those properties prior to signing an agreement. It all depends on the wording of the agreement. If you decide you are comfortable working with this agent, make sure you understand the terms thoroughly, and that it includes an escape clause in case you become dissatisfied with the services the agent is providing.

Dual Agency

Your agent may ask you to sign a Dual Agency agreement. Dual Agency rules are not the same everywhere. In some states, Dual Agency means that if an Agent shows you a property where she is the Listing Agent (the Sellers listed their house with her), then she would be advising both you (the Buyer) and them (the Seller), trying not to disclose any confidential information to either party. In other states, and at least some of Canada, Dual Agency exists where the Listing Agent and Selling Agent work for the same Real Estate company, even if they work out of different offices of that company. A Dual Agent does not exclusively represent either the Seller or the Buyer, and that may present a conflict of interest.

It may be difficult to *avoid* entering into a Dual Agency transaction, especially if there's a large real estate company in the area with a sizable percentage of the listings. But it can be a tricky situation and one in which you may not feel you should be totally open about your personal circumstances or rely on your Agent's advice during negotiations. That's not good, because their guidance is one of the reasons you're using an Agent in the first place. One *good* thing about dual agency is that if an agent is getting the commission for being the Listing Agent *and* the Selling Agent, occasionally he may be willing to cut his commission a bit, giving you a better price on the property. You might want to consult a Real Estate Attorney in the area before deciding to agree to Dual Agency. You'll certainly want to read the document and ask questions until you understand exactly what it means in that state and can determine whether or not this is something you would be comfortable with.

Share your thoughts: Give your agent as much information as you can about what you are looking for—the things that are essential, and the things which would be nice. As you look at homes, in person and online, you'll probably find there are other characteristics which are equally important. Tell your Agent. As soon as you realize what you don't like about a particular home, let your Agent know. The more they know about your preferences, the easier it will be to show you homes which you will like—and this is a good thing. It will save you time and energy, and make the whole relocation process a lot more efficient and a lot less frustrating.

Searching For Homes on your Own

Some builders of new homes and some homes being sold By Owner will not "cooperate" with Real Estate agents. This means that if an agent takes you to see one of these homes, and you purchase it, the agent will not make any commission. Obviously, since they're doing this to make a living, if there's no commission involved, Real Estate agents will not choose to show you these properties.

Note: If you want to consider a new home where the builder does cooperate with Real Estate Agents, **your Agent must be with you the first time** you look at the development. Otherwise, the builder will not pay a commission and you will not have the advantage of your Agent's guidance in the negotiations and throughout the rest of the building and purchasing process.

If you decide not to work with a real estate agent to search for a house, or if you feel it's important to do some looking on your own, there are a lot more resources available to you than ever before. Maps of the area and additional information can be obtained from the local Chamber of Commerce, or AAA (if you're a member, it's free—although you may have to request it from the local office). If you can determine what areas you might want to live in, that will be helpful because one of the big challenges is to zero in on those neighborhoods, and not waste time and energy evaluating homes in inappropriate parts of town. While Real Estate agents are very familiar with the areas they sell in, and can quickly eliminate those neighborhoods which don't meet your criteria, if you're looking on your own you'll probably have to visit the areas in order to figure this out yourself. If possible, figure out what towns or counties you're interested in, as well as zip codes and area names. These will at least let you narrow the field somewhat in order to start your search.

- **Newspaper Classified Ads**

  You can look at the printed version of the Real Estate section of the newspaper, but most large cities now post their classified ads online, including homes for rent and for sale. In fact, the sites are usually set up so that you can search for houses which meet your parameters, including county or area, price, number of bedrooms and bathrooms, and type of property (single family home, townhouse, etc). You can even opt to look at "new homes".

  The sites often offer additional information about buying and selling homes, which you may find helpful. Some large metropolitan areas have more than one major newspaper, so the following is not a complete list, but are just some websites to get you started.

  Websites are modified quite often, so here are some general guidelines for where to go once you get there. Look for headings such as Classified or Marketplace, Real Estate and Homes. You may find search tools for finding a home within your parameters (price, number of bedrooms and baths, etc.), helpful advice for buying and selling, and/or a listing of classified real estate ads.

  Atlanta GA: www.AJChomefinder.com

Baltimore MD: www.BaltimoreSun.com
Boston MA: wwwBostonGlobe.com
Chicago IL: www.ChicagoTribune.com
Dallas TX: www.dallasnews.com
Denver CO: www.denverpost.com
Detroit MI: www.freep.com
Houston TX: www.chron.com
Los Angeles CA: www.LAtimes.com
Miami FL: www.Miamiherald.com
Milwaukee WI: www.jsonline.com
Minneapolis/St Paul MN: www.startribune.com
New York city area: www.NYTimes.com
Philadelphia PA: www.philly.com
Phoenix AZ: www.azcentral.com
San Antonio TX: www.mysanantonio.com
San Diego CA: www.signonsandiego.com
San Francisco CA: www.sfchron.com
Seattle WA: www.seattlepi.com
Washington D.C.: www.WashingtonPost.com

- **Free Publications**
  Publications with Homes for Sale and Homes for Rent are available at many locations, usually found in stands near the door in restaurants, pharmacies, gas stations, convenience stores and grocery stores.

- **Websites**
  Check out Realtor.com, the website of the National Association of Realtors created for home buyers, or any of the websites for individual real estate companies. Usually the name of the real estate company, ending in ".com" will get you to their website; otherwise, just do an online search for it.

  Many of the "For Sale By Owner" types of companies have their own websites. I'm not vouching for the good practices of any of these; that's up to you to research. However, for starters, try:

www.buyowner.com
www.ByOwner.com
www.HomesByOwner.com
salebyownerrealty.com (select "Buyers click here")
www.ziprealty.com (you'll have to register to use this)

Additional sites are listed in Chapter 17, under "For Sale By Owner (FSBO) Assistance Companies".

Tools of the Hunt

When you go to look at homes, there are a number of things you should take with you. If you're taking young children along, see Chapter 11 for additional items.

- **Measurements:** Measure important pieces of furniture. Unless you're willing to replace your bedroom set, you'll want to make sure it fits into the Master Bedroom of a new home. The same goes for your couch or sectional, piano, etc. Include items in your basement, attic, or storage facility, if it's important to have them in the new place.

  When you tour prospective homes, take these measurements *and a tape measure* with you. This way you can verify that the furniture will fit...and you can record measurements to take home in case you have questions about other pieces of furniture. You may also want to measure your current closet, so that you can compare the hanging space to what you currently have. If you do this, take into account how much space is double-hung. This is something easy to fix if the new closet is large enough.

  P.S. Try to find a lightweight tape measure so that it's easy to carry in a purse or pocket, but a metal one which measures at least 12' would be best. It's difficult to measure the height of windows or ceilings with a soft fabric measure. (Just don't leave a metal one in your pocket when you go through airport security.)

- **Digital Camera**: Most homes which you visit will have information sheets about the home available for you to take with you, and these usually have color photos. However, there may be a particular feature about the house which you want to remember, so having a camera will allow you to capture that feature. Anything which will make that particular house stand out in your memory will be helpful. It might be an outstanding kitchen, a charming patio, or built-in bookshelves in the office. Make a note on the information sheet about the specific photo you took, or take a photo of the information sheet before shooting photos of the house. Otherwise, after looking at homes all day, you may get confused about which homes offered which features.

I strongly suggest that you take multiple interior photos of a home you plan to purchase, and take measurements of wall space between doors and windows as well. These can prove extremely helpful in several ways:

- ☛ They will guide you as you work on furniture arrangements before the move.
- ☛ They will remind you of how the house really looks. It's amazing how your perception and memory of a house can change between the time you view it before making an offer until the time you see it again, especially if you're moving from out-of-town and there's a time gap.
- ☛ Photos can answer many questions about how a particular area was used or accessorized, which can be helpful even after you've settled into the house.

➻ Photographs of particular items you care about, such as a chandelier which is to be included in the sale, can be very important. Take the photos with you when you do your Final Walk-thru before closing to verify, for instance, that the chandelier hasn't been replaced with another. The photo will help your case in the event that it is. We'd like to think that no one would replace faucets or other hardware or curtains with less expensive ones, but it has happened.

➻ You will enjoy having photos to help describe the house to friends & family.

➻ They will serve as "before" photos, if you're making changes to wall color, floor coverings, etc.

These tangible records will be invaluable.

- **Checkbook**: If you decide to make an offer on a house, you'll need to attach a check for earnest money to the offer. These funds will be applied towards your down payment at closing. The check won't be cashed until your offer is accepted, but it would be safest to have extra money in your account to cover this when you're going on a serious house hunting trip. Otherwise, be prepared to move money into the account within a couple of days, and make it clear when the check will be good. Ask your agent what amount you should consider putting down as earnest money. Typically it is about 3% of the purchase price, but in more expensive areas can be up to 10%. If you choose too small an amount, this may indicate to the Sellers that you're not as serious a Buyer as another.

- **Comfortable clothing, snacks, and a positive attitude**: If you're out for an intensive day of house hunting, you may need to take a break after awhile for a meal or coffee or ice cream. Other than that, it's helpful to bring along water and some granola bars or whatever to keep your energy up between meals.

If you have the right fuel in you, and you're dressed comfortably—in layers—and stay hydrated, you'll be able to focus on your task: finding the right home for you and your loved ones. Plan to have a good time looking. Your attitude is very important—keep an open mind.

• **House Hunting Form**: Make a form (or use the Sample House Hunting Form in the Appendix) where you can write notes about every appealing property as you view them. Personalize this form to include things important to *you*, which may not be on the listing sheet, such as a large pantry, hanging room in the laundry area, or a desirable area in the back yard for the screened-in porch you want to build. The handout which you pick up in each house will give you a lot of information, but this form will remind you to look for the certain features *important to you*, and note how the house measures up. By the time you have seen 8 houses in one day, you will most likely be confused as to which home had what features. This form will help you to evaluate the properties you're viewing, and will help you sort out the properties you're most interested in at the end of the day. You'll want to make enough copies of the form to last you through your first few days of house shopping. At that point, unless you've already found your house, you may want to modify the form to include other things you've thought of.

When viewing a house, make sure you've looked at all the items on your sheet, because it may be easy to forget to look at one or two of the characteristics otherwise. Also, give it an overall rating, which means something to you. Some examples could be "Great" "OK, but small" "NO" or "Best yet". At the end of the day, you'll want to review what you've seen and come up with the top 1-3 homes to consider. As you continue your search, these will be the standards you'll be comparing other homes to. *It's important to physically go back* to your favorites periodically, to refresh the details in your mind. It's amazing how your memory of a house can shift, once you've viewed a number of others. If that is the standard you're comparing others to, you'll want to be sure you're comparing them to a reality.

Things To Consider—For Yourself and For Re-sale

Obviously, you want to make a wise decision when you select your new home, and there are a number of things to look for which you may not be aware of. Some of these may affect how livable your home is, and some may affect your pocketbook. So consider the things below for your own comfort and well-being—but also, for resale.

Resale—how the house will do when *you* try to sell it—is definitely something you should consider. You may choose to live in this house for many years, or something may happen and you may wind up needing to put it on the market in a year. You want to give yourself the best chance of being able to sell your house when it's time, without undue delay or loss of funds. The things below are not carved in stone. I just want to make you aware of them in order to give you the best chance possible of making a good decision, both for yourself now, and for down the road when you are ready to sell the house.

If possible:

- Avoid homes very close to high voltage power lines. Although the jury is still out as to whether these may actually be harmful to people, there is enough doubt that you may find it more difficult to sell the house.

- Avoid homes on, or backing up to, busy streets. There are exceptions to this—obviously some city dwellers prefer to be right on a bus line or as close as possible to the action. However, half a block away may be much quieter, cleaner, and allow easier access when pulling your car into the street.

• Avoid homes on much lower ground than others in the vicinity—there may be a greater chance of water seepage into the home.

• Beware of illegal additions. If a room was added or a basement finished, for instance, you want to know that there was a permit issued for the work. Generally, when the work has been done with the required permits, you know that there have been inspections done by professionals, to verify that the work was done properly and that the addition sits on land acceptable for building. If a permit was not issued when an addition was done, you (as the new owners) may be required to submit "as-built plans" and have it inspected. If it's not up to code (licensed electricians, plumbers and builders know what the local building codes require), you will be required to see that it's brought up to code. Also, if the enlarged kitchen, for instance, was built over or too close to the property line, you may be required to tear it down, or pay thousands of dollars for a zoning variance.

An illegal addition is the kind of thing which should make bells go off in your head, and it certainly is an issue you want the Sellers to clear up before going forward. Otherwise YOU may be liable for those costs right away or somewhere down the road, when you apply for a permit to replace the roof or build a deck or do some other minor or major improvement—or sell the house. The city may never find out about it and people interested in buying the home later on may not care, but are you willing to take that chance?

Other things to consider:

- **Layout:** Is the floor plan one which will work easily for you? Is there adequate space for your family to do what they typically do? Is the Master Bedroom a good distance from the other bedrooms? Often, parents will want to be close to the bedrooms of young children, so they can hear them at night, but farther from the bedrooms of teenagers, whose music might be annoying.

- **School System:** Find out about the quality of the local school system even if you don't have school-age children. This is important because the school's reputation will affect the resale value of your home when it's time to sell it.

- **New Subdivision:** Make sure you find out what the plans are for the rest of the subdivision. Beware of promises for coming attractions. The developer could go bankrupt and stop building; additional roads into the subdivision may never be paved; the remaining property may be sold to other developers. The promised tennis courts and/or pool may not materialize. On the other hand, if all goes as planned, a subdivision where everyone is new can be ideal for forming many lifelong relationships.

- **Surrounding Vacant Properties:** If a treed area exists, even if you're told it will stay rustic forever, it's up to you to make SURE whether that's true. You don't want to pay good money for a home where you believe the deck will always provide a wooded seclusion, only to see those trees chopped down 2 years later, and apartment buildings built, providing 16 balconies which overlook your deck. I'm not trying to scare you. I just want you to be cautious when you purchase property in an area which has not been built out yet.

If there is a vacant lot nearby, find out who owns it and what building plans, if any, exist for the lot. You probably want it to be a house consistent with the look and quality of existing homes. If the vacant lot is next door, or backs up to the lot you're looking at, you may even want to consider purchasing it yourself to ensure that it remains undeveloped.

The way to research vacant property is to talk, either by phone or in person, with someone in charge at the planning department or building and zoning office, at the county or town the property is in. The name of the department and the political entity it falls under varies according to location, but it should be fairly easy to determine with a phone call or two. Once you find the appropriate person to talk with, they can advise you of how the property is zoned and if there are any current plans to develop the property on file. A word of caution: zoning can change and variances can be granted, so there are no guarantees. However, it's still worth doing your homework before you put your money down.

- **Home Owner's Association (HOA):** Is there an HOA in the development? What is their annual fee? Will you be required to join the golf club or swim/tennis club, even if you don't plan to use the facilities? If major repairs are required, have funds been set aside to cover them, or would each homeowner or member be accessed a fee? Are there any major expenses looming at this time?

  You'll want a copy of the entire by-laws of the HOA prior to making an offer, so you can decide if you're willing to live with their rules. Some HOAs offer an abbreviated version; insist on a copy of the entire, most recently revised, document. Although these rules are generally meant to protect the value and ambiance of the neighborhood, some HOA's restrict even the color of pot you put plants in outside your house, and impose a fine on homeowners who don't mow their lawn often enough to please the officers of the HOA. If the by-laws aren't available before making an offer, be sure to include reviewing and accepting them as a contingency in your contract. It would be very stressful and expensive to back out of the transaction after seeing the rules for the first time at closing.

- **Crime:** Read the police report column in small community newspapers, or check with the local police department, to learn how much and what type of crime is occurring in the area. Crime seems to be increasing everywhere, even in "nice" areas, but there may be significantly more of it in one area you're considering than another.

- **Area idiosyncrasies:** Check into what's "normal" and what's a "concern" in the area. For instance, in Florida, it's rare to find a basement, so lack of one is no problem. In the suburbs of Atlanta, a home without a basement or one which is very contemporary in style may be difficult to sell. In California, homes of a certain vintage in particular areas may have aluminum wiring. It is important that aluminum wiring be either totally replaced with copper or else be "pigtailed', to avoid an increased chance of fire. (This is something you may be able to get the Sellers to pay for.) Finding out about these idiosyncrasies will allow you to make an informed decision. The main way to find out is to *ask*. Ask real estate agents or anyone else in the real estate industry. Area homeowners may be good resources for this information, too, but homeowners who have always lived in the area may not realize that these things are done differently elsewhere.

- **Water:** Determine if the home has city water and sewer, as opposed to well and septic system. If you are comfortable with a well and septic system, and the upkeep and maintenance that they require, that's fine; but you should still be aware of what you're getting. As Real Estate Agent Leslie McDonnell says, "City water sells better".

- **Neighborhood Upkeep:** Drive through the neighborhood, and note how the properties are cared for. Look at the shutters, paint, landscaping, garage doors. Is everything in good repair and not in need of a good coat of paint? Are the lawns mowed? Are things kept clean and neat, or is junk strewn on the yards and driveways? These things DO affect property values.

- **Typical Home:** You want a home which is typical of the surrounding homes. If many of the homes have 3-car garages, don't buy one with a 2-car. You also don't want to have the most expensive home in the area. Even though the kitchen and bathrooms may be far nicer than the ones in surrounding homes, you'll find that it's difficult to recoup your money when you go to sell the home, if it's listed at much more than recent selling prices of other homes in your neighborhood. In fact, if you buy one of the least expensive, but high potential, homes in the neighborhood and you make improvements, you're more likely to recoup your investment when you sell.

- **Bedrooms:** In most cases, I would suggest you not consider a house with less than 3 bedrooms. Each bedroom should have a door leading directly into the hallway (rather than through another room). Many prospective homeowners insist on master bedrooms with abundant (preferably walk-in) closet space and a connecting roomy bathroom including tub.

Although many find a whirlpool tub a luxurious feature, they do require a bit of maintenance to keep the jets clean, so factor this into your decision.

- **Bedroom Closets:** Make sure every bedroom has a closet. We looked at one house where the people had eliminated the closet in a bedroom they were using as a den, in order to create a larger linen closet in the hallway. The problem comes when you go to sell the house, and it's not really considered a bedroom because it doesn't have a closet.

  In another case, it wasn't until a few nights before our move, when I was laying in bed, mentally figuring out where various things were going to be placed in the new home, that suddenly I realized the gorgeous wood built-in bookcase in one of the bedrooms was actually built in the space where the closet was supposed to be! Although that gave us a welcome space to display items and store our photo albums, it meant that the things which were currently in our spare bedroom closet would need to be stored someplace else, and when we had guests use the room we had to bring in a free-standing clothes rack. It also could have hampered us in re-selling our home, since again, it could not be used as-is for a bedroom. Fortunately, in that case, the house was such a sought-after model in a sought-after subdivision that it didn't hurt us.

- **Bathrooms:** In addition to a bathroom off the Master Bedroom, there should be at least one bathroom on each level of the house (except in the basement, where it is still a plus). An exception to this rule is in split level houses, which typically have a bathroom on the upper (bedroom) level and lower level, but not the one in between (which has the living room, dining room, and kitchen).

- **Dining Room**: Here's a guideline to see if everything will fit comfortably—allow 3-4 feet between the table's edge and other objects (china closet, sideboard, serving unit, or a wall) in order to allow room for someone to sit in a chair at the table, and for others to walk comfortably behind them.

  If the room is not large enough to accommodate the furniture in the way which first comes to you, consider alternatives. Perhaps a piece could be angled into a corner or placed on a wall next to, or near, the dining room instead of actually in it. I've even seen a server placed by the front door, looking very attractive as you enter the home, but near enough to the dining room to be wheeled into there for a party. (Yes, this server had wheels.) Be creative.

- **Kitchens**: Eat-in areas are important. Light and bright is important. Look at the layout to make sure it's workable for you.

  One house we looked at, which was really very nice in most aspects, had the refrigerator located in a short hallway between the kitchen and the laundry room. There was no counter right next to it, and we couldn't imagine fixing cereal every morning with the kitchen counter over here and the milk & juice way over there. It just didn't make sense. On another note, if you have a strong preference for gas range vs. electric, note what exists in the house. Many homes are all-electric, and it could be very expensive or impossible to convert to gas. Note the number of ovens (two can be very useful) and whether there is a built-in microwave. Some microwaves have a built-in turntable, and some don't. I tried to purchase a turntable for a microwave oven which didn't come with one, and learned that they either come with one or not—you can't purchase a turntable and expect it to work.

- **Swimming Pools:** Homes with in-ground swimming pools are more difficult to re-sell in many areas of the country. Ask your real estate agent for advice, if you're considering a home which has one.

- **Pets:** Some people are very allergic to cats, among other animals. If someone in your family has a significant cat allergy, you may want to think twice before purchasing a home where a cat has lived.

  It's the animal dander that people are actually allergic to, not the fur, so even after the animal has left the premises, what's left behind could still trigger an allergic reaction. You could have the carpets cleaned, and possibly the ductwork (though probably not if it's the soft aluminum-wrap-type of ductwork) and hopefully that would eliminate the problem. However, we have a friend who is very allergic and purchased a townhouse where a cat had resided. After doing all the cleaning they could, he was still miserable with allergic symptoms until they moved to a new house.

- **Home Maintenance and Improvements:** Notice how modifications have been made in the home. If you see a sloppy repair job in the wallboard of a bedroom, for instance, this is a clue that other repairs may have been done sloppily, as well. You may not be able to see the plumbing or electrical repair as easily, but there's a good chance these owners took short-cuts in those repairs, also. If you see a home which appears to be very well tended, it's not a guarantee, but it is a clue that things have been done the right way.

- **Use Your Imagination:** Don't automatically turn down a home because the carpet is awful, or the wallpaper or paint colors are not your taste, or the window coverings are old-fashioned and make the house dark.

Even dark paneling can be painted a light color, or removed and the nail holes patched and repainted. (We had the latter done in one house, and it sure did brighten things up.) On the other hand, if the house is situated so that sunlight wouldn't be abundant even with updated window coverings...or the house would need major remodeling in order to fit your desires and needs...then perhaps another home would be a better selection.

- **Odors:** If any part of the house smells damp or musty, you may want to eliminate it as a possibility. At the very least, have a good inspection to pinpoint the source of the problem and verify that it is an easy fix. You do not want to buy a home where mold may be growing inside the walls, and/or water is leaking/ seeping in undetected.

- **Walk Around the Exterior:** Look at the roof, gutters, drainage (water should drain away from the house), siding and trim. This inspection will give you clues as to how well the house is being maintained, and also will help you determine what expenses you might incur to get the exterior in good shape after you purchase it. Also look at the condition of the landscaping, to determine what upkeep would need to be done regularly, and whether an initial investment would be required to bring it up to your standards.

- **Talk with the Neighbors:** A great thing to do when you see a home or area you're very interested in, is to ask people in the neighborhood how they like the area. Leave the question open-ended at first because you never know what may come up. They may discuss a potential building project on a treed area in the neighborhood (one which you might otherwise assume was going to stay that way) or flooding concerns...you just never know. After they've answered your open-ended question, you might want to follow up, specifically asking about any concerns you may have—school, traffic, builder, etc. Probably the best way to have these conversations is if you're able to go back to the one or 2 neighborhoods you're interested in, after you're finished with the real estate salesperson for the day. Then you can take a walk in the neighborhood, get a better feel for what it's like (noise level, children, etc), and hopefully run into residents you can chat with.

- **Check out the commute:** You may want to drive to and from work, at the times of day you would normally be doing it, to get a realistic picture of what the commute would be like.

Making an Offer

When you're comfortable that you've found a house for which you want to make an offer, see Chapter 8 for information on purchase offers and negotiating the purchase of a home.

After an Offer Has Been Accepted

Once an agreement has been reached, and all parties have signed the contract, there are some things the Seller and Buyer each need to do in order to fulfill the terms of the contract. For you, this includes removing contingencies you've written into the contract, such as applying for a mortgage (*see Chapter 6*) and hiring a professional to do a home inspection (see below).

Hint: Ask if the Sellers have a layout of the house (with room measurements, window/doors, etc.). If they bought the house when it was new, they'll probably have one—and they may have it even if they didn't. If it's not available, use the opportunity to take these measurements while you're in the house for the inspection. It will help more than you realize, when you figure out where things will go and what will fit into the empty spaces (you may find a wonderful piece of furniture between now & then and wonder if it'll fit into a particular place). You might also ask if they happen to have a small scrap of carpet and/or wallpaper (if any), so that you'll be able to match colors as you prepare for the move.

Home Inspection

- The inspection is done by a professional home inspector, usually within a week or 10 days after acceptance of the offer to purchase.

- According to The American Society of Home Inspectors (ASHI), "the physical inspection is an objective visual examination of the physical structure and systems of a home, from roof to foundation. It includes a visual inspection of the home's heating system, central air conditioning system (temperature permitting), interior plumbing and electrical systems; roof, attic, and visible insulation; walls, ceilings, floors, windows and doors; foundation, basement, and the visible structures of the home. When problems or symptoms of problems are found, the inspector may recommend further evaluation or remedies." More detailed information is available at ASHI.com, and I encourage you to check out their "Standards of Practice" so you'll understand what is and isn't examined during inspections.

- You can find an inspector on ASHI's website, but the best way is to get a recommendation from someone (such as your real estate agent) who has used a particular inspector and been satisfied with them. I strongly recommend that you be present for the inspection. If that is impossible, try to line up a trusted friend or family member with a fair amount of building or real estate experience, or at least a great note-taker who will communicate well with you. Your real estate agent will probably be present for the inspection, and her feedback will be valuable, as well. I do NOT recommend using your real estate agent as your sole representative, however, even if you have developed a trusting relationship. There is a potential conflict of interest there, and it's important that you not only receive the report but the unwritten feelings about the urgency of some issues.

Most of the inspectors we've worked with are terrific, but here are some things to make sure are considered, in case yours doesn't catch everything.

- For additional information about home inspections, go to www.HomeDepotMoving.com. Search for "home inspection"; then select "Taking a Closer Look at a Potential New Home". There is a wealth of information on the website about other moving-related topics as well.

- Take a pen and pad with you to take notes. Most of what the inspector finds will appear on his report, but often there are additional hints he will suggest which you'll want to make a note of. You will learn a lot about the house, and perhaps some hints on how to care for it, if you have a good inspector and listen well.

- Take a working nightlight with you. In case the inspector doesn't check every single electrical outlet in the house, this will be an easy way to check them out yourself, to make sure they all work. Sometimes wires have been connected incorrectly and an electrician needs to be called in to correct the problem. Sometimes it's more complicated. In either case, you will want to either have the Sellers pay an electrician to do the work, or have an electrician check things out and give you an estimate to do the work. Once you know what you're dealing with, you'll have the opportunity to negotiate with the Sellers so that they pay to have the work done.

- Open and close every door and drawer in the house (except, obviously, not in furniture which will be moving out). Open and close every window. If the window won't stay up, that's a safety hazard which needs to be fixed. Have insulated windows become cloudy? Is there a screen in every window? Do any of them have holes or tears? The inspector will probably spot-check windows, but I recommend that you take the time to try them all. Also, he will probably not be looking at window coverings, but you may realize as you go through your check, that some of the mini-blinds or shades don't work properly. You'll have to pick your battles, and may choose not to even mention some issues. On the other hand, it would not be out of line to request that the Sellers replace those things which don't work or are falling apart.

- Check each faucet to make sure it works, and that the hot is really hooked up to the hot water line. Check each tub and sink drain to make sure the stoppers work and that the water drains. In one house, after we moved in, I went to run a sink of water and when I pulled up on the stopper handle, it pulled right out of the sink and there I was holding it in mid-air. (I laughed at how silly I looked but then had to call someone to repair it.)

- Make sure that all exterior doors are hung in the right direction. We had a house recently in which the back door was hung so that the hinges were on the *outside*. Anyone could have walked up to the rear of the house and pulled the pins on the hinges and walked right in, despite a lock and deadbolt on the other side of the door. As obvious as this sounds, the inspector did not catch the error.

- If you haven't already taken photos of the home, this would be a good time to do it.

- <u>What if the report reveals problems?</u>

- No house is perfect. When the inspector identifies problems, it does not necessarily indicate you should not buy the house.

  Unfixable problems, however, should make you think seriously about whether this is a good investment. If the roof has been leaking, for instance, and the attic smells very musty, there's a good chance that mold and/or mildew is growing on wood surfaces and it may be very problematic to completely eliminate. Since this may lead to health issues, I would certainly proceed with caution. We attended one inspection in California, where a 1-story home was built with just a 10" space beneath it, in which to access pipes or the foundation. This space was less than the minimum currently required, and prevented the inspector from evaluating some of the foundation and plumbing. Also, if the house needed repairs on those pipes or the foundation in the future, the owners would have needed to shop around for a *very small person* to do the repairs. There was nothing which could be done to increase that 10" clearance, and other issues were also present in the house, so the prospective homeowners decided that this house (which was no bargain in the first place) would be a very risky investment.

The inspector's findings serve to educate you in advance of the purchase about the condition of the property. In some cases, another professional (such as a roofer, drainage expert, or contractor) may need to be called in, to evaluate an issue and determine if it is fixable, and at what price. A Seller may be willing to adjust the purchase price or contract terms if major problems, which you are willing to deal with, are discovered during an inspection. If you are not convinced that the problem can be fixed to your satisfaction, or if it can't be fixed by the Sellers and you do not want to be involved in future repair work, you may decide that this is not the house for you. In any case, the information you obtain from the Home Inspector will be extremely valuable, and well worth the fee for the inspection.

When you've made the final decision that this is where you'll be living, enter the full address into your address book or Blackberry or whatever, because you'll refer to it many times over the coming months. Then prepare to apply for a mortgage (see Chapter 6) and review the other Seller's Obligations at the end of Chapter 8.

Chapter 8

Preparing A Purchase Offer & Negotiating The Purchase

If you use the services of a Real Estate Agent, they will walk you through the process. However, it's still a good idea to familiarize yourself with the information in this chapter so that you fully understand what your options are. In the end, only you can decide how much you're willing to offer and on what terms.

Purchase Offers

A written **Offer to Purchase** is usually completed by the Buyer's Real Estate Agent or attorney. Obviously, a very important part of the purchase offer is the price, but there are other items of great significance, too—some of which may make an offer more attractive than another offer, even one with a lower price. Some other elements are: the amount of earnest money, contingencies (financing, physical inspection, sale of another property, etc.), closing and possession dates, and what is included in the sale.

You may want to request a blank Offer to Purchase form from your Real Estate Agent ahead of time, so that you can familiarize yourself with it and ask any questions you have, while you're not rushed. This way, when you find a house and are ready to make an offer, you won't spend precious time trying to understand the document but can move forward with completing it in the way you want, and hopefully make a deal before another offer comes in.

It's important to realize that once the offer is accepted in writing, it's legally binding on both the Buyer and the Seller. Instead of accepting the first offer you make, the Seller may present a counter-offer (the same contract, but with some modifications). You can choose to accept that contract, reject it, or counter with additional changes. Once an agreement has been reached and a "clean" contract (one with all of the terms both Seller and Buyer has agreed to) has been signed by all parties, it's a valid contract, so you'll want to be sure you understand the contract, and that it says what you want it to, before you sign on the dotted line.

Before making a Purchase Offer, it's helpful for Buyers to learn what they can about the Sellers—why they're selling, how quickly they want to move, how much they paid for the house how long ago—and how long the property has been on the market. Any defects in the property should also be considered, since it may cost money to make them right, either now or in the future. These bits of information may be useful in crafting an offer which will be acceptable for the Sellers, and good for you, as well.

I do need to mention that it is not uncommon for Selling Agents to say that if you're interested in a property, you should make your offer quickly because there's another Buyer interested in the house. Sometimes this may be true, but it's a ploy utilized by salespeople in many fields. Don't allow yourself to be pressured. What you need to do is decide if you really want the house, and if you do, at what price (after educating yourself about current home prices in the area) and with what contingencies. If someone else offers more and gets the house, they may have paid too much for it. And it may take some looking, but chances are you *will* find another one.

- <u>Price</u>
  First, understand that despite what they may or may not say, real estate agents are required to present *any offer*. If all you are willing to pay for a property is $50,000 less than the listing price, for instance, don't accept the agent's protest that this offer would be "insulting" to the seller. If you really want to purchase the property and are willing to pay a lot closer to the asking price, then perhaps you should discuss your strategy (*see below*). However, if you would only want to purchase it at a given price, by all means make the offer. They can either accept the offer, reject it, or present a counter-offer.

  If the house is listed for $200,000 and you really don't want to pay more than $185,000, you might want to offer $170,000. They may counter the offer with a price of $190,000, allowing you to come back with $180,000. In this way you can compromise and settle on a price of $180,000 or $185,000. However, you really need to consider the market before you try something like this. If houses are selling quickly in the given market (geographical area and price level at that time), then it's very possible that another offer for the listing price, or close to it, is waiting in the wings to be presented. In that kind of market, well-known during real estate booms in southern California, for instance, it may be only the "clean" offer of listing price *or even above listing price* which will be accepted. A "clean" offer is one with no contingencies (although I still would not make an offer without it being subject to a physical inspection by a professional).

  Your Real Estate agent can do a Comparative Market Analysis on the house to help determine a fair price for the property. Obviously, you don't want to pay more than you need to for it—both because that would be wasting your money, and also because when you apply for a mortgage, the lender may require an appraisal. If the appraised value of the house is too low, the lender probably won't approve the mortgage. So, when determining how much to offer for the house, consider how much similar homes in the area have sold for recently, the neighborhood (and how well-kept the properties are), the condition of the house (will you need to make major investments?), how many homes are currently on the market (if there are many similar ones, you may be able to get away with a lower price) and how much you can comfortably afford. Your agent is required to present your offer no matter how low it is, but if it's too low, you may be outbid by another Buyer. If it's way too low, the Seller may refuse to negotiate and just say "No".

BE CREATIVE! If you don't have the cash readily available for closing costs, offer a little more than you want to, but include "Seller to pay closing costs" in your offer. If you know that the house will need new carpeting and don't have an extra chunk of money sitting around to pay for it right away, increase your offer by the amount you estimate carpeting will cost—let's say $5,000—and include "Seller to provide a $5,000 carpeting allowance" in the offer. That way the cost of your carpeting will be included in the mortgage. This practice is sometimes frowned upon, since it artificially inflates the sales price of the house, and others will use that price when making appraisals and marketing assessments of homes in your area. However, it can be a good tool if you are able to use it. A good real estate agent will help you craft the appropriate clause.

One more reminder while we're talking about money: to make sure you're not offering more than you can afford, remember you will be responsible for certain costs associated with purchasing the house and other costs associated with owning it. Those associated with the purchase can include: appraisal fee, survey fee, a homeowner's insurance policy with the first year paid in full, service charges (for utilities, if they require an installation fee or deposit), legal fees, and land transfer tax.

Some of the costs associated with owning a home include property taxes, maintenance (a ball park figure might be 1% of the purchase price per year), mortgage loan insurance (if required or desired), and a homeowner's insurance policy (your mortgage provider will require that you keep this in force). In many cases (such as when the mortgage is for more than 80% of the Purchase Price), the lender will require that each mortgage payment include an additional amount, which is placed in an escrow account and used for your property taxes and homeowner's insurance each year when they're due. If this is not required, you would be smart to set those funds aside yourself, through an automatic withdrawal from your checking account each month. The funds should be placed in a separate interest-bearing account, so that the money is there when your homeowner's insurance and tax bills come due.

- Earnest Money (Deposit)
  The amount of earnest money attached to the offer indicates how committed one is to completing the transaction, since the funds would be forfeited if the Buyer backs out for a reason not provided for in the contract. In the event of an issue related to the contingencies—such as the physical inspection revealing major problems with the property that the Buyer is unwilling to accept—the earnest money would be returned. Discuss with your Real Estate Agent what an appropriate amount is for the earnest money, and

under what conditions it might be returned. Your earnest money check is attached to the Offer to Purchase, and is cashed upon acceptance. The funds are kept in an escrow/trust account and are applied towards the down payment.

- Inclusions
  There are things which are almost always included in the sale—if they're present in the house—such as the dishwasher, oven/range/stove, garbage disposal, tacked down carpeting, smoke detector, built-in shelving, garage door opener, sump pump(s), central air conditioning, central humidifier, ceiling fans, existing storm and screen (windows and doors), window blinds and shutters and everything else physically attached to the house.

  Items which vary sale-to-sale and are frequently negotiated include the clothes washer and dryer, refrigerator, TV antenna or satellite dish, and curtains, valances and draperies.

  It is acceptable for a Buyer to include and negotiate some furniture which is "made for the space", such as book cases, barstools, or even a patio set, in the offer, especially if the offer is close to the asking price and there are no other offers coming in at the same time. If the listing shows that the Seller is not including the washer, dryer and refrigerator, those are almost always open for negotiation. If included in the offer, the Seller can always counter, excluding those items. And the Buyer can always counter offer including them again, if he's willing to take the risk. However, if you're really interested in the property, I would not suggest risking the deal by being too greedy with the small stuff. In some cases, Sellers are willing to sell much of their furniture, but unless they list the property as "furnished", these would best be dealt with separately, after the purchase contract has been negotiated.

- Closing & Possession Dates
  There's no right or wrong answer to this—it depends on the Buyer's and Seller's situations. It can make a big difference to either one if the other is flexible—so if the date isn't crucial to you, try to find out through the Real Estate agents what the Seller's preference is. Generally, possession takes place immediately after closing, but in some states or situations, this can differ. For example, it has been common in Michigan for the Seller to stay in the house for 30 days after closing, although this practice is changing now.

  If you can avoid moving twice, or putting your things into storage, the move will be easier on you and your family. In most cases, that means arranging the closings within a few days of each other. Sometimes, people prefer to own the new home for awhile before moving in, so that remodeling and/or redecorating can take place in an empty house. If you can afford to do that, it does make things easier.

  In some cases, the Buyer agrees to let the Seller pay rent to remain in the home for a given time. I don't generally recommend this due to the risks for the Buyer. However, these risks can be minimized by keeping some of the Seller's funds in an escrow account, to be returned when he has moved out and the property proves to be free of damages unseen in the walk-thru. Whether a family is trying to time their move to the beginning or end of the school year, waiting for their new home to be completed, or eager to move out-of-town so the family can be reunited with the spouse who's already begun his new job there, closing and possession dates can be very important to both Buyers and Sellers.

- <u>Home Owner's Warranty</u> (HOW)
  In some states these are called "Home Service Agree-ments" or "Home Protection Insurance".
  You may want to include a stipulation stating that the Seller is to provide a one-year Home Owner's Warranty policy (you can name the company you prefer) including HVAC not to exceed $(*insert an appropriate top figure for what this should cost*). You can search online to find companies which offer this service, or ask your real estate agent for a suggestion. I strongly suggest you check the warranty company's record through the Better Business Bureau (www.BBB.com). Some haven't been in business very long and others seem to have a very high number of consumer complaints. Purchasing a policy of this type is not an unusual thing at all to ask for. The policy covers the Buyer for the first year of home ownership and typically covers major systems (heating, air conditioning, electrical, plumbing), water heater and major appliances. But *read the fine print* on the policy for specifics.

  To check out what it should cost, go to www.ahswar-ranty.com and select "get a quote". You'll need to provide zip code, whether the house is less than 5,000 square feet or more, the year the home was built, and dwelling type—single family house, condominium, etc. You'll want to use an amount slightly higher than the premium quoted for your Offer to Purchase (in case it costs a little more than you anticipated). Including an upper limit for the cost of the policy will ease the Seller's minds so they know they're not committing to an expensive extra. A typical home policy at this writing runs about $250, but do verify the cost before including the amount. Purchasing the policy for you may make Sellers more confident that you (the Buyers) won't come back to them if the furnace, for instance, suddenly stops working a week after closing.

Having the HOW will ease your mind, as the Buyer, because at a time when your finances may be stretched pretty thin, at least you know you won't be responsible for funding a major repair on covered items for the first year. Although it's a good thing to have, and will offer you some protection and peace of mind, you should note the following:

(a) Coverage is limited to the items and systems stated in the policy. Not everything in your house is covered. Also, there may be an additional fee to cover water wells.

(b) There is a "trade service call fee" which you will need to pay each time a serviceman is dispatched to your home. The amount of this fee varies policy to policy. There also may be additional charges for specific repairs and replacements. Read the policy when you get it for details.

(c) When something malfunctions, most policies require you to go through the insurance company and deal with the repair people they select. If you do it on your own or have an unauthorized repair company make a service call and do a repair or replacement, this may not be covered by your policy.

(d) Understand that when there's a problem with something in your home, the company will pay for what is needed to keep things going. If your furnace is near the end of its useful life, for instance, they will pay for a minor repair to keep it functioning rather than for a replacement unit. If it absolutely needs replacing, they will authorize an adequate replacement...but not necessarily the fuel-efficient, higher-end unit you might select yourself. You may be able to work with the repair service and pay the difference to upgrade the replacement, if you want, but if you want any of it covered by the insurance policy, you'll still need to do it through the authorized service.

(e) Call a warranty company you'd like to use, to ask questions or clarify coverage. Use this as an opportunity to see how they treat you, because this will give you an idea of how they'll respond once you need service on your policy.

- Seller's Responsibilities
  A good sales contract will include Seller's responsibilities, such as maintaining the property in its present condition, conveying good and marketable title to the property, a Termite Inspection letter in some states (*see below*), and providing a valid property disclosure (if required in the property's state). *More extensive information about property disclosures is located in Chapter 3, under "A note about disclosures...".*

- Title
  You'll need to indicate who will hold title, and if there is more than one owner, *how* you will hold title. Some of the choices are: "Joint Tenancy with Right of Survivorship", "Tenancy in Common", "Community Property", "Tenancy in Partnership" or in a "Living Trust". These options may vary state to state, and it's a good idea to consult a real estate attorney to determine which is the best way for you to own the property, considering your personal circumstances.

- Mortgage Contingency
  It's very common for an Offer to Purchase to be contingent on the Buyer obtaining an unconditional written Mortgage Commitment for a certain amount of money, within a given amount of time, at an interest

rate not to exceed a certain amount, at a term not to exceed a given number of years. It also specifies the size of the Buyers' down payment. Many of the newer sales contracts are much more specific about the type of loan you intend to apply for, also including whether the rate is fixed, adjustable or interest only. The Buyers are required to diligently pursue approval of this loan in good faith. If you are turned down, you need to immediately notify the Seller, and provide the Seller with a letter from the lender denying the loan and detailing all of the reasons for the denial. This is to help prevent Buyers from using this contingency as a way out, if they get cold feet about proceeding with the transaction.

If you have been pre-approved, the chances of this contingency being satisfied are excellent, but it's not a done deal until you apply for THIS mortgage for THIS property, and get approved. Among other things, the lender will want to make sure the house is worth at least as much as you're borrowing (they'll do an appraisal to satisfy this requirement) and they'll review your credit, to verify that there have been no significant negative events since you were pre-approved. If a Seller has a choice between two otherwise identical contracts, it would be a no-brainer to accept the one where the Buyers are paying cash (in which case, there would be no Mortgage Contingency), or lacking that, one in which the Buyers have been pre-approved for a mortgage.

• Attorney Review
Often, an Offer to Purchase will state that the respective parties have five days in which their attorneys may review the contract, and approve, disapprove, or make modifications to the contract, other than the purchase price. If an agreement is not made within a given period, say ten days after signing of the

contract, then the Offer is null and void and earnest money is refunded.

Try to get recommendations for a good attorney who has a lot of real estate experience. It's not fair to any of you, if you use a cousin who usually deals in divorce law or litigation. In many areas, it is not common practice to involve an attorney in a real estate transaction, but it does offer you a layer of protection. Even if there is nothing problematic in the Offer to Purchase, something may arise later on during the process of purchasing the home, such as a problem during the final walk-through. In this case, it would be helpful to already have an attorney, who has approved the contract, to ensure that you are protected in any agreements required to complete the transaction.

- Home Inspection
  Another contingency typically included in an Offer to Purchase is that the Buyer has five days in which to have a professional Home Inspector examine the property in depth. I can't stress enough how important this is, and it is WELL WORTH the cost. Please note that this is not a way for Buyers to get out of a contract when they've just changed their mind. *See the end of Chapter 7 for more information on Home Inspections.*

Reasonably-timed visits to the house are usually also included, so you can bring in a decorator to order window coverings, for instance, or measure room sizes to verify whether furniture will fit in given places. I recommend you keep these to a minimum, and be considerate. Being thoughtful and considerate is not only a nice way to be, but also if issues arise (as they often do, in a home sale transaction), they will be resolved much more easily and equitably if you haven't already alienated the other party.

A final inspection (usually called a "walk-through") is also done by the Buyers immediately prior to closing, to verify that the house is in the same condition it was when the contract was signed, and that items which were supposed to be left in the home are, in fact, there.

- Appraisal
  If you're going to apply for a loan, in order to purchase the property, it's probable that the lender will require an appraisal. However, to be on the safe side, it wouldn't hurt to have the sale contingent on an appraisal showing the house to be worth at least the amount you're offering for the property.

- Termite Inspection
  In parts of the country where termites are an issue (is there anywhere they aren't?), the Sellers will usually be required to provide proof of inspection by a licensed pest control operator, showing no termite infestation. If infestation does exist, or has in the past, the treatment needs to be documented and any damage to the property needs to be repaired and disclosed to the Buyer. There are time limits for all of these actions to take place. If a recent inspection has already been performed, the report can be provided by the Seller when the contract is accepted.

- "Contingent on the Sale Of"
  It is very common for an Offer to Purchase to state that the offer is "contingent on the sale of" the Buyers' current property. If there is a great demand for the property you're trying to purchase, there's a good

chance the Seller will not accept a contract with this contingency. However, you never know for sure, so if that's the only way you could purchase the property, it's worth submitting an offer with a contingency.

- Time Limit of Offer
  You may limit the amount of time which the Seller has to respond to your offer, by naming the time and day until which the offer will be open to acceptance. Do your homework first and make sure the Sellers are not on an African Safari, returning in a week, before you put a 2-day limit on a response. Among the advantages of a time limit, is that if you have a second choice which you like, you would be free to enter into a contract on another property without undue delay.

Before you make the offer...
- Have you included all the contingencies you want to? (*See above*)
- Do you understand everything in the contract?

Evaluation of Purchase Offers

The Seller will be evaluating your Offer to Purchase, and will respond to you (or her Real Estate Agent will respond to your Real Estate Agent, who will contact you) within the allotted time. The Seller will either accept the contract as is, reject it, or make a "counter-offer". A counter-offer will modify the price and/or some of the terms of the contract. In order to respond appropriately, the Seller will need to evaluate all of the details, as well as how solid the offer is, before they decide how to respond.

Offers and counter-offers

Every time an offer is rejected or countered, one runs the risk of the other party deciding to exit negotiations, and possibly consider someone else's offer. It's a gamble. If they don't come back with an acceptance or counter-offer, you have no deal. If they come back with that counter-offer, you have to accept it (in which case you have a deal) or counter it (in which case you'll have to wait to see if *they* accept the counter to see if you have a deal). Or you can decide not to accept it and walk away. It can be very nerve-wracking for the typical homeowner, although some people (including those who negotiate for a living) have mastered the concept of not getting attached to a particular property, and are very good at this skill. It's often said that in order to negotiate a good deal, you must not be "in love" with the property. If you care about the property so much that you MUST have it, you're probably not going to be willing to take the chance of not getting it. The result is that you may pay more for the house than you need to, or give up some of the other terms you might have liked.

If it's a "hot" real estate market at this point, and Sellers know that lots of buyers will be competing for the property, they may want to counter the offer *removing* any contingencies they don't want to live with, and altering the sales price or any other terms to which they object. You, as the prospective buyer, may be in a position where you are able to purchase the home while still owning another one or be willing to accept the other changes made to the contract. You always have the option of countering the counter-offer, putting the conditions back in. Often, verbal negotiations between the two agents, each communicating with their client for responses, will result in an agreement and then the final contract is prepared and signed by all parties. On the other hand, when you receive a counter-offer (as opposed to an acceptance), you may decide that you no longer want the house, for any reason, and just walk away. Each party has to be willing to take that chance if they choose to counter an offer rather than accept it as written.

3-Day Release Clause

A popular response to an Offer to Purchase containing a "Contingency on the Sale of" the Buyer's current property, is a counter-offer, which includes a 3-Day Release Clause. With this clause in the contract, if the Seller receives another offer which doesn't contain a "Contingency on the Sale of", they advise Buyer #1, who now has 72 hours (basically 3 days) in which to remove her contingency. If she does remove it, she proceeds with the purchase at the agreed-upon terms and price in the original contract, even if this price is lower than that offered by Buyer #2. If Buyer #1 sends the Seller notice that they will not be proceeding, Seller is free to proceed with the sale to Buyer #2. Without this clause, the Seller takes the chance of tying up the property for months, not knowing if the sale is going to go through or not. In many cases, the 3-Day Release Clause really is a good option for both parties.

Negotiating

There are whole books devoted to negotiating, and I wouldn't presume to cover the topic in a few paragraphs here. The purpose of this chapter is to make you aware of some aspects which pertain particularly to buying and selling houses and condominiums.

One thing which can be helpful is learning what is motivating the other party. Have the Sellers already started new jobs in another location so they may be willing to accept a lower price to accelerate the sale? Or have they put so much love into this house that it's important to turn it over to someone who will treasure and care for it? It doesn't hurt to gently explore what is important to people you're negotiating with, without giving away your bottom line. A great sale is when both parties feel they have gotten what is important to them.

It is also said that, in negotiations, "He who cares least wins". If you let on that you're in love with this house and absolutely have to have it, you're not going to get the best deal you could. Whatever your negotiating style, consider what is important to you and think through each response (within a reasonable time frame) to make sure you're comfortable with all of the contract terms.

During the time the contract is being negotiated, but also afterwards when other issues may arise, it is important for all parties (Buyers, Sellers, and Real Estate Agents, where used) to work towards a solution. If your Real Estate Agent doesn't seem to be focused on working things out, go to his/her manager and let her know you need immediate help. This is one of the big reasons for using a Real Estate professional—they have the experience and the will to see that the deal is consummated.

Occasionally, if the parties are very close on price and agreed on all other terms, real estate agents have been known to adjust their commission slightly in order to make up the difference. This is especially true if the agent is both Buying and Selling agent for your property, or even if both agents work for the same broker. In these cases, their commission percentage is higher than it would be during a typical sale, so they may be willing to give up a little bit in order to see that a deal is made. Real estate agents often work hard for their commissions, however, so don't enter into negotiations expecting this to happen.

After a Contract Has Been Signed by all Parties

First, breathe a sigh of relief that you're well on your way to completing the purchase of your home. And then...

BUYERS' OBLIGATIONS
Of course, there are many things you'll be doing during this time besides those listed here, but these are some of

the things you'll need to do in order to fulfill some possible requirements of your contract:

1. <u>Set up a Home Inspection.</u>
See Home Inspection at the end of Chapter 7 for how to select a home inspector, additional things to keep an eye out for, and who should be present during the inspection.

2. <u>Shop for mortgage rates and terms</u>, if you haven't already. *See Chapter 6.*

3. <u>Apply for a mortgage</u>
Even if you've been pre-approved, you still need to apply for a mortgage for *this* home and for *this* amount.

4. <u>Obtain a Homeowner's Insurance policy</u>
Contact your current insurance company regarding coverage of your new home, to become effective on the date of closing (which you'll advise them of later, since you may not know the closing date until the financing is approved). Consider using your auto insurance provider because there are often discounts for multiple policies (such as auto and homeowners) with the same company. You may want to contact several other insurance companies, as well, to compare prices. Just be sure to compare the same coverage when you compare prices, and make sure you deal with a company which is highly rated. You may want to consider selecting the highest deductible possible, if you can afford to, because of the way the insurance companies now often penalize homeowners for placing (or, in some cases, even asking questions about) claims. At the closing of your new home, you'll need to provide proof that you've paid the annual fee for this insurance and that it is currently in effect.

A standard homeowner's policy provides coverage if your property is damaged by fire, lightning, wind, storms, hail, explosions, riots, aircraft wrecks, vehicle crashes, smoke, vandalism, theft, breaking glass, falling objects, weight of snow or sleet, collapsing buildings, freezing of plumbing fixtures, electrical damage and water damage from plumbing, heating or air conditioning systems, according to the Insurance Information Institute, a Washington, D.C. based non-profit group for the insurance industry. It insures the home itself and what you keep in it. It also covers your liability or legal responsibility for injuries and damage you, or your household pets, cause to other people. These policies generally cover damage due to everything except earthquakes, floods, poor maintenance, war and nuclear accidents. Some policies, however, exclude trampolines and certain breeds of dogs, among other things. Be sure to read the policy thoroughly, to be certain exactly what it covers and what it excludes.

A basic policy can usually be expanded to include additional coverage, such as for floods and earthquakes. Riders are also required to cover jewelry or other expensive possessions above the limits stated in the standard policy, but this is for your own protection and is not necessary for your real estate transaction. A wealth of information about homeowner's insurance policies and some free home inventory software are available at www.iii.org/individuals/homei, the Insurance Information Institute's website.

If you're purchasing a condominium, the condo association typically provides some of the coverage but you will still need to obtain coverage for your personal effects and some other items. Consult your homeowner's association and insurance provider for more information.

SELLERS' OBLIGATIONS

Depending on the terms of the contract, some of the things Sellers might be required to do at this point are:

1. <u>Obtain a termite letter or report.</u> Sellers will need to set up a termite inspection, unless one was done very recently. Hopefully the inspection will find no active infestations and no damage, and the company will provide a document attesting to that. If a problem does exist, the infestation will need to be treated and any damage repaired. The Sellers will need to disclose this information to you and any other potential Buyers. This is not necessarily something to panic over. In Georgia, for instance, they say that there are two kinds of houses: ones which have had termite infestations, and ones which will have them in the future. You do, however, want assurance that there are no current infestations when you purchase the property, and that any damage already done is someone else's responsibility to pay for.

2. <u>Cooperate with you as you make appointments</u> to have the Home Inspection performed, and any other necessary visits to the house.

3. <u>Continue to keep up the property</u>, by mowing the lawn, repairing anything which breaks, and generally taking good care of things.

4. <u>Purchase a Home Owner's Warranty</u>, if this was in your contract. Once contingencies have been removed from the contract, and the closing date is set, the Sellers can proceed with this.

Chapter 9

Scheduling The Move
And Other Tidbits

In this chapter, you'll learn the busiest time for movers (so you can avoid those times, if possible), how to select and work with movers, services available, and what *not* to send in the moving van.

Scheduling the Move

- <u>How do we coordinate the closings of the new house and the old one?</u>
  Ideally, you will close on the sale of your house and the purchase of the new one on the same day, or within a few days. If you close on the house you're selling first, you will have the funds needed for the other closing, and will just need to convert them into a certified or cashier's check for the next closing. Your mortgage broker or lender will advise you of the amount and type of check (usually certified or cashier's check) required. The exact amount is usually not available until a day or so before the closing. If you close on the purchase of your new home *before* the sale of your old home, you may need to arrange interim financing in order to complete the purchase transaction. In some cases, the employer relocating you may supply funds for this "Bridge Loan".

An advantage of closing on the purchase of your new home before the sale of your old one, *as long as the latter deal really does go through,* is that you'll have some time, while the new house is empty, in which to have work done. Painting, carpeting, bathroom and kitchen updates are all easier to do when the house is empty. On the other hand, you'll be paying the mortgage on both homes for the overlap period.

If you close on the sale of your old home more than a few days before closing on the new one, you may need to stay in temporary housing until you're able to close and take possession of the new home. Usually, this means putting at least some of your things into storage temporarily. If you have things put into storage, there will be additional charges for storage, warehouse valuation coverage (or insurance) and delivery charges from the warehouse to your new home. I've heard a number of "war stories" about items being lost in transit to or from the warehouse, or sustaining water damage from a leak in the storage facility. If you need to put things in storage, try to check out the facility first to make sure it seems sturdy and watertight. Another option, if the Buyers are agreeable, might be to remain for a short time in the house you've just sold, paying the Buyers rent until you gain possession of the new house or have work completed in it.

- <u>How long will it take for the moving van to arrive at our destination?</u>
Ask the moving company for an estimate of how long it will take from the time they leave your old house until they're ready to begin moving things into your new house. They will take into consideration how many days drive it is, appropriate rest for the drivers, and whether your belongings will fill up the moving van. If you fill up the van, the delivery time will be

much more predictable. If they need to load other people's possessions onto the truck in order to take a full load, they'll have to consider where they're dropping the other load off, and whether it makes sense to deliver that load before your own. They may not know these answers when they give your estimate, so it may be a wider range of dates than you'd like. It will become firmer when the time gets closer and they know for sure who else's things will be on your truck, where the other pickup is, and where the other shipment is going.

• <u>What if one spouse needs to remain in the house for awhile after the other begins working in the new city?</u> While there are definitely some negatives to living apart, you may feel that some of you should remain in the house until it sells, or until the end of the school year, or whatever. In most cases, companies moving an employee will expect to pay for the employee to be in temporary housing for some amount of time. Often, this is in the form of a suite hotel, because it has a kitchen or kitchenette and feels more like an apartment. It also may be large enough to accommodate the whole family when they go for a visit. Often, the relocation package allows the employee to fly home periodically for a 2 or 3 day weekend, until the rest of the family has moved.

There is an up-side to the family not moving when the job first starts. For the first four to six weeks, acclimating to a new job and new working environment can be pretty intensive. Although coming home to an empty hotel room (or apt or house) can be dismal, at least the employee can take the extra hours needed to get up to speed with the job, without feeling guilty about shortchanging his or her family. Once that initial period has passed, the working partner can hopefully be much more supportive and available to help as the family gets settled into a new home and begins to acclimate to their new environment.

- <u>How soon should we consult with moving companies, and what moving dates should we avoid, if possible?</u> It is to your advantage to schedule movers as soon as possible, so that they are available for the dates you want. From mid-May until mid-September, when children are out of school, movers are busiest. If you're able to schedule your move during the months of October to April, you'll find it easier to lock in the date you want, and in many cases you'll pay less and have a better experience. Also, many people want to move at the very beginning or end of the month, so moving in the middle of the month might also be easier and better. *See Chapter 11 for additional thoughts on when to schedule your move if you have school-age children.*

- <u>Are there any restrictions on moving days or times we should be aware of?</u> If you're moving into or out of an apartment building, condominium, assisted living facility or senior community, inquire about any rules for moving days and times. Some buildings have restrictions, mostly to avoid tying up elevators and access to the building and parking lots during high-use times, but also to assure that a staff person is available to ensure the safety of residents and the building. When you contact the building administrator, ask whether it will be possible to block an elevator for your movers' use during the move, since this will shorten the amount of time they'll need to be in the building. When you talk with your mover, they'll be able to tell you whether they can commit to a particular day and time, or whether they will have to wait until the shipment has arrived in the new city before they can schedule an exact time. Whatever information you are able to provide, let your building administrator know, and keep the communication lines open so that things will go smoothly when your moving day arrives.

Other questions to ask the building coordinator include: "Where is the best place for the movers to park the moving van?" and, if appropriate, "Who should they check in with when they arrive, for assistance in controlling the elevators and gaining access into the building?". By taking these steps ahead of time, you will save time and frustration on moving days. This can also save you money, if this is a local move which you are paying for by the hour.

Determine What Will Be Moved & What Won't

- Furniture and other large or heavy items
  Walk through your house and note what items will not be moved. When a mover comes to give you an estimate, he'll need to know which items to exclude from the estimate. It may be helpful to obtain a layout of your new house to figure out what furniture will actually fit. *See "Arranging and Decorating Your New Home—Steps To Take Now", in Chapter 10.* If you're moving to a much larger home, you can postpone figuring out what will go where, and just decide which items you simply don't want to move to the new house.

  Keep in mind, if the new home has stairs or elevators, some bulky items may be difficult or expensive to deliver. The problem arises when furnishings can't fit into the elevator, or can't be manipulated at the landing or top of the steps, or even through a contorted hallway. It isn't always size that's the problem. For instance, king size mattresses can be bent, but queens cannot. Queens usually do not have split box springs, either, as all kings do. If the movers can't do it any other way, they can often arrange to raise the item up on the outside of the building and bring it in a large window or doorway. This is where the extra expense comes in.

- Food
  Movers will not move perishable food, including frozen and refrigerated food and produce. Other food is acceptable, but it makes sense to minimize what you take. The packers will seal containers which have been opened, so don't worry about an open box of graham crackers or cereal.

- Items which cannot go in the moving van include hazardous materials, such as: acid, aerosol cans, ammonia, ammunition, batteries, bleach, charcoal, charcoal lighter, cleaning fluid, cooking fuel (including Sterno®), fertilizer, fireworks, frozen or perishable foods, gasoline, kerosene, lamp oil, lighter fluid, matches, motor oil, nail polish remover, oily rags, oxygen bottles, paints, paint thinner, pesticides, poisons, pool chemicals, propane tanks, and weed killer. Your mover should provide you with a complete list. Use them up, give them away, or safely dispose of them—just have them gone before the movers come to pack or move your things. Don't forget to drain fuel from lawnmowers and gas-powered weeders, or run them until all the fuel is used up.

Federal regulations permit movers to transport plants if the trip is less than 150 miles and under 24 hours. However, some states won't allow plants to be moved from out-of-state, and others require plants to be quarantined. Even if you're not moving to one of those states, in extreme weather conditions the plants may suffer inside of a truck, so in most cases giving your houseplants away, selling them, or moving them inside your car if you drive it, will be the best choices. If you really want plants moved, check with the moving companies you get estimates from, to see if they will take them.

Years ago, we had accumulated an extensive collection of matches, from various restaurants we visited during our travels. I still remember sitting on our family room floor, scissors in hand, opening up each matchbook and cutting off the tips of the matches, so that we wouldn't have to give them up. We destroyed the flammable tips, and finally convinced the packers that they were safe to move. Since very few restaurants today use matches as promotional materials, you may never have thought about collecting them—and that's probably good, if you're planning to move.

- <u>Items you'll want to take with you, rather than have them go in the moving van,</u> include address books, airline tickets, back-up computer disks, bank account and investment account numbers, car keys (except those for a car which is being moved or driven by a professional), car titles, cash, cell phones, Certificates of Deposit, checkbooks, deeds, documents and contact information pertaining to the move and the closing of both homes, insurance policies, your moving estimate, precious jewelry (whether expensive or sentimental), laptop computers, medical and dental records, passports, irreplaceable photographs (printed or digital media), prescription medications, school records, stocks and bonds, and wedding albums. Needless to say, you will need to be very vigilant while transporting these items, to make sure they arrive safely with you at your destination. If you're flying, make every attempt to include these items in your carry-on baggage, rather than checking them, so that you're sure they won't be lost or stolen while out of your sight. If you're driving, try to keep your eyes on the car whenever you're not in it, selecting restaurants where you can sit watching your vehicle through the window. If at all possible, put tempting things out of sight in the trunk, or hidden in the back of your SUV.

- <u>Phone Books</u>
These are something people usually leave behind, but they can be very useful. Take one book from your old location, and hang onto it for a year or 2. It may save you a lot in Directory Assistance charges, because not every person or business is easy to find on the internet. Also keep phone lists of groups or organizations you belong to and church or synagogue directories. Many times you'll want to reach out to people listed in these directories, who you haven't bothered to enter into your personal address book. Make a folder to place these in, and keep the folder in a logical place in the new house. We keep ours in our file cabinet.

- <u>Should your car move to your new home? And if so, how?</u>
If you're planning to sell your car in the near future anyway, it may make sense to sell it before you move, unless for some reason you believe it may sell better or for more money in your new location. Obviously, you'll have to time the sale so that you're not without a vehicle during the busy pre-moving days, although you could consider renting a car for a short time if that would ease the transaction.

If you're planning to keep your car and it's in decent shape, you may decide to drive it to the new city. Perhaps you have pets or other precious possessions you'd like to transport in the car...or perhaps you'd like to take advantage of the move to take a car trip and show the kids some of the country, or visit friends or family in locations along the way. If you have the time, inclination, and a dependable vehicle, go for it. As before any road trip, make sure your car is checked out and serviced, if appropriate, before leaving on the trip.

Should you decide not to drive the car yourself, there are several options for how to get it to the new location. One, the easiest for you, is to have the movers move it. They can put the car right on the moving van with your belongings. It's fascinating to watch how they get a car on and off the van, and we've done it more than once. Another option is to hire someone else to drive the car for you (you can find companies on the internet who do this, but be selective) or have the car moved on a car carrier. We have had someone else drive a car for us or family members on two occasions, and had no problems in either case. Be sure to verify the cost and form of payment required before you seal the deal. You may get recommendations from your moving coordinator (although if you have one, chances are your company will cover the car being moved on the moving van) or word-of-mouth. If you find a company online or in the phone book, be sure to check them out with the Better Business Bureau and anyone else you can think to check with.

Hint: If you have your car moved by truck, on the racks like you see new cars moved...try very hard to have your car be one of the ones on TOP. This advice is from an acquaintance whose car was below another car, one which leaked oil onto hers, damaging the paint. Anything you can do to avoid being inconvenienced at the other end of the move is well worth it, in my opinion. You'll have enough to deal with.

Selecting a Moving Company

- Get recommendations
  Ask neighbors, friends, family, co-workers, and real estate agents if they can recommend companies they've been happy with during past moves. It's essential to find a reputable company, one which won't hold your possessions hostage at the destination for a much larger sum of money than agreed upon, or which will just disappear with your possessions. I'm not trying to scare you...well, actually I am trying to scare you just enough to make you realize it's important to do your homework so that you use a legitimate moving company. However, you do *not* need a Moving Broker.

- Check them out
  Always check out potential moving companies with the Better Business Bureau at www.bbb.org or phone your local BBB office and ask whether the mover has any complaints against them, how many, and whether they have been resolved. Keep in mind that what looks like a large number of complaints for a large company may be comparable to a smaller number for a small company. Besides verifying that they are registered and insured, and investigating their complaint history, check the company's background and references. Find out how long the company has been in business (preferably 10 years or longer). Be aware that some national van lines actually are manned by local franchises. Be sure to check out the particular agents (or franchises) in the area you're moving from as well as those at your destination.

  For interstate moves, you can verify that a mover is registered by going to www.protectyourmove. gov. This is a website provided by the Federal Motor

Carrier Safety Administration (FMCSA), whose mission is to "decrease moving fraud by providing consumers with the knowledge and resources to plan a successful move". There's a lot of helpful information on this website, including specifics on what constitutes an interstate move. (It's not as simple as you might think.)

For intrastate moves (generally, moves within a state, unless the route requires some out-of-state travel), check with your local consumer affairs agency or your state attorney general. If you're considering a local company, it wouldn't hurt to visit their office, to see if it seems to be run professionally. Verify that they have liability, workers' comp, cargo and vehicle insurance by asking to see their Certificate of Insurance.

Also verify that a moving company uses dedicated trucks and vans which have their name permanently painted on the vehicles. An exception to this is that sometime moving companies purchase additional vehicles and if they need to get them right into service they may use magnetized signs on them temporarily. However, if a moving van or truck with bald tires or peeling paint or a rental truck pulls up to your house, *do not* let them take your things.

The American Moving and Storage Association (AMSA) can also be of help. Their website, www.moving.org, has a lot of helpful information about movers and moving, a Mover Referral Service, and a list of ProMovers and Van Lines. If you have a good recommendation for a particular moving company, it doesn't hurt to verify that they're listed here. AMSA also administers an arbitration program, which is limited to losses of $1,000 or less. For larger claims, you would need to go to court.

- <u>Have several movers come to give you free written estimates.</u>
  It is important that this be in person, not over the internet or over the phone. Unless they see your things with their own eyes, they cannot give you a legitimate moving estimate. Try to do this as soon as possible after you have determined, for the most part, what you will be moving and what you won't. Once you have met with several movers, you will make your selection based partly on cost, but also on how you feel about the company, how dedicated they are to service, how well you believe they will take care of your possessions, and how good a reputation they have with others who have used them. Obviously, if the price is much less than other estimates and sounds "too good to be true", it probably is. Legitimate movers do not usually request a large deposit prior to the move, so be wary if a company requests this. In fact, professional movers usually don't require a deposit at all, although it's possible they may request a small "good faith" deposit. As with any contract, be sure everything you've been promised is in writing on the estimate. Also, <u>read and understand everything you sign.</u>

Get prices for packing and unpacking services, and ask whether supplies for packing are included in the quote. And remember: **As with so many other relationships, good communication is vital for your move to go smoothly.**

The best move we ever did was with a company which assigns one team to do the move from start to finish—including packing, hauling, unloading, etc. They establish a rapport right at the start, are very motivated to avoid any damage claims at all, and have learned that when the homeowner feels good about the people who have packed their belongings and know they will meet them at their new home, it makes a big difference. These movers know which items might be worrisome to the homeowners, and make the effort to verify that all is well before they leave.

- Packing
  Having movers pack our belongings is a luxury we sure hope we don't ever have to move without. It makes a huge difference—your home looks much more normal until very shortly before the move, your possessions are packed the right way so that they have the best possible chance of arriving intact, and you don't have the strain of having to pack everything. I strongly recommend using this service if at all possible. *For further discussion, see "Do-It-Yourself?" in Chapter 13.*

- Unpacking
  Unpacking is something we prefer to do ourselves. If we are concerned about a few particularly fragile items, we might have the movers unpack those, just to verify their condition while the movers are still there. We also have the movers set up anything they took apart, such as televisions placed on wall units and plugged in, bed frames reassembled, and mattress and box springs put in place.

  If movers unpack *everything*, then all the surfaces in the house will have "stuff" on them. We find it difficult to deal with all that clutter until we can get it put away (not to mention, keeping the kids out of it). Instead, we prefer to systematically put things away, as we unpack one or 2 boxes at a time. We do know someone, however, who finds it physically difficult, due to a medical condition, to open the boxes and unwrap every item, and for him it is extremely helpful to have the movers unpack everything and haul away the boxes and packing materials right away. It's a personal decision, partly based on your physical condition, whether you have young children or pets around, how many adults you have to put things away (more will hopefully speed up the process), and whether you're willing to pay for this service the movers can provide.

- <u>Wooden crates</u>
  Movers can custom build crates for chandeliers, glass lampshades, antiques, large vases, large mirrors, statues, some televisions—anything large and bulky which requires extra protection. Show these items to the moving company representative who comes to do your moving estimate. The moving company will need to arrange for the supplies, and may well want to crate your item prior to moving day.

- <u>Other large, very fragile things </u>which are best left to the professionals include large glass table tops and glass shelves in china cabinets.

- <u>Show it all</u>
  When the representative from the moving company comes to do your estimate, you'll need to show him everything which needs to be moved, including things in your basement, garage, attic, storage shed, etc. He/she will probably look in your closets, in and above your cabinets, and under beds. They can't give you an accurate estimate unless they see everything they'll be responsible for moving. Make sure you advise them which things you will NOT be moving, especially large items such as furniture. Be consistent, and tell each mover the same thing, in order to compare "apples to apples" when you review the estimates. In some cases, you may not be sure yet whether you'll be taking some items, such as a washer and dryer. You can tell the mover you're not sure about these items, and ask how much you'll save if you don't move them, but do have them included in the estimate. It's much better to have the

price come down at a later date than worry about it being increased, especially if your employer is paying for the move.

If you tell the moving estimator that you're going to clean out the garage or basement or shed, so most of those things will not need to move with you, try really hard to be realistic and then to actually get rid of those things. If it all winds up moving with you, the cost of the move is going to be higher and you may be wondering why, or getting angry that you didn't get a good estimate. If you can, get rid of the stuff before you put your house on the market, so your property looks better and you don't have the project looming over you when you have so many other moving details to attend to. The move will go much more smoothly if you only move what you indicated, or you advise the mover well in advance of any significant changes.

- Pricing
  Local moves are charged on an hourly basis. Charges for interstate moves are determined by the weight of the load and the distance it will travel. To determine weight, the mover will weigh the van on a certified scale before and after they load your shipment, or before and after they unload it. The difference between the two weights is the net weight of your shipment. Besides this transportation cost, there are charges for additional services (see below) and valuation coverage (depending upon the type you select). The prices are based on Tariff Rate Schedules, which are price lists used by interstate moving companies.

- Additional services
  These include packing, unpacking, servicing your appliances (preparing them to move and installing them after the move), and crating (enclosing

special items, like an extremely large mirror, in a crate). There is also an additional fee if the move involves stairs, elevators, carrying your belongings long distances, and shuttle service. Shuttle service is required when the moving van can't pull up to your building and a second, smaller truck is needed to get your things from the van to the building. It would be a good idea to gather the information about your destination, including the number of steps, so you can share it with movers when they come to give you an estimate. If movers get complete information about what services you want and need, they should be able to give you a good estimate.

- Types of estimates
The estimates moving companies give you can be binding (the mover guarantees the price prior to the move) or non-binding (the mover estimates the price and provides final charges after the shipment is weighed). In some states, a mover has the option to give you a "Not-to-exceed Estimate". The estimator can include known Additional Services in the binding estimate, but if any further Additional Services are required or requested on moving days, the total will need to be increased. Whether you select a binding or non-binding estimate, you'll still want to confirm, in writing, the method of payment. You'll also want the mover to confirm the date(s) they will pack your household (if you're having them pack it), the date they will load you (onto the moving van) and the date they'll deliver your shipment. In fact, it's possible to include a penalty in the contract, if the mover fails to deliver your belongings on or before a date that you specify.

- Paying for the move
All charges will need to be paid before your shipment is unloaded at your destination, unless arrangements

have been made for your employer to be billed for the shipment. Don't expect a mover to take a personal check. Some movers accept credit cards, and using one is an excellent way to get yourself a little extra protection, because the credit card company will probably help you in case there's a disagreement about the total of the charges. **In most cases, you'll be required to pay in cash, by certified check, or money order.** If you have a non-binding estimate, the mover is required by law to deliver your possessions for no more than 10% above the price on the estimate, so be prepared to pay 110% of the estimate. *Be sure the method of payment is established prior to the day your belongings are loaded onto the truck.*

* Valuation Coverage
  Valuation is not insurance. If a moving company says that your possessions are covered by their insurance, that should warn you that they are probably not an ethical company

  Moving companies offer two types of Valuation Coverage: Released Value and Full Extra Care Protection. If you select Released Value, there is no cost to you. It provides only minimal coverage and will pay you 60 cents per pound per article if lost or damaged. So if a 10-pound stereo component worth $1,000 was lost or destroyed, your mover would only be liable for $6 (10 lbs x 60 cents). If your Homeowner's Insurance covers the replacement of your household goods during the moving process, this Released Value protection may be just fine.

  Full Extra Care Protection or Full Replacement Value provides that things which are lost, damaged or destroyed will, at the mover's option, be either repaired, replaced with like items, or a cash settlement will be made for the repairs or replacement of the articles at their current market value, regardless of their age. There is a charge for this type of coverage, although it may be reduced if you select a deductible. Ask each Moving Company how their program works.

Note: The coverage you obtain may not include the contents of boxes packed by yourself, or other things the movers don't see. Check this out to be sure, and don't accept assurance that things are covered unless it's in writing.

- <u>High Value Items</u>
Very valuable items, generally those worth more than $100 per pound, such as jewelry, silver, antiques, china, crystal, oriental rugs, fur coats, sound systems, video and digital cameras, and stamp collections, are considered to be articles of "high" or "extraordinary" value. You should definitely consider carrying irreplaceable and expensive articles with you, if you feel you can protect them while doing so. If you do have the movers transport high value items, be sure to itemize them on the appropriate document, sometimes called "High Value Inventory" or "Extraordinary Value Article Declaration". If you neglect to include valuable items on this list, any damage or loss will be limited to the valuation which covers the rest of your shipment, which will probably not adequately compensate you for your loss. It would be helpful if you have an appraisal of valuable items, as well as photographs of them. Be sure to transport the photos and appraisals separately from the actual items. Have the moving representative explain how his company deals with High Value Items.

- <u>Servicing of Appliances</u>
Most refrigerators, washers, dryers, and some other appliances will need servicing prior to moving. This

may involve bolting down a motor, securing washer drums, or protecting icemakers before shipping them. This service can be provided, upon special request and for an additional charge, through your mover, or you can arrange it through your appliance dealer or regular serviceman. Gas appliances also need to be serviced and disconnected prior to moving them.

Hot tubs and flat screen televisions may also need to be serviced; inquire whether this is something the mover can arrange for or whether you'll need to get them serviced on your own.

- Wine Collections
  If you have a precious wine collection and will be moving during very cold or very warm weather, you may want to consider either moving the wine in your car (if the collection is small enough and you can control its temperature) or request an estimate for moving it on a climate-controlled moving van. We've always just let the movers pack our wine with the rest of the household goods and never had a problem, but if you're very particular about your wine, it will be more important to you. If the collection is very valuable, it would be appropriate to get an appraisal prior to packing. You can ask your local wine merchant if he can recommend a good appraiser. Most wine bottles with corks are properly packed on their side, in appropriate boxes and with good packing materials.

- Moving Company Responsibilities
  Your interstate mover must provide you with a booklet entitled *Your Rights and Responsibilities When You Move*. Read it for more details, including what to do if you have claims, complaints, or questions. It can also be accessed at www.protectyourmove.gov/consumer/awareness/rights/rights.htm.

Once you select a moving company, they will prepare an Order for Service. This is a written confirmation of the services requested, the pick-up and delivery dates, the valuation you requested, the costs for the move (the maximum if you got a non-binding esti-mate), and how you can be contacted during the move (very important).

Obviously, movers have many other responsibilities, but the booklet and Order for Service are the impor-tant ones for now.

* Additional questions
  1. Ask the moving representative whether you need to pack items which are in dresser drawers. Some movers say if the drawers just have clothing in them, and nothing fragile or very valuable, that the contents do not need to be packed. Others believe it would be best to empty all drawers.

  2. Hopefully you won't have to use it, but it's best to understand *now* what the claims process is, and what to do if something does wind up being lost or damaged in the move.

  3. Inquire about any items you're not sure whether the mover is allowed to take, such as plants, and ask about setting up your beds and wall units, etc.

  4. Do they require any deposit to hold a date for you? (You're not ready to give it until you inter-view other moving companies, but it's good to know the answer.) If they request several hundred dollars to hold the date or give you "premium ser-vice", seriously consider using another mover.

Once you've received several estimates, consider the prices, the other terms and details, and the impression you got of each company and its employees. You already checked the movers out before you set up an appointment (*see earlier in this chapter*), so add that information to the equation, and select the mover you feel will be the best one to work with. Finalize the moving dates with the company you've selected, and they should provide you with the Order of Service. Make sure you understand everything in it before you sign the document.

Chapter 10

Getting Ready For The Move

In this chapter, we cover many of the things you'll need to orchestrate in order to have the move, and the weeks or months before it, go smoothly.

Food, Glorious Food

Take an inventory of your freezer contents, to make it easier to use as much of your perishable food as possible. It makes sense to use up other food as well, especially those in cans which will add weight (and, therefore cost) to the shipment. You'll inevitably be moving *some* food products, and that's OK, as long as they're not perishable.

Hint: As you begin using up things which you don't plan to replace until after you've moved, enter the items onto a shopping list. Keep this in a handy location, so that you can keep it with you when you move, and purchase the items on the list when you do that first major grocery shopping for the new house. Your grocery and household purchases will probably cost much less as the move nears, since you won't be replenishing stock on many items, but plan to invest more than normal on them within the first 2 weeks in the new location.

Satisfy Responsibilities as Seller & Buyer

Consult the Contract of Sale for both the home you're selling and the one you're buying, to determine what actions you need to take. If you're using real estate agents, they should walk you through these steps.

- Seller Responsibilities
As a Seller, you need to maintain the home. This includes keeping the lawn mowed, repairing any-thing which breaks before the closing, and generally taking good care of the property. Depending on the terms of your contract, you may also need to set up a termite inspection, purchase a Home Owner's War-ranty, and cooperate as appointments are made to do a Home Inspection, etc. Once the Home Inspec-tion is complete, you and the Buyer may negotiate who is responsible for certain repairs. Perform—or hire someone to perform—any repairs you've agreed to do.

- Buyer Responsibilities
As a Buyer, you will need to purchase Homeowner's insurance on the new house—effective on the date of closing—and be prepared to provide proof of the prepaid policy at closing. You will also need to do whatever's required in order to remove the contin-gencies in your contract. This may include setting up a Home Inspection; evaluating the inspection results; negotiating what, if anything, the Seller is responsi-ble for fixing; having your attorney review the sales contract; shopping for mortgage rates and terms, if you haven't already; and applying for a mortgage. If there are any other contingencies you included in the contract, you need to do whatever's necessary in order to satisfy those contingencies, such as sell-ing your current home. Once financing is approved, make sure closing is scheduled on a date which goes along with the terms of your contract, and during the time that your mortgage commitment—including any interest rate lock—is active. If your closing will

occur on the day you're moving into the new house, schedule the closing for early in the day.

Additional responsibilities may be spelled out in your contract.

Make Travel Arrangements

- <u>When</u>
  Try to schedule your departure on the day *after* the moving van leaves your "old" house, if possible. That way, if the movers take a lot longer to load your things than anticipated, you're not stressed out about making your flight or getting on the road in time to get to the hotel where you have reservations that night. You can take your time, make sure everything's out of the house that should be out, and be able to leave the house in the condition in which you'd like to find it (tidy, swept, and with owner's manuals and garage door openers where the new owners will find them easily). Moving days are exhausting, so getting a good night's sleep will certainly be helpful.

- <u>Plan your drive</u>
  If you are driving to your destination, you'll want to have directions from AAA (www.AAA.com), if you're a member, or www.Mapquest.com or other routing vehicles. Be sure to do this in advance because AAA requires lead time (if you're getting a hard copy of your routing) and because you may not have access to your computer, internet connection or printer the night before the move. Even if you have a Global Positioning System (GPS), it always helps to have real maps of the areas you'll be in, as back-up in case of construction or accident delays on the highway or errors in electronic routing. Unfortunately, these things do happen.

Have your car serviced (oil change, if appropriate; check headlights, brake lights, signal lights, turn signals, tires, brakes, windshield wipers, fluids, etc.).

- Air transportation
  If you're flying, you'll want to be at the airport about two hours before departure for a domestic flight (unless security issues change significantly), so select your departure time accordingly. If you will be traveling with a child under 2 years of age and will not be purchasing a separate seat for him, you'll need to let the airline know. Sometimes there are special fares for children who do require a seat, and they may not be available online, so you'll need to call the airline to ask. If you are planning to have your pet fly on a plane—check it out well ahead of time. There are restrictions due to weather conditions and type of pet, and some states require quarantine for animals entering their state. More information about traveling with children or pets is included in Chapters 11 and 12. If you have any special needs (such as wheelchair, oxygen, or service animals) do tell the airline well ahead of time so that appropriate arrangements can be made on their part, or modifications made on yours.

- Rental Car
  If your car is leaving town before you are, you may need to rent a car for a day or two in the city you're leaving. Likewise, you may need a rental car at your destination until your car is delivered to you. Check with your employer to see if they have corporate rates with a particular car rental company which you can take advantage of—they may be lower rates than you can get with other discounts (AAA, AARP, and so on).

- Accommodations
  If you're planning to make hotel reservations for the move, consider the possibility of getting a room or

suite with a kitchen or kitchenette, especially if you have young children with you. It may make a big difference, to be able to eat while other family members are sleeping, without having to get dressed and go to a restaurant. This may be especially helpful if you're going to be in the accommodations for several days.

Depending on the time of day the movers finish placing your things into your new home, how organized you are, and other factors, you may need to stay in a hotel for an additional day or two. When you make your hotel reservation, ask about their policy for canceling the last night or two. It may make sense to reserve the room for an extra couple of nights, to reduce the pressure on yourself, especially if you know you can shorten your stay with no penalty. Also, if there's any chance you won't check in until after 6pm on the first day of the reservation, you'll want to "guarantee your reservation for late arrival". If you guarantee your reservation, you'll get charged even if you don't show up at all, but you'll know that if you get there late, there will be a room waiting for you. If stale smoke bothers you and you don't smoke, request a No Smoking room. Not all hotels offer this but many do, although they may not be willing to guarantee it.

Keep in mind that in order to stay in your new home semi-comfortably, you'll need to have heat (if it's cold out), functioning bathrooms with soap, towels and toilet paper, and either a cold refrigerator or a cooler with ice or cold packs. Sleeping bags or inflatable mattresses, blankets and pillows are also pretty important, unless your beds are there, made up with linens, and ready to use. Also, you'll want a telephone and an alarm to wake you up before any telephone, cable, or appliance service people arrive. If you have a good cell phone signal inside the house and your charger, you'll be OK in the telephone and alarm department.

Medical/Dental Appointments and Records

- Scheduling appointments
  You may want to schedule appointments before the move with your physicians, optometrist or dentist, especially if there's a problem you'd like to have resolved with someone you know and trust. However, if all is well, we like to schedule appointments with physicians and dentists soon after the move, because then we and the medical professionals get to know each other while there are no big problems. If we're comfortable with them, then when a problem *does* arise, we know who to call and they know what we're like when we're feeling good. Plus, it's always easier to get an appointment at a doctor's or dentist's office if you're an established patient. If you're not comfortable with the medical professional, you can continue to ask around for references, and hopefully have someone good lined up by the time they're needed. *For more information on finding health professionals in your new area, see Chapter 16.*

- Obtain Your Medical/Dental Records

  ↳ Contact your physicians and dentist, and ask them for an **Authorization for the Release of Information** form. You'll need to complete and return this to them, in order to receive copies of your health records, or a summary of the information. These records should include vaccine and immunization records. Often, a letter requesting that your records be forwarded to the new professional will suffice, as long as it has your signature on it. Be sure to include the new doctor's name, address, and phone number. A copy of your prescription for glasses or contacts should also be obtained from your optometrist.

☛ **Be aware that physicians routinely forward only the records their office has generated.** So if you had surgery 15 years ago using a different physician, and those records were then forwarded to your current doctor, they will not automatically be forwarded to your next one. Try to get copies of everything in your file so that you can take them with you. Then give copies to your new doctor, but maintain copies in your own medical file, so you can reference them if & when you change doctors again. In some circumstances it may also be appropriate to take x-rays to your new physician—ask your doctor if you think this may apply to you.

☛ **It's common for medical offices to charge a fee for these copies**, although not every doctor does. They are only permitted to charge an amount to cover the cost of copying, including labor and supplies, plus any postage required to send it to you. Some medical offices take up to 60 days to send out records, so ask how long it should take when you call. Follow up to be sure the records have arrived, preferably *before* your first appointment with a new provider.

☛ **Keep your eyeglass prescriptions** with your medical records. If you don't have a copy, ask your ophthalmologist or optometrist for a spare prescription in case your glasses or contacts are lost or damaged.

☛ **If you have a particular medical condition** which might need special attention, you can ask your doctor to write a letter of introduction to the new doctor. It would be a one-page summary of your situation, the treatment you have had and are currently undergoing, and anything special your doctor feels your new doctor should know. Rather than sitting with an inch-thick file to review at your first visit, this will bring the new doctor up to speed quickly and will help him to treat you appropriately from the beginning. Not every physician will be willing to take the time and effort to write a letter like this, but it doesn't hurt to ask, and it could be very beneficial for your health.

Notifications

- <u>Be organized</u>
  If you haven't already done so, start a file folder and label it CHANGE OF ADDRESS. You'll want to begin notifying others of your new address as soon as 6-8 weeks before the move. Magazines are a prime example of those who need a long time to make the change.

  <u>Keep a list</u> of who you've notified and when, for easy reference. As you get monthly bills and statements, notify these companies so that they will make the changes to your account. Advise them of the effective date, so they don't send mail to your new address TOO soon. Believe me, you will wonder as the move progresses, whether you've notified this company or that, and keeping good records will save you the time of sending duplicate notifications. Sometimes, companies fail to note the change of address, and 3 months down the line it can help to tell them exactly how you notified them (mail, phone or online) and when. Keep in mind that mailing labels are often generated 4-8 weeks in advance, sometimes longer.

- <u>Change of Address Forms</u>
  The U.S. Postal Service (USPS) offers Mover's Guides at no charge, available at any Post Office. They contain one card to give to your local Post Office with your

new address, and quite a few postcards you can use to send to magazines, and other places. Of course, you can accomplish all of this online if you prefer. You can change your address with the Postal Service at www.usps.com using your e-mail address and your credit card (which will be charged approximately $1). For magazines, check the title page for the publisher's website. You'll need to have the mailing label from the magazine in front of you when you do this online, because you're required to enter the name and address exactly as it appears on the mailing label. If you choose to mail the change-of-address postcard, rather than doing it online, cut your label off of the magazine cover and tape it onto the postcard where it asks for "old address".

The USPS will forward first class mail for one year after the effective date of a change-of-address. Also, many bulk mailers pay for and automatically receive address updates from the post office when a forwarding order is in place. If you see "Address Service Requested" printed on a piece of forwarded mail, the post office is probably notifying the sender of your new address.

- Automatic debits
  Notify companies and organizations which regularly debit your checking account, and give them the information for your new checking account (if you're switching banks). Find out when the debit change will be effective, so you know which account to keep those funds in, during the transition. If you receive direct deposits, such as Social Security, be sure to notify these depositors as well, and find out when the first deposits will hit the new account. This information will help you determine how much to keep in which account in order to prevent insufficient funds and associated fees.

- <u>Utility companies</u>
  Make arrangements with your current utility companies which provide **gas, electric, and water & sewer**
  to take final readings as close to your closing date as
  possible. You probably don't want these utilities to be
  disconnected, but rather to switch the billing name
  on a given date (usually the date you close the sale
  of your house). The Buyers may need to call with this
  request before the utility will honor the transfer. If your
  buyers are moving from out of your area, they might
  appreciate being given the names and phone numbers of the utility companies, so that they can do this
  notification.

  If your home is heated by oil or propane gas, discontinue your automatic refills. In some areas, you or the
  utility will do a final estimate of the fuel remaining, and
  using your last bill, calculations will be made so that
  you are reimbursed for the remaining fuel which you
  purchased. It is often *not* recommended that you fill
  the tank prior to closing. Check with your Real Estate
  agent to find out how this is handled in your area.

  If the house is going to be vacant for awhile, consult with your Real Estate agent about the advisability
  of disconnecting service. Probably it will be difficult
  to show the house properly without lights, and you
  may need heat if it's going to be vacant during cold
  weather, to avoid having pipes freeze. Under some
  circumstances, such as when a relocation company
  is involved, it may be appropriate to temporarily
  transfer these services to the real estate broker until
  it's time to transfer them to the new owner. Your listing agent can explain if this is appropriate for you. If
  the services are to be disconnected, try to have that
  done right *after* moving day.

You'll need to provide utility companies with your new address, so that they can forward your final bill. They may even owe you a refund or the return of any deposit you made when you initially signed up for their service.

Your **home telephone** will also need to be disconnected, if you have a land line. Once your new phone service is connected, I suggest you give the number to your old phone company so that they can include it in the recording people hear when they call your old number. You've probably heard these recordings before. They say, as an example, "The number you have called, 222-555-1111, has been disconnected. The new number is 555-222-1111. Please make a note of it." If you have a cell phone as back-up, have your land line disconnected on moving day. Often, phone companies won't promise what time of day this will take effect. If you don't have a cell phone you can count on, request that disconnection to take place at the end of moving day, but accept the following day if there's any doubt that they might turn it off too early. It's important for you to be able to communicate at this important and potentially stressful time, but at the same time you'd like to ensure that no one is going to make long distance calls using your phone after you've left town.

Hint: You will probably be using your cell phone a lot more than normal during the moving days. Be sure you have enough minutes in your contract to cover the additional use. It may make financial sense to increase your package to add minutes, rather than spend $60 in additional minutes for one month. Before you sign any contracts, though, verify that your cell company has good service in your new area. If not, it may be time to switch carriers.

Additional utility companies are included in the list below.

- Other companies/organizations to notify
  1. Credit cards (and close any local charge accounts)
  2. Insurance companies (including Life, Health, Automobile, Long Term Care and Disability)
  3. Bank* (see additional info below) and other financial institutions
  4. Investment accounts
  5. Vehicle finance company (auto loan)
  6. Accountant
  7. Attorney
  8. Financial consultant
  9. Stock broker
  10. Physicians
  11. Dentist
  12. Chiropractor
  13. Employer (even if you're leaving the job, because they'll need to send your W-2 in January)
  14. Telephone providers for long distance and cell (for home, see above under "utility companies")
  15. Internet service provider
  16. Cable or satellite TV
  17. Trash collector
  18. Home Security Service
  19. Lawn Service
  20. Home cleaning service
  21. Health club (You may be able to transfer membership if they have clubs in your new city; in some cases you're required to provide written notice a certain number of days in advance to cancel. Consult your contract.)
  22. Organizations
  23. Magazine subscriptions
  24. Professional journals
  25. Newspapers

26. Newsletters
27. Schools and alma maters
28. Church/Synagogue
29. Social Security Administration (if you receive benefits)
30. Veteran's Administration (if appropriate)

*Before closing your checking account you'll need to allow time for checks you've written to clear. This may take a month or 2 (and you may have to call some folks who are slow at depositing their checks). Make sure you have enough in each account to cover the checks and debits which will occur, and to hopefully avoid bank charges for falling below the minimum balance for your type of account. Check with your bank before the move, to find out the best way to close the account. Some banks charge a fee (ours charges $20) to close the account by mail.

- Moving announcements
  Prepare moving announcements and a list of family and friends you would like to notify. The labels can be made up ahead of time. You can use custom printed announcements, generic ones (which you purchase at a card store and fill in the blanks), announcements you generate yourself (using your computer or artistic abilities by hand), or you can even notify most of the people by e-mail (obviously the "greenest" way). We recently received a very cool "We've Moved" announcement from friends who used a small photo of their new house with the address in the return address section on the front of the postcard, and new contact info along with a small photo of them on the reverse side. This is especially good for sending to clients or acquaintances who are potential clients.

  Be sure to list the effective date of the new address. When you list your new phone number, be aware that sometimes a phone company will give you your new number but not guarantee it. If you're concerned about this, you may want to have the announcements all prepared in advance (you won't have the time and energy when you first move in) but wait until the phone is connected and you definitely have the right phone number, before actually putting the announcements into the mail. You can always change the phone number by hand, if necessary. If you notify friends & family TOO long before the move, they may either lose the announcement, or change your address immediately and then send things to the new house weeks before you're there to receive it. In that case, your mail may be returned to the sender.

Establishing Accounts in the New City

- Bank Accounts
  Open bank accounts in the new city, if possible, about a month or more prior to your move. You can use your current address in the beginning or, if one of you is beginning the new job at that point, you could use that spouse's temporary address. The bank can supply you with temporary checks (they will probably be able to print out the quantity you'll need at no extra charge). Then, after you've closed on the new house, you can simply change the address on the bank account and order permanent checks.

  When ordering permanent checks, request that the number begin with 500 or 1000, or even whatever number your current checks end at. Some businesses require additional screening when you write a check with a low sequence number, so this may save you some hassle when you write checks around town or at the grocery store. Also, consider having your check order sent directly to the bank, for security reasons. The bank employees will hopefully call when they're in, so you'll know when to take your photo ID and go to pick them up.

One of the reasons for establishing a checking account in advance of the move is that many businesses will only accept a local check. (This is not much of an issue anymore, since so many of us carry debit cards.) Also, it will be a lot easier to just notify the bank of the change of address and order checks, rather than take on the project of selecting a bank and opening an account while you're trying to get all your worldly belongings put away in your new house. Another advantage of doing this ahead of time is that once you know what bank you're going to do business with, it will be a no-brainer to figure out where to open a safe deposit box. That's important, because you don't want to keep those valuable things laying around the house for long after you move in. It will be much better if they're put in safekeeping as soon as possible after your move. The rate that you pay for the safe deposit box may be less if you have an account at that bank.

Do your research to get the best account for you. You want a bank which has locations convenient to home and/or work, and whose deposits are protected by the FDIC Some banks have branches which are in grocery stores and have non-traditional hours. Also, you'll want to check out the terms of various accounts so that you select the best one considering: whether your employer will be using Direct Deposit for your paychecks, the number and types of accounts you'll be maintaining (and possibly the total balance in those accounts), which accounts offer free checks, online bill paying, and other perks, and whether it's important to you to earn interest. Also, inquire about overdraft protection. Banks often have several products to offer, which will serve that purpose, and even if you're not ready to pursue them right now, at least you'll know what's available.

- Utility companies
  Telephone, internet, cable or satellite TV, trash collection, and gas and electric companies are among the services you may need to arrange for in your new home. To find out which utility companies operate in your new area and how to reach them, consult your real estate salesperson, the website of your new town, the local phone directory, or even your new neighbors. In some cases, there may be more than one provider you can use for some of these services. Knowing about your options is important because you'll want to evaluate the cost as well as the service provided. Waste removal companies are one example where prices and service (quality as well as how often and what they will pick up, and what they recycle) differ widely. Some cities and towns list this information on their website. You'll probably need to request that the utility companies begin service or transfer the account (if they're already providing service there) into your name, on the date you take possession.

For phone service, it's important to place your order as soon as possible. Some areas have a 2-3 week waiting list—or longer—to get new phone service installed. And you won't be 100% assured of the number until it's actually installed.

Utility Company Brokers: When arranging for services in some areas, there are "brokers" who can sign you up for all of your utilities, offering a one-stop service. It definitely saves some time on your part, however you may not be given all of the choices available when you go that route, and the prices may not be the best ones. We used one of these brokers, offered as a convenience service by our relocation team, when we moved back to Atlanta. After being in our home for several years, we found out that we were paying our trash collection company significantly more than our neighbors down the street were paying for the same service from the same company. In that location, residents are free to select any trash removal company which services the area, but we didn't realize the companies might charge inconsistent rates and that if we called them directly we might be able to negotiate a better rate. If you're inclined to use a broker for this service, remember to *ask questions* about your options, and verify prices with your neighbors when you get a chance.

- <u>Cell Phones</u>
  Check to see if your cell phone company services your new area. If not, many companies allow you to terminate your contract with no penalty. You'll want to explore which companies have the best service in your new area, as well as the other places you expect to spend time in, when you travel. Note that even if a cell phone company has service in the area, you may not get good reception in your new home. Check it out when you're there before committing to a contract you can't cancel without a penalty.

  Some people like to keep their old cell phone number so that friends and family will be able to reach them by placing a "local call". More and more people have cell phone contracts which include "anywhere minutes" or home phone service with "flat rate long distance", so that may or may not be an important issue.

- <u>Communicate Adjustments to Moving Company</u>
  If you change your mind and decide, for instance, to move the dining room table instead of selling it, or if

you need to alter the moving date—let the moving company know right away. They can usually make adjustments to accommodate your needs, if they know about any changes well in advance.

Inventory Your Belongings

- Appraisals & Photos
  Get an appraisal of antique items or pricey artwork to verify their value. If you don't have a fairly current appraisal of valuable jewelry, get that, too. Also, take photos of any items of great value. The appraisals and photos will be helpful in case of loss or damage. As they say, a picture's worth a thousand words. Keep the appraisals in a safe place and not with the valuables themselves. If anything is damaged or stolen, it's important that you be able to get to the appraisals.

- Take inventory
  I don't want to overwhelm you, so don't feel that you *have* to do this, but if you're able to take an inventory of your belongings it will prove extremely helpful, not only for this move but for whenever you might need to place an insurance claim in the future. It's also helpful so that you can make sure you have enough insurance to cover your possessions. If there was a fire in your house, would do you have any chance of remembering all the things you have? Probably not. If taking a thorough inventory is not realistic, just include the most valuable things—it would certainly be much better than not doing one at all.

An inventory can be done by taking photos of your things and writing or recording information about each item, especially valuables like jewelry, silver, art work, and collectibles. Digital photos can be downloaded and other photos can be scanned; then both can be saved onto a disk. Or you could use a camcorder and tell appropriate information about each item while you're recording. The information which should be included are where you bought it (if you remember that), the brand name and model number, and where available, the serial number. For clothing, it may be sufficient to simply list how many pants, blouses and coats etc. you have, unless the brand names will establish high dollar values. If you have receipts and/or appraisals for valuable items, attach these to your inventory record.

Home inventory programs, worksheets, and advice are available at a variety of real estate and insurance company websites, as well as in some personal finance software programs. **Very important: keep the completed inventory in a safe deposit box—or with you during a move,** while you travel to your destination. It's essential that it NOT be on the moving van. After the move, it would be wise to update your inventory annually, or after any major purchase for your home.

Inventory hint: This has nothing to do with moving, but as long as you're doing an inventory, you may want to include sentimental information, such as that the diamond butterfly necklace belonged to your mother's Aunt Freda, or the little box was purchased by your parents when they visited Italy for their 30th anniversary. These details may be helpful for your heirs some day, as they wonder what of your things are valuable or are precious family heirlooms. We actually did this type of inventory for my in-laws several years ago, and placed the photos in a small photo album we named "Cal & Fran's Treasures". I labeled each item in the photographs with a number, and created a list, giving information about each numbered item. Later on, when my mother-in-law passed away, we were extremely glad to have this record of the history of various items.

Miscellaneous Hints

- <u>Wood furniture</u>
  Avoid waxing or oiling wood furniture before the move, because some products may soften the wood, making it more likely to incur damage to the finish.

- <u>Don't move the dust</u>
  Put aside a few old cloth diapers or other dust rags for the moving days, because you'll inevitably see surfaces you normally can't get to, which you'll want to wipe clean before things are moved and put together again.

- <u>Address labels?</u>
  Don't worry about ordering address labels. Unless they've moved on to another giveaway idea, charitable organizations will find you within weeks and supply you with enough address labels to last at least a decade. If you'd like a small quantity to use in the meantime, office supply stores carry blank return address labels which are fairly easy to print, using your computer. If you don't have access to a computer or a friend who will do it for you, you could also order a stamp at your local office supply store. This will only take a week or 10 days, as opposed to 4-8 weeks for personalized labels you order to be shipped to you. You can always order those in addition, if you prefer them; but you may need something to use in the meantime, if you'll be moving before they will arrive.

- <u>What should we leave in the house?</u>
  You are expected to remove everything from the house except those items included in the sale, and things such as extra keys, garage door openers, owner's manuals for major appliances (and information about anything else which is part of the sale, such

as ceiling fans, carpeting, security system, etc., if you have it). It will be helpful to leave a note about trash day, and what items are collected for recycling. If you have wallpaper, carpet remnants or paint which matches what's currently in the house, your Buyer will appreciate having them. What will *not* be appreciated is trash, cans of old paint, or anything else which the new owners would have to dispose of. There are laws about disposing of hazardous materials, including paint, so check with your community to find out how to handle these items for everyone's safety.

- <u>Any special advice for those of us with children or pets?</u>
  YES. *See Chapters 11 and 12.*

- <u>Medications</u>
  Prescription medications should travel with you, rather than in the moving van or even in checked luggage. If you have drugs which need to be refrigerated, plan on bringing a cooler with you, whether you fly or drive. There are no refrigerators on board commercial aircraft, so you'll need to use ice or blue ice in your cooler, which should be as small as possible (like the size of a lunchbox). Full-size coolers are too large to carry onto a commercial airplane. If you use needles or syringes to administer prescription medications (such as insulin), be sure to have appropriate documentation with you for the folks at airport security.

- <u>Selling large appliances or equipment</u>
  If you'll be using a lawn mower, snow blower, clothes dryer or other large appliances or equipment up until the move, you may be able to sell the item ahead of time, and possibly collect a down payment, with the understanding that the balance will be due and

possession take place right before the move. If, by some chance, the purchasers back out at the last minute, it's often possible to have a charity pick the item up within a day or 2, and you'll at least have a tax deduction and be released from the responsibility of disposing of the item.

We once had someone agree to purchase our washer and dryer, but the day before the move they didn't come to complete the purchase and we weren't able to reach them. Fortunately, we were able to locate a non-profit organization which helps battered women and children to get set up in apartments. They were thrilled to send a couple of men with a truck to pick up the donation. We got a thank you note from the recipients a couple of weeks later (they sent it to our old address and it was forwarded to us) and we were really glad it had worked out that way.

- Moving Expenses
  These may be deductible from your taxes, if you moved due to your job. Check with your accountant or the IRS to see if your move meets the requirements. If so, you may be able to deduct costs including the movers, hotel, transportation costs, meals, automobile registration, and driver's licenses. Be sure to save your receipts!

- Plan to use disposables the last couple days
  We know it's not "green", but there's a time and place for everything, and when you've got to get your dishes and glasses and cutlery packed, this is the time for paper plates and plasticware. You might want to keep out one pot and one microwaveable container until the end, for various needs.

- Use it or gift it but don't waste it
  Check coupons and gift certificates for local establishments, so you can be sure to use them or share them with friends rather than move them and have

them be worthless. Gift certificates or gift cards for businesses which have locations in other cities are often usable at any location.

- Don't lose sleep over the details
  You'll sleep easier if you keep a pad & pen by your bedside, so when you think of things you can write them down and then clear your mind for sleep, instead of worrying that you might not remember it in the morning.

Arranging & Decorating Your New Home – Steps to Take Before the Move

- Pre-arrange for services such as carpet cleaning or replacement, wallpaper hanging or stripping, and/ or painting. These services can be done much more easily when the house is vacant, so if you have that luxury, it will be much easier on you and the job will be done more quickly.

  I strongly suggest that improvements be made after you own the house, however, because otherwise you put yourself in a poor bargaining position should any problems arise at closing. In the worst case, the sale falls through and you've lost any funds you invested in the property—and you may even need to pay to undo the work you've had done.

- Arrange the furniture
  Figure out ahead of time how you'd like to arrange your furniture. You can make scaled drawings of the rooms in your new home, cut out scaled drawings of your furniture, and play around with them that way. Or you can go online and find software which will help you to do it on your computer. Or you can even spring for a magnetic furniture planning kit, such as that offered through Scale Space Planning Products

(www.furnitureplanning.com or 877-215-4420). However you choose to do it, it's especially helpful to figure out where the heavy pieces will go. You may wind up moving them afterwards, but it really helps if you can have the movers place things properly as soon as they bring them into the house. Remember to note where doors and windows are before you start this project. Inevitably something in the house will need to be moved, despite your best planning, and you can have the movers do a minimum of this before they leave. (It would be nice to tip them a bit additional for this service, because they're not actually *required* to do it.) The more prepared you are, the better.

Make sure to allow enough room between your dining room table and other furniture, to allow people to sit at the table and others to pass behind them. Approximately 3-4 feet between the table and the other piece of furniture, or a wall, is usually sufficient. Also, make sure your traffic paths are wide enough to walk around comfortably.

- Color schemes
  When selecting color schemes, if you'll want to purchase bed linens, towels, curtains and/or rugs, look in stores to see what current accessory colors are, to make sure you'll be able to find accessories in the right colors. Just because mauve towels were everywhere when you decorated your last home, doesn't mean you'll be able to find any now.

  There are some great sites online which will help you select paint colors, such as www.benjaminmoore.com and www.glidden.com. At www.behr.com you can upload photos of your own rooms and view them in different paint colors using their Paint Your Place™ feature. You may also want to check out paint and other materials from www.healthyhome.com. This company has earned several green certifications, and among other products, it offers paint which has low or no odor, and no VOC (gassing off).

Some of the sites also let you look at external colors, but we prefer driving around the area looking at similar houses, to see what appeals to us. Some colors which look great on the outside of a house in Pittsburgh really don't fit in on a house in Florida or New Mexico, so check out what colors are typical for your area and try to stay in character.

- New purchases: be prepared
  Years ago, an interior designer gave me this hint: You never know when you will see something which might be perfect for your home, so be prepared. Collect small samples of fabric from your furniture (obviously from places which won't be visible or damage the integrity of the piece), window coverings, carpet remnants, or anything else which will be in your new home. Place them in a small plastic bag and tuck it in your purse or bag. Then, when you unexpectedly run across something that you think might work for your new home, you'll be able to compare it immediately with your swatches and see whether the color or pattern really goes with your things.

Appliances

Refrigerators and freezers which are being moved should be turned off one to two days before the move, and defrosted, dried and aired out, with the door open. Take appropriate safety precautions if you have children around. To absorb odors and make the appliance smell fresh, place baking soda in a dish or charcoal inside a nylon stocking, knot at the top, and place inside the appliance. All removable parts should be individually packed. Check with your Owner's Manual or consult the manufacturer for details.

You may want to load up a cooler for the few items you'll need between the time you turn off the refrigerator and moving day. Unless you plan to drive with the cooler in your car, you can dispose of any remaining contents and get the cooler onto the moving van before it leaves. Ask the driver when he comes to load the van, when you'll need to have it emptied. Remember to keep a towel or some paper towels available to dry out the cooler before it gets packed.

Computers

- Original packing materials
  Even if the movers will be packing your belongings, it will be helpful if you have the carton and packing materials in which these items were originally packed. If not, extensive use of bubble wrap and a large, sturdy box should hopefully keep them safe.

- Back up your computer
  Make sure that you have a computer back-up strategy in place. If you don't, then figure one out prior to the move. Besides the normal back-up, also back up your most important files onto something easy to access (for example, an external hard drive or memory stick) and be sure to keep the back-ups with you during the move, or send them to your destination using an insured, traceable method.

Saying Your Goodbyes

- Plan get-togethers with close friends, and consider hosting a party a few weeks before the move. Take photos of relatives and special friends, possibly making them into a collage after the move. If you have children at home, you might want to do a separate party for them and their friends, in a setting where they can interact and you can take photos of your children with their friends. *See more suggestions for kids in Chapter 11 under "Before Moving Day"*.

- Use a camcorder (borrow one if you need to) to record a tour of the house while it's still intact (before pictures are removed from the walls, etc). Include family members, especially the children. Shortly before one of our moves, we had our second grade daughter give the tour, which we captured on video. That made it a very special keepsake, and a real treat to watch years later.

- What places in your area did you really enjoy going to, and believe you'll miss when you don't live there anymore? Try to find the time to revisit them before you leave.

Prepare Survival Kit

It's important to put aside everything you and your family will need during the last day or two before moving, when final packing is taking place, until you are partially unpacked and staying in your new home. You also need to gather valuable items which you should keep with you rather than send on the moving van, and many of these are listed in Chapter 13, under "What Not To Pack". Obviously, you'll have to think about what items are appropriate for you, but here's a list to get you started.

- Clothing, including outerwear if appropriate

- Cosmetics, personal hygiene items

- Medications (in original containers), vitamins and supplements

- First aid kit

- Flashlight

- Snack foods to hold you over between meals

- A roll of cellophane tape and masking tape, and a pad of paper (for making notes and "Do Not Move" signs and for labeling rooms in the new house)

- Travel documents including your ticket and/or itinerary if flying, rental car reservations, hotel reservations, and maps to your destination if driving

- Contact information for your real estate agents (in both locations), moving company representatives, mortgage broker (if you have one) and real estate closing information for both homes (including phone numbers, directions, date and time)

- Phone numbers for utility companies for old house and new, so you won't have to look for them if you need to contact them regarding connection or disconnect issues

- Documents relating to the sale of your house, the purchase of your new house, and those relating to the move. Remember to take with you the inventory sheets the mover gives you before the van pulls away—they're very important.

- A list of all your medical professionals, including their office addresses and phone numbers

- Map of your new area, and directions to your new house and closing location and accommodations

- Your address book or planner or whatever you keep all of your current contact information in, including your new address and phone number (even if it's not active yet)

- Cash or traveler's checks and major credit card (if you rent a car you'll need to use a credit card for the rental to avoid paying a huge up-front deposit)

- If you have children or pets, see Chapters 11 and 12 for additional items.

Before Moving Day, Remember To:

- Return materials to the library (and school library) and pay any outstanding fines.

- Return any movies or games which you've rented or borrowed.

- Empty and close your Safe Deposit Box.

- Pick up items from the Dry Cleaners, shoe repair, jeweler, and/or tailor.

- Gather Owner's Manuals and warrantees for major appliances which will remain in the house (oven, cook top, refrigerator, furnace, washer, dryer, etc.), as well as those for house siding, carpeting, windows, and so on. Place in an envelope or clear plastic bag, with a big "DO NOT PACK" sign on it.

- Collect spare house keys from family, friends, neighbors, and under that rock in the backyard. Place with other items you don't want packed, but will give to the new owners. Also write down the code for the security system, and give to the new owners.

- Gather money or other valuables which you, or your family, may have hidden in or around the house.

- Return any keys for other people's houses, if you'll no longer have a need for them.

- Drain the fuel from your lawn mower, gas weeder, and leaf blower (or let them run until there's no fuel left).

- Properly dispose of any hazardous materials, such as paint which is not a current color used in or on the house, and gasoline.

- Collect any belongings you keep at the gym or other recreational facility. Be sure your children have cleaned out their lockers at school and collected any clothing or other items they've lent to their friends. Check the Lost & Found at school, place of worship, and recreational facilities. Retrieve or return any tools, books, or other items you've exchanged with others.

- Gather items for your Survival Kit (*see above*) and things which should stay with you during the move. *See "What Not To Pack", in Chapter 11.*

- Settle all current bills, so that they don't get overlooked in the busy-ness of the move.

- Advise a close friend or family member of your itinerary and contact information during the move, in case of emergency.

- Unplug electronic equipment, such as TVs, computers and stereos, and allow them to reach room temperature before they're moved, to avoid causing damage to their components.

- Drain waterbeds prior to moving day. This sometimes takes hours longer than you think it will, so allow plenty of time. Remember to unplug the mattress heater and allow it to cool before you begin draining the mattress. Check manufacturer instructions for further details.

Make sure you have mattress conditioner, the adapter, and anything else you'll need to get your mattress set up in your new home, so that you won't have to go looking for a store which sells waterbed supplies while you're busy unpacking that first week. (We've had to do this.) Pack these things together, if possible, to make life easier for you to refill the mattress, as you begin to get settled in your new home.

- Have fruit and other snacks available for you and your family, and beverages for yourselves and the movers. Put ice or blue ice into a cooler to keep things cold if your refrigerator is disconnected.

- Be sure to have any packing you're doing yourself completed before the packers come. If you'll be packing *all* of your possessions, you'll need to have everything ready to go by the time the movers arrive on moving day. If the mover determines that any of your packed boxes are not safe for transport, they will want to repack them before taking responsibility for moving them.

  Even if you have the moving company pack your belongings, there may be a few things you'd rather pack yourself—personal items you may be uncomfortable about strangers handling. If you do pack your own box or 2 for the movers to take, be sure to use a marker to label what room it should be placed in. Your movers will probably mark "PBO" on those boxes. That stands for "Packed By Owner" and releases them from responsibility in case the contents are damaged. *See Packing on Your Own, in Chapter 13.*

- Be prepared with cash to tip the people who pack and move your goods, if you decide you'd like to tip them. The amount will depend on the size of your move and how much the movers set up for you (wall units, bedroom suites with light bridges, etc), as well as how comfortable you are with the movers and the services you received...anywhere from $40-60 for a small, local move to $100-200 or more for a distant move which takes up a full trailer. At least one moving company I contacted said they do not condone tipping their personnel. However, those I have tipped have really appreciated it, and I have *never* had a mover turn down a tip.

- Take the garage door opener out of your car(s)!

Chapter 11
Moving With Children

"As a child, leaving friends and familiar surroundings was sad and frightening at first. But after some time in our new city, I would make friends whom I never would have otherwise met. As an adult, I'm now thankful for the varied experiences that broadened my world." Michelle Fradkin

In this chapter, we will discuss when best to move schoolchildren, communicating with your children about the move, how to put a positive spin on the move, traveling with children, and getting children established in the new environment.

When to Move

Check out the calendar for the school districts in your new area. School may begin or end much earlier or later than you're used to. Some school districts, for instance, begin the fall semester by mid-August, while others don't begin until well into September. If your children are fairly young, it doesn't matter a lot when you decide to move. Some children find it easier to meet others when they move during the school year and are the "new kid". However, if you have the choice, and especially if you have older children or teenagers in your household, you may not want to uproot them in the middle of academic courses. That can be very disruptive to their education, so moving during the summer—or during winter break, if summer's not feasible—might be the best solution. Also, older children (and some younger children) often have very strong ties with their schoolmates, and get very upset if moved during the school year. Juniors and Seniors may insist that they want to stay at their school until graduation. It's a pretty important time in a person's life, so you may want to consider that request (whether it means one spouse staying back with the kids until graduation, or having the high schooler stay with trusted friends or family until the school year is over). That said, children do usually adjust very well to a move, especially once they've established at least one new friend in the new community. And it *is* very important, for your marriage as well as you and your children, to get you all living under the same roof as soon as possible.

Discussing the Move with Your Children

- **Don't keep it a secret**
  You may need to bounce the situation off a close relative or friend while you're making the decision, but try very hard not to share the news with others before you talk with your children. They have a way of overhearing conversations or seeing nonverbal communications and will know something's going on.

  If you will actually take your children's input into consideration when you make the decision about moving, obviously you'll talk with them as you're considering it. Otherwise, try to tell them as soon as you've made the decision and done enough research to be able to give them some basic information about the move. If you delay telling them and they find out another way, they could feel betrayed by you, and their resentment could delay their adjustment to the idea of moving.

- **Call a Family Meeting**
  Discuss the move with all of your children at the same time. Pick a time and place where you can all be

comfortable and you can take the time to address all the questions and concerns which come up immediately. This is going to be a process, and many more questions will come up as time goes by. It may be helpful to have a map with you, to show the children where you live and where you're moving. If you have not made the final decision yet, and will truly take their feelings into account, by all means lay it out for them and listen to their opinions and the reasons behind them.

- **Tell your children why you're moving and why it's good for *them***
  Talk openly about the move. Explain why you're going to relocate, and be prepared to point out why it will be a good thing for your children. Perhaps there are more sports opportunities, or the weather is nicer, or it's near mountains where you can all go skiing in the winter. Maybe you're moving to a state where college tuition is free for local high school graduates who have earned good grades. Perhaps there are family members who live in the new area (this may or may not be seen as a good thing, by the way). Maybe this will be an opportunity for your children to have a bedroom of their own or even a pet. Think these things through before promising them—and *please* don't suggest you might be getting a pet unless you seriously believe you will take good care of it for life—but whatever you truly believe is realistic and something they will see as a good thing may help their outlook about the transition.

- **Watch your attitude**
  If you approach the move in a positive, excited way, it will go a long way toward your children having the same attitude. Even as they may be protesting it, they're watching how you're handling things.

They may well adjust their initial attitude to coincide with yours, once they get used to the idea and get more information about what's ahead.

- **What's going to happen when**
  Discuss the timetable and the process—when the new job will start, when you will look for a new home, whether they will be included in that adventure, and when you expect everyone to move. Explain that you will be driving or flying to your new home, while most of your things will be going in a moving van.

- **Involve your kids in the process**
  Children (and even adults) may become anxious because of the unknown, so give them an appropriate job to do, and do what you can to put them at ease.

    - **Take them househunting, if you can.** It may help if they're able to tag along when you visit the new area.
    - **Research online.** Research the area online with your kids, if they're old enough, or even assign them the job of researching particular areas of interest themselves, if they're capable.
    - **Check out written materials.** Look through the literature and brochures you've received from your real estate agent and/or the Chamber of Commerce in your new town.
    - **Let them make some decisions.** Allowing children to have some input in the process will help them buy into the concept of the move, and even get excited about it. Be careful to only ask opinions on things about which you may actually follow their suggestions. This can be as simple as offering your kids a new style of bed in the new house (bunk bed or waterbed, for

instance), or allowing them to help pick colors for their new bedroom or work on furniture arrangement. Making a floor plan and using it to arrange furniture could even become a school project.

A great way to let them be part of the decision-making process is to come up with some choices, all of which are acceptable to you. An example is asking whether they would like their walls to be painted sky blue, taupe, or off-white. You will then hopefully avoid the answer we got when our daughter was about 13. We asked her what color she'd like her bedroom walls and wood-work to be, and she responded "All black". (We did paint the baseboards and trim black, but kept the walls white.)

- **Ask their opinion.** If you do ask their opinions on other matters, tell them up front that you may not wind up going with their suggestion, but you would like to get their input on what-ever it is, so that you can consider it. Having influence over some of the decisions which are made at this time will help everyone in the fam-ily to feel that they have some control over the situation.

- **Have them help plan the route** you'll take, if you'll be driving to your new city. Depending on the amount of time you'll have, they might even be able to suggest a place of interest, to see along the way.

- **Allow them to grieve and encourage them to express their feelings**
  In many cases, children will be unhappy at the thought of leaving their friends, as well as their famil-iar activities and home. Very young children may not even understand that their friends and neigh-bors will not be in living in the new city. Make sure

your children know they can talk about the move and its ramifications with you. They may be angry (especially older children) and sad. Allow them to express their feelings, and resist telling them they don't—or shouldn't—feel that way. They're *entitled* to those feelings. Try to be patient and understanding. Tell them that they can keep in touch with people by e-mailing, texting, tweeting, and/or talking on the phone (if you will let them do these things), and that they can visit each other once in awhile during the summer or school breaks (if this is feasible). After awhile, they should adjust to the coming changes, and will complete this process after they've lived in the new area for long enough to establish friends and a routine and feel comfortable in the new area.

- **Make it as positive as you can**
  Discuss the good things in your child's life right now, and try to recreate similar ones in your new location. Try to have them meet (in person, via Skype or electronically) some kids their age in the new city. These could be potential new neighbors, schoolmates, or members of a church or synagogue you plan to attend.

- **What about a teenager's job or child's special interests?**
  If your teenager has a job now, and is concerned about where he might be employed after the move, work together to find out about job possibilities in the new town. A lot of this research can be done online. In many cases, potential employees can even fill out a job application online. Also, research activities or groups which are similar to what your child participates in currently, be it Tae Kwon Do or community theatre or whatever.

Once you have determined exactly where you will be living, look into sports teams if your children are interested in playing. In many cases, these teams are formed months before the first practice begins, so it may be important to register even before you are actually living there.

- **Understand the control issues**
  Especially for teenagers, school and friends and perhaps jobs are vital parts of their lives. All of these things are going to change, and it's understandable if they're feeling upset at the lack of control they have over their lives right now. Keeping them involved in the move will help overcome these feelings. It won't be magical, but it will help. Try to understand what they're going through, even when they're not being especially sweet.

Use Books to Help

There are a number of books which you can use, to help address the concerns of children of various ages and teenagers. Explore what's available and select the ones which work best for you and your children.

Encourage Their Creativity

My daughter painted a rock in art class when she was in elementary school. We moved that rock from house to house, always placing it in the yard near the front door, where we could appreciate it. That was always part of making the new home our own.

Whether they decorate a light switch cover for their new room or the cover of a new address book, paint a small rock, or paint a piece of pottery at one of those stores which will bake it in a kiln for you, let them create something they'll look forward to seeing in the new home.

Househunting

Our children always enjoyed looking at houses with us. They would immediately figure out which bedroom they wanted to be theirs, and what else they liked, in each house. It certainly helped to fuel their excitement about the move. However, if you're planning a day of intensive househunting (8-10 homes or more), especially two days in a row, we suggest that everyone might be happier if the children visited with friends or relatives, or played with a babysitter instead, for at least part of the time. Then, when you're closer to making a choice, you can bring the kids along on the next house shopping trip. Obviously, this depends on your children's personalities and needs, whether you would be able to concentrate on the job of selecting a home if they were with you, and what alternatives there are for their activities or care, if they *don't* go househunting.

When you do bring children along, remember to bring something to amuse them (handheld video games, reading material, iPod, puzzle books) as well as non-messy snacks. If your real estate agent is driving you around, ask if it's ok for the kids to eat that snack in the car before offering it. If it's something likely to leave crumbs or worse, have them eat their snack outside. If the children have excess energy to work off after sitting in the car for awhile, have them run up and down the sidewalk or do Jumping Jacks. One of you can stay outside with the kids while the other looks inside a house. If the house looks good, then you can trade places and have the other one go in, or calm the children and all go inside.

Try to stop at appropriate time intervals for bathroom and food breaks. Any of us (including me) can get grouchy if we haven't eaten in too long and our blood sugar drops.

Visit the New Community and New House

If possible, plan a trip to visit the new community and house you've selected with your children, if they weren't along on the househunting trip. The unknown is usually more feared, and if they have a mental picture of the house they'll be living in and their room and the neighborhood, they will be able to handle the coming change much less fearfully.

If you have school-age children, be sure to include them in any decisions about which school to attend and what courses to register for. Also, it would be helpful for them to visit the school they'll be attending. You might be able to meet some of their teachers, or even get a tour of the school. While you're there, keep an eye on how students are dressed and what kind of tote or backpack they're using. Two of the great fears children have when moving is fitting in, and making friends. Despite the merits of being an individualist, they will feel more at ease if they're able to fit in with how the rest of the students look, when they start at the new school.

Plan Some Bonding Time Before the Move Takes Place

We always found it helpful to take a short family vacation before the new job started and the move was made. It helps to pull you together as a family, and is especially helpful if you're going to have to endure some weeks or months of living in separate cities. If you can't afford the time or funds to make this happen, maybe you can manage to spend a day hiking together or having some other adventure. As you're preparing mentally and physically to leave friends and family, it's good to know you can depend on each other as you all adjust to your new environment.

Be Prepared For School Registration

Be aware that different states have different ways of doing things. Kindergarten may be half-day or full day. The date by which a child must turn five in order to enroll in kindergarten may be September 1 or December 31 or some other date. (Often, though, if a child has already started school elsewhere, they will be allowed to continue in the same grade in the new school district.) Gifted programs, if they exist, may operate quite differently in other school districts. Just be aware of this and try not to assume things will the same as what you're used to.

It's important to find out what items and forms are required *before* attempting to register your child. If you do this well before moving day, especially if you're moving during the school year or right before school starts, you'll be prepared and have the right documents available when you need them.

Items you'll need may vary with your school district, but a survey of several different states seems to agree on the following:

1. **Birth certificate**
Must be government issued. Hospital certificates are not acceptable.

2. **Proof of residency** in the school district
These might include utility bills, homeowner's or renter's insurance, or lease. These must have your name and address on it. Contact the school district to verify what they require.

3. **Social Security number or migrant number**
These may be optional.

4. **Emergency contact information**
You'll need someone in your new area, other than you and your spouse, so consider who you might trust with this responsibility, and ask their permission before including their contact info. This is a person who might be contacted if, for instance, your child was involved in an accident, and you couldn't be reached; so pick

someone you feel your children would be comfortable with, and whom you feel would be there for your child and behave responsibly. You can certainly change this contact as you get to know other people better. And if you really don't have anyone to put down at registration, you can get back to them as soon as you do.

5. **Placement information**
It will be helpful if you bring your child's most recent report card, withdrawal form from previous school, and/ or transcripts and any testing results (for gifted or special needs students).

If your child receives special education services or accommodations of any type, through either an IEP (Individualized Education Plan) or a 504 Plan, request a special review meeting with the current team, to update present levels. At the end of that meeting, request copies of the file. Take the copies with you when you enroll your student, and request that a transition meeting be held. It is to your child's great advantage to have this in place before he enters his new classroom.

6. **Immunization records**
Completion of state forms by a physician may be required—if so, try to get the forms ahead of time from the state you're moving to. Many school districts will accept a generic form completed at the doctor's office. Check with the new school to verify requirements.

7. **Physical examination**
Often a physical examination, either shortly before the move or shortly after, must be documented. Most important, besides immunizations, are screening tests for hearing, vision and sometimes dental problems. You may be able to download the appropriate form from the school district's website. If not, they should be able to mail or fax it to you.

Unless there's a particular reason why it's important to use the pediatrician from your old town, I would suggest using this visit as an opportunity to get established with a new one. In Chapter 16 there are guidelines on finding a new physician. After you've narrowed your choices, this is a chance to actually have an office visit with a physician to see if this is the one for you, at a time when your child is well. You'll get the required form completed, and then when your child gets ill or has a problem, the physician is already familiar with him/her. Alternately, if you do not like your experience with this office, you may decide to establish yourselves with one of the other choices.

If you're Packing Household Goods Yourself

Try to pack the children's things as close as possible to the move date. This will help them to feel less disrupted. Of course, you can certainly pack away toys or arts & crafts supplies which aren't used frequently and out-of-season clothing without them noticing it. But try to keep their favorite things available as long as possible, and try not to dismantle their room until very close to the move.

Before Moving Day

- **Give kids time to say goodbye** to the house and the area before moving day. Take, or have them take, photos of them with their friends, and photos of your current house, including their room. Or use a camcorder to record a tour of the house. Or work with your children to make a scrapbook including favorite activities and locations in the area, as well as photos of friends and close relatives. Collect addresses, phone numbers, and e-mail addresses of friends. You can even host a "Going Away Party", complete with a "Friendship" cake. We once hosted a party at a local skating rink so everyone could focus on having a good time together rather than their upcoming separation.

- **Pack a Survival Kit** for each of your children with some of their favorite things (small stuffed animal, blanket, toy, book, or music) and snacks for the trip and to occupy and comfort them until their things are un-packed in their new room.

- **Involve the kids.** When boxes are packed with their belongings, let children decorate those boxes with crayons or washable markers and/or stickers. A great idea is to have them write their name and new ad-dress on each box. That will help them to learn the address, as well as involving them in the process of the move. You could even let them pack a box them-selves, although I would suggest picking something like stuffed animals, which are not fragile at all and wouldn't be damaged by being improperly packed.

  Older children and teenagers are certainly capa-ble of doing some meaningful tasks to help with the move. Don't over-burden them, but assigning them some things to do will help them feel a part of the process and will help them to feel better about it. Be sure to show your appreciation for their support.

- **Determine what school your child will be attending**
  If your children will be attending public school, you may be able to determine which one by looking at the listing form for your new home or searching on the internet, using the city, state, and "schools". Some school districts have maps online, indicating school attendance districts. Otherwise, you can phone the Board of Education in your new area, or ask your real estate agent or leasing agent. Wherever you get your clues from, it doesn't hurt to phone the school to verify that your information is correct. Also note that

in some cases students can elect to attend a magnet school, so you'll need to find out about all of your student's alternatives.

- **Request school records.** Complete a form to request that your child's school records be sent to the new school. If the new school is within the same district or county, they can often transfer the original records. At least some schools are required to maintain permanent records for 60 years, so they'll send photocopies. Obviously, you'll need to provide the address of the new school.

Moving Days

Set your children's Survival Kits where they won't be packed by the movers. Include clothing they'll need until their boxes are unpacked in the new house. Also, remember to set aside any medications or first aid supplies you think you might need for the family, and place those in your own Survival Kit.

- **What will the kids do?**
  Consider getting a babysitter for young children on the days when things are being packed up and moved, both out of the old house and into the new one. Safety is the most important issue. You will need to concentrate on the move, and it could be dangerous for the movers and the children if they're in the mover's path. When you're moving out, you'll be making sure everything has a moving sticker, pulling picture hooks off the walls, checking high shelves to be sure everything's been removed, picking up items which have been hiding under or behind furniture, and vacuuming empty rooms. In the new house, you'll be checking items off the inventory list as they come in the door, directing where items are placed, and when there's a lull, trying to unpack some of the

boxes so the movers can haul them away when they leave. It would be extremely difficult, if not impossible, to do all the things you need to do, while ensuring that your children are entertained and safe at the same time. It's well worth it to have someone come to the house to be with the kids (especially if the weather's good and they can play in the yard), or find some-place you trust for them to hang out until the major tumult is over.

Even after the movers have left, things need to be unpacked before the place is "livable". If you have small children, you'll want to have something to amuse them early in the process. Chances are, your computer will not be set up, and the cable TV or sat-ellite dish will not be working yet. So you'll have to resort to handheld electronic games, books (if they're old enough to read on their own) or games they can play themselves (if there's a place they can do this safely), and so on.

Flying with Babies

- **Keep their ears comfortable.** Bring a bottle or other drink for babies and toddlers, and time it so they are thirsty during descent. It is during approximately the last 30 minutes in the air that the cabin pressure changes to adjust for the decreasing altitude of the plane, although some people experience mild dis-comfort during ascent as well. Most of the time, you can clear your ears by swallowing or yawning. These fixes don't come naturally to little ones, so encour-aging them to swallow frequently during this time by drinking will help to equalize the pressure and make them more comfortable. Older children and adults usually find that chewing gum during this time is a big help. If your young one (or anyone else) has a cold, then nose spray and/or a decongestant should be used so that it is most effective during the descent. Discuss medications with your doctor ahead of time, if you have any questions.

- **Be prepared for irregularities.** Bring plenty of extra diapers/wipes/food with you on the plane, "just in case" of a delay or unscheduled landing. Baby food & diapers aren't easy to find in an airport and don't exist onboard. Better to be prepared. Also, if you can get seated at the bulkhead, there will be extra leg room, so your little one will have some room to hang out other than on your lap. You can request these bulkhead seats—airline employees can look at a diagram of the plane you'll be on, and figure out which seats they are. Generally, they are the first row of first class and the first row of coach, but if it's a wide-bodied plane there are additional bulkheads. Note that since bulkhead seats do not have a row of seats in front of them, you will need to store all carry-on bags overhead for take-off and landing.

- **Let the airline know the baby's coming.** Be sure the airline knows ahead of time if you will be bringing a baby who will be seated on your lap, rather than sitting in his own seat. In case of an emergency, it's important for there to be enough oxygen masks for every person sitting in each row. Although many rows have one additional mask, usually there are not two extras. So, the second adult (even if it's your spouse) with an infant would need to sit across the aisle or in a different row. If you purchase a seat for your baby, this isn't an issue, but then be sure to check that you have an approved child seat to use onboard.

- **Know what you can bring onboard.** Rules have been changing in recent years, as to what you're allowed to take through Security and take onboard. Check ahead of time so you know the rules. Currently, large amounts of liquid (in containers larger than 3 oz.) are prohibited, so if you're bringing baby bottles with you, you'll probably want to bring them with just the powder in them and add water after you've gone through security, using a water fountain or water bottles purchased on the concourse. As of this writing, each person is only allowed to bring containers of 3 oz. or less, as long as they all fit into a quart size plastic zipper bag. Go to www.tsa.gov or phone (866)289-9673 for more information.

Traveling with Children

It's important, when traveling with children of all ages, to bring things to amuse them, as well as snacks. Snacks are important because you never know for sure when you'll be able to eat, and this will help when the need for nourishment comes at an inopportune time, such as during a flight delay or a stretch of road without a restaurant. Chewing gum can help keep the pressure in everyone's ears equalized and comfortable, in the air (especially during the last half hour), as well as when driving up and down mountains. Playing games with little pieces can be tricky in a moving vehicle, but there are some travel games which have magnetic pieces. Electronic games are good, but can't be used in airplanes during take-off and landing. In restaurants, a game of tic-tac-toe or hangman can keep everyone involved while waiting for food to arrive, and it doesn't require anything more than a pen and paper placemat or napkin. You could bring a pad of art paper (or just some copy paper) and crayons or markers, and periodically tear off a sheet for each child and assign a theme for their artwork, such as a house and tree or flowers and bees or things with wheels or a dress. Coloring books, sticker books, puzzle books, or a little wind-up toy can all be purchased ahead of time and brought out when you sense the need for a distraction. One caution, though: don't leave crayons in a closed car in hot weather. (We made that mistake once, and learned our lesson when we returned to the car and found pools of color spaced around the back seat of the car.)

Safety in the New Home

Remember to install child locks on cabinet doors, if your youngsters are of an age where that's appropriate. Store harmful substances where young children can't get to them until these child locks are in place.

Establish right away how to escape from various parts of your new home, and make sure every family member knows the one spot outside the home where you will all meet, should a fire or other emergency require evacuating the house. Try to communicate this without scaring the children, but by telling them it's good to be prepared "just in case". Do a practice run—everyone will remember it better if you do.

Register Your Child in School

If you haven't already done so, register your children in school.

- **It will be good for all of you**
  If school is in session, it will be good for them to be making new friends quickly and jumping into classes and homework, rather than worrying about what it will be like. You'll also get a lot more done while they're gone. If you have preschoolers or babies, this time will be more of a challenge for you, but just do the essential things first and the rest will get done little by little. If you're fortunate enough to find quality babysitters or preschools quickly, splurge and use them so that you can have some hours to get lots of unpacking done and get yourselves settled sooner.

- **School Supplies**
  Find out what school supplies your child should take to school, and try really hard to see that he takes them the first day. (*This* may test your organization skills.) At a minimum, a spiral notebook, pens and pencils should get your student through until he comes home from the first day with a list of additional supplies to be purchased.

- **Physical Appearances**
  Help your child to fit in by allowing him to wear clothing which is similar to that which local students wear, *if he wants to*. Styles are often somewhat different in different parts of the country. Unless the clothing and hairstyles are very offensive to you, try to be understanding about your child wanting to "fit in" and not stand out by looking different. I am not referring to pierced body parts or tattoos when I'm talking about styles, by the way. Hair does grow out and clothing can be changed in a minute. Permanent changes to your child's body obviously need to be considered with much more thought than fitting in at a new school.

- **Getting Involved**
  Encourage your children to participate in one or two activities at school which interest them. They'll get to know more people, feel more comfortable at school, and become more engaged academically.

Priorities, Priorities

With so much going on during the moving process, it's easy for adults to get wrapped up in the move and—without realizing it—minimize the time and attention they're giving their kids. Don't do it! Make sure to spend time with your children. Listen to them, play as a family, explore what your new area has to offer, pick some new favorite places, and make some good memories.

Throughout The Move

Try to continue family traditions, such as having waffles on Sunday mornings, reading a book to the kids at bedtime, or going for a walk after dinner. This will help all of you to feel less unsettled. Also, realize that even when it's a positive thing, moving can be stressful. Remember, "Don't sweat the small stuff."

Adjusting To The New Surroundings

You can expect some regression in children's behavior, including toddlers who have recently been toilet trained. (I hear your moans.) And, even for adults, it's not unusual for it to take 6 months to a year before feeling really "at home" in a new city. However, if you find your child is upset about the move for an extended period of time, it might be appropriate to get some outside help to assist in the adjustment. Hopefully, you'll all grow to love your new area and new friends, and look forward to sharing them with family and old friends when they come to visit.

Plan a Visit

After you've had a chance to get settled, explore the area, and make some new friends, try to plan a visit back to your former area. It'll be good to see old friends and your old neighborhood again, but it will probably be equally good to get back to your new home when you return. If possible, have friends and family come visit you and your family, too, so you can show them your new home and city. Your children will enjoy showing guests around and will feel pride in their new surroundings.

Chapter 12
Moving With Pets

It's vital to plan ahead for moving pets. In one case, a couple who moved from southern California to Milwaukee in December had to find a foster home for their 2 cats for several months, because the airlines refused to fly them east until the temperature at their destination could be counted on to be over 40° F.

In this chapter, we'll discuss how to select a home and an area where you and your pets can thrive, information you need to find out from the state where you're moving, and what you need to do at the vet before the move. We'll also cover many of the things to keep in mind so that your pets are transported safely to your destination, and stay safe during the move-in, plus we'll give you hints to help them adjust to their new environment.

Selecting a Home for You and Your Pet

One family we know specifically selected a home where the front door was not by a sidewalk, since their dog routinely barked—loudly and long—at anyone who walked by the outside of their home. They lived much more peacefully in a 2nd-story apartment for awhile, and then in a home with the main entrance on the side of the house, while the rural mailbox was at the front by the street.

In some neighborhoods and buildings, especially condominium and townhome communities, there are restrictions on the number and type of pets. Some ban certain types of dogs or exotic animals, while others ban every type of pet. Here are some things you should consider while searching for a new place for you and your pet(s).

- **Are pets allowed?**
  - ↪ Check out the covenants of the Homeowner's Association, if there is one.
  - ↪ Verify that your particular breed and species can live there, and find out if you are limited to a certain number of pets.
  - ↪ Look into local government restrictions, especially if you have an unusual pet or a breed of dog which has a history of violence.

- **Are fences allowed?**
  Some communities only allow electric fences. Some allow particular types of fencing, but not 6' privacy fencing. If you can't legally have the type of fence you feel is appropriate for you and your pet, you may need to keep looking. Also, in some cases, existing fences are allowed but if it has deteriorated, it can't be replaced due to changes in the local building code. Do your homework, so you don't have any negative surprises.

- **Is the area good for pets?**
  - ↪ Do many of the neighbors have dogs? Dog owners are more likely to be tolerant when your dog barks.
  - ↪ Are there good places nearby for you to walk your dog?
  - ↪ Do a lot of the neighbors walk theirs in the neighborhood?
  - ↪ Is it a safe area for you to walk your dog at night?
  - ↪ Are the streets not too busy, and do they have sidewalks?

- ↜ Are annual vaccines required for pets? You may or may not have a problem with this.
- ↜ Are there play groups for dogs in the neighborhood?
- ↜ Are there good off-leash parks for dogs nearby?
- ↜ If you don't have a car, a good vet within walking distance could be a big bonus.

- **Is the home a good one for your pet?**
  - ↜ Will your cats have an interesting view out of the windows?
  - ↜ Is there a good place to put a litter box for your cats?
  - ↜ Will your older or blind cat or dog be able to move about inside and outside the home without having to navigate (or fall down) a flight or more of stairs? If you have animals which shouldn't or can't navigate stairs, would it be possible to install a baby gate at the top and/or bottom of the stairs, in order to protect them?
  - ↜ Is there a good place to install a doggie door? It might be important to you to have your pets enter a mudroom or garage, instead of your living room.
  - ↜ Is the inside space appropriate for the size and number of pets you have?
  - ↜ Are the floors good for traction, or will your pets slip and slide on a smooth surface? Some people would rather have tile, linoleum, or similar, and use area rugs, which can easily be replaced periodically. Obviously, floors can be changed, but depending on what exists in the house, you may want to consider the cost before you make an offer to purchase the property.
  - ↜ Can the kitchen—or mudroom—be baby-gated, to keep your pet in when company is over or when your pets are muddy or whatever?

↷ Is the yard fenced in, and safe? A terraced yard might present dangers for pets.

Obviously, you need to select a home which meets your needs and those of your family. However, since many people consider their pets to be part of the family, these are all things which should be considered as well.

State and Local Regulations

If you're moving to another state, contact the animal health authorities there, to determine what the state requirements are to travel or relocate there. Go to www.usaha.org/ StateAnimalHealthOfficials.pdf (or go to www.usaha.org, click on "Reference Links", and select State Animal Health Offices) to find contact information for these officials. Also, if your pet is flying, check with the airline; they may have different requirements. Be sure to do this as soon as possible, so you'll know what you need to do before your move. Hawaii, by the way, requires a 120-day quarantine for dogs and cats.

Health

Take pets to your veterinarian before the move, to make sure their shots are current. Some states require health certificates and proof of rabies inoculations. Also, get a copy of vet records to take with you to the new veterinarian. Have the health certificate and proof of rabies inoculation with you when you travel.

If your pet is high strung, ask your vet about a short course of anti-anxiety medication for the trip, and to help with the first few days at your new home. Opinions are mixed about whether or not it is good to tranquilize pets when they're flying, so ask your vet for his advice.

Identification

Make sure current ID tags are attached securely to your pet's collar or leg band (for birds). *See "Hints from a Professional Show-Dog Owner" below for an alternative to ID tags.* If your pet has in ID implant, remember to update your contact information. ID tags should include: your name and cell phone number(s), as well as your destination address and phone number.

General Tips

- **Consider boarding your pet or having someone watch him** during the days just prior to your move out, and for a few days while your things are delivered and you get somewhat settled. It may be much less stressful for you *and* your pet(s). If you decide not to do this, you might want to at least confine him to a crate or an out-of-the-way room. This will avoid having your 4-legged dears get underfoot while boxes and furniture are being moved, or maybe even bolting out of an open door. Remember, many kennels require a "kennel cough" vaccine prior to boarding your dog.

- **Take a photo of your pet** so you have something to show in case he escapes. Write down a description of his coloring and any atypical features, and make a note of his size and weight. This is helpful whether your pet is flying or you're driving him in your car. It also might prove important if he takes off from your new house and doesn't immediately find his way home. Don't pack this—keep it with you as you travel. You probably won't need to use it, but in case you do, it will be invaluable.

- **Get enough medications** to last until you get settled and find a new veterinarian.

- **Make sure any hotel reservations are at places which welcome pets.** There are quite a few websites to help you, such as www.petswelcome.com or www. officialpethotels.com. You can search on the internet for "hotels with pets" and you'll find others. Of course, you can call any hotel directly to find out whether your type of pet will be welcome, what the weight limitation is, and how much they charge per night for each pet. Petswelcome.com has additional information, such as fun places to go with your pets.

- **Put aside plenty of food.** You'll obviously want enough food to feed your pet at appropriate times before you get to your new home. Also, if you aren't sure you can easily find the food your pet is used to once you're there, you'll want to bring along some extra to tide you over until the moving van arrives. In addition, put at least some of the food in a moving box clearly labeled so that you'll be able to find it as soon as you move in. It will add a little bit to the weight of your shipment, but will be easier than running around on moving day or the day after, trying to locate the type of food you're used to providing.

- **Transporting your pets.** It may be obvious, but animals cannot be transported on a moving van—so generally, the choice is whether they will fly or you will drive them.

Travel by Car

Cats, dogs, and other animals can be taken in your car. Dogs, especially, will require frequent stops and walks along the way, and any of the animals can get car-sick. Unless you have successfully traveled long distances in the car with your pet, you might want to try some short rides with him, working up to a longer trip. Considering how these rides go, and your animal's temperament and size, decide whether it would be best to transport him by car or have him go by air instead.

If you drive them, remember to take along the following items, as appropriate:

- Food, water, and containers to serve them in
- Can opener, if needed for pet food
- Any needed medications
- Toys & Grooming Tools
- Your pet's bed
- A leash for letting your dog out of the car, and possibly a halter for your cat
- Scooper and plastic bags for clean-ups
- Newspaper or sheets to keep your car clean

You will probably not want to feed your pet for at least three hours before leaving on a trip, and will want to walk a dog right before beginning the trip.

See "Hints for Specific Pets" below, for additional information on specific pets.

Travel by Air

The following are just guidelines and hints. Contact the airlines directly for complete information.

- **Can your pet be accommodated, and in what part of the aircraft?**
  Some pets can be carried into the aircraft cabin with you, in an approved pet carrier, and some must be shipped in the cargo section of the airplane. Some airlines won't accept animals at all. When animals *are* permitted in the cabin, the number per flight is extremely limited, so it is vital for you to check with the airlines as soon as possible, to determine what the possibilities are and to make a reservation for you

and your pet. When animals fly as cargo, sometimes they are to be brought to the terminal and checked as baggage there; in other cases, they must be taken to the airlines' cargo facility. Be sure to inquire about charges and insurance fees for your pet, and about the specific regulations and procedures which apply.

Airlines which do transport animals caution that, even with advance reservations, there is no guarantee that your pet will travel on a specific flight. Irregularities occur, as they do with people-passengers. Airlines also reserve the right to refuse to transport an animal for a variety of reasons, including illness or aggressive and/or violent behavior on the part of the animal. They also will refuse to fly animals during extreme weather conditions. Ask the airlines what their procedures are, and prepare a back-up plan in case Plan A falls apart.

- **Increasing the safety aspect**
  Try to only fly animals who are in good health, not too old, are mentally stable and relaxed in temperament, and only on direct (no change of plane) flights, if you can't get a non-stop flight. Avoid flying them in very hot or very cold weather. If you absolutely must take a flight with a connection, try to be very proactive, to ensure that your pet makes it onto the connecting flight. Some experts caution against flying a "pushed-in nose breed" of dog at all, and some airlines will not fly them during hot weather.

- **Crates/ pet carriers**
  The airline may provide a crate for the pet which flies as cargo, or you may be able to purchase it from the airline. Even if you purchase it elsewhere, there are specific rules about the crate, so contact your airline for their guidelines.

- ☙ Your pet should be able to stand, turn around easily, and have good ventilation in the crate.
- ☙ It would be helpful to have the crate *ahead of time* so your pet can get used to it before the stress of travel.
- ☙ Comfort your pet by including a piece of cloth with your scent on it.

- **Hints from a Professional Show-Dog Owner**

  - ☙ Use an embroidered collar with your cell phone number and the word "REWARD" sewn onto it, and use no hanging tags which could get caught. *If you aren't able to purchase these collars through your vet or animal supply store, search the internet for "embroidered dog collars", and you will find multiple choices.*
  - ☙ Pad the bottom of the crate with many single sheets of paper towels—this provides a good cushion and they're easily disposable when soiled.
  - ☙ Use a crate fan for air circulation, such as the one you'll find at www.caframo.com/specialty/pdf/737PFpetfan_infosheet.pdf. Drill a hole in the side of the fan, and padlock it onto your crate so that it won't fall off in the plane or get "lost". Besides providing ventilation, this keeps prying eyes from "peeping" in at pets and keeps fingers out of the crate.
  - ☙ Put a cute photo of your pet and a short bio on the outside of the crate, so that ground handlers will empathize with your animal and treat him with more care. For example: "My name is Henry. I am a field spaniel puppy. Please keep me warm in winter and cool in summer. My Mom is onboard and she worries about me." Also say, "Please keep my crate closed unless there's an

emergency. I won't bite," (if this is true) "but I might run away if frightened."

☛ Tape your itinerary on top of the crate, just in case there is a mix-up or the baggage tag falls off. Use a good-quality, clear packing tape, which covers all the wording and attaches it securely to the container. For example: "June 6, SW3664 BNA/LAS; June 6 SW2490 LAS/ONT", lets the reader know the date, airline and flight numbers, and departure and arrival cities for all flights.

☛ Also tape names of contacts on top of crate. These can be written on a large index card. Make sure you include your cell phone number, and the phone number of someone who is usually at home. Also include someone in each connecting city who can help you if your dog misses a connection. Use clear tape to attach and protect this information as well.

☛ Tape an old leash to the top of the crate, if you're transporting a dog. (Don't put one *in* the crate.)

☛ Inside the crate, put a Coop Cup water bowl that is at least 10 oz, so that if there's a delay, there is a way for people to give water to your pet without opening the crate. Some airlines require you to have two such bowls in the crate.

☛ If something does happen, and your pet is left behind or not picked up soon after arrival, airlines generally have contracts with local kennels which will pick up your pet and board it. You (or your appointed friend or relative) just pick the animal up and pay the bill. This can prove helpful in situations when unexpected incidents occur.

- **When your pet flies without you**
  If you ship your pet by air, make sure someone can meet your pet at the destination airport and take care of him until you arrive. A kennel can do this for you and keep your pet until you have completed

your move, if necessary. You'll need their contact information when you make the arrangements with the airline.

Again, the above are just guidelines. Consult the airlines directly for complete information and regulations.

Adjusting your Pet to the New Location

- Make your pet's new home area comfortable and inviting.

- Use common sense about building habits in the new surroundings.

Hints for Specific Pets

- **Dogs**
  - ☛ Take your dog for walks to become familiar with the new neighborhood, allowing plenty of time for sniffing around.
  - ☛ Be sure to use a leash when walking, especially until they've adjusted to the new neighborhood.
  - ☛ Have your dog meet neighbors, service people who come to the house, and your mail carrier.
  - ☛ You and your dog may need to adjust to a different routine if your move involved a change from one type of living to another, such as city to suburbs or a rural area. If you're now in the city or suburbs, you'll need to bring a pooper scooper and plastic bags along when you go for a walk. If you now have a yard, you'll need to train your dog to do his thing in the specific place you've decided on.

- **Cats**
  - ☛ Cats don't walk on a leash unless they're trained to. If you want to try, use a halter instead of a

leash, because a leash can be dangerous when they jump off of things.

🐾 Cats will usually not use their litter box on the road. Wait until the evening, when you're settled in a hotel room, or wherever, and things are calm. Then take the litter box out, and chances are your cat will use it.

🐾 Felines know something is up as soon as boxes start getting packed, so try to keep your cat's routine as normal as possible during the moving process to lessen the stress. Give her lots of affection (if she'll let you) and attention.

🐾 Try to pack your cat's belongings right before moving, and if you're driving, be sure to take her bed, food dishes and some toys with you.

🐾 If you don't board your cat for moving day, then put her in a room with her bed and toys and food, and put a note on the door so the movers don't open the door. You don't want her to run away due to the commotion of moving.

🐾 In your new home, keep your cat in one room to start with, and introduce her to other rooms one by one. As your cat adjusts, you can move her bed and feeding dishes to their new permanent location.

🐾 If yours is an outdoor cat, wait until she's comfortable in the new home before you let her out.

🐾 If you've moved to a condo or apartment building, be sure that all of the windows have screens which cannot be pushed out by your cat, to prevent her from falling.

🐾 Be cautious about things your cat may not be used to, such as elevators or traffic. You may want to consider changing an outdoor cat to an indoor cat, if you feel the area might be too dangerous for her.

- **Birds and other small caged animals**
  Hamsters, birds, rabbits and other small animals generally do well traveling in your car. Cover their cage
  to avoid drafts, and to help keep them calm and
  quiet. Try not to expose them to sudden changes in
  temperature. Be sure they get fresh water when you
  make stops, so they don't get dehydrated. Ask your
  vet for advice on whether to feed them during the
  drive, or wait until the evening when you're settled
  for the night.

- **Fish**
  Moving is very stressful on fish, and quite risky. Unless
  you are moving a very short distance, you would
  probably be better off selling or giving away your
  fish, and getting new ones at your destination. If you
  really want to move them, check with professionals
  for advice.

Obviously, you can't explain what's going on to your
pets, so you need to be aware of their needs and anticipate
what will make them comfortable. Just as with children, if
you are calm around them during the moving process, and
give them a little extra attention and affection, along with
discipline-as-normal, you can help to minimize the stress the
move will have on these precious family members.

Chapter 13

Packing Tips

In this chapter, we discuss whether to have the mover pack your belongings, do it yourself, or some of each. You'll learn some useful hints for any of these options, and find more extensive information in case you're doing it yourself.

Professional Packing or Do-It-Yourself?

- <u>Professional packing</u>: If you are able to have the movers do the packing, it will be a fantastic help. Your possessions will have a much greater chance of arriving intact, you will have much less work to do, and you'll be able to live much more normally in your house up until the day the packers arrive.

- <u>Do-it-yourself</u>: If you're trying to save money on the move, you may consider doing the packing yourself. If you have a lot of possessions (and many of us seem to have a lot more than we think we do), it's a huge job which takes a lot of time and energy, and you will have weeks of living around packed boxes. Remember, too, that the mover is not responsible for damage to the contents of cartons you pack yourself, unless there is damage to the carton itself, which has caused damage to its contents. But yes, you could save a fair amount of money by doing the packing (or even, most of it) on your own. The big goal, of course, is to protect your things so that they arrive in your new home without being damaged or destroyed.

- <u>Some of each</u>: A third alternative is to pack most of the non-breakable things yourself and have the mover pack fragile and valuable items. This might be a good solution if you have to pay for the packing yourself, and need to cut down on costs. In order for the mover to give you a realistic estimate, you'll need to give him a good idea of which items they'll be packing, so they can estimate the labor and packing materials required.

  If you decide to pack some of the boxes yourself, your boxes will stack better with the rest of the truckload if you use the same size boxes which will be used for the rest of your belongings. Your mover may be able to provide you with boxes ahead of time, and certainly can tell you the sizes of the various boxes they use.

  Even if you have the movers pack all of your belongings, you may, for the sake of privacy, want to pack a few things yourself. As long as you're willing to assume responsibility for packing them properly, that's no problem.

No Matter Who's Doing The Packing...

- <u>Put aside things which should stay with the house</u>: keys, extra garage door openers (and a note to include the ones in your cars on moving day), owners manuals for major appliances (oven, microwave, furnace, etc), warranties (or at least the company name and contact information) for major items such as the roof you replaced last year. Put "Do Not Pack" notes on carpet remnants, extra kitchen or bath tiles, wallpaper and paint, if they match what is currently being used in the house.

- <u>Put collections together</u>
  If there are things you'd like to have packed together, such as children's toys or arts and crafts supplies, putting them altogether in one location will help that happen.

- <u>If you're moving things to more than one location</u> (perhaps because you will be living in temporary housing for a period of time, and need to put some things in storage), use colorful tags to indicate what is going to which destination. This will give you a much better chance of everything ending up in its proper location.

- <u>Keep track of connectors</u>
  Be sure to pack power cords and other connectors with the equipment they belong to, to avoid a big headache when you try to hook things up on the other end of the move. Use masking tape to label each cord and indicate where it goes.

  <u>Electronics</u>
  If you're moving locally, you might want to move the computer's CPU unit yourself. A turntable needs to have the pick-up arm fastened for moving, so it doesn't flop around. Check your Owner's Manual or contact the manufacturer for advice on how to move electronic equipment safely.

- <u>Plants</u>: for a short move, especially when the weather is mild, you can probably get away with moving your plants and having most of them survive. Movers may agree to take plants, but will not guarantee their survival. Also, some states (the most notable being Arizona, California and Florida) have restrictions on bringing plants into their states, to prevent importing harmful bugs or pests. Check this out before deciding to cross state lines with them. For longer moves, you may want to give your plants a better chance at survival by giving them away to friends, family, or nursing homes and just starting over in your new house. If you do decide to try moving them, and have room in your car or your mover is willing to transport them, consult your local nursery or the websites listed in the back of this book for detailed guidance.

One thing I *will* suggest: for floor plants, soil should be slightly damp. Place the pot in the bottom of a large plastic trash bag. Then use packing tape to fasten the bag tightly around the bottom of the plant, where it meets the soil. Tape the bag, not the plant, to avoid damaging the plant. The bag will hopefully prevent dirt from spilling and water from leaking onto the truck and your other possessions.

- Large rugs: you may want to have these cleaned before the move. They'll be returned to you rolled and wrapped, ready for moving. It will be easiest if these are among the first items unloaded from the truck, so that furniture is placed on top of them as it is brought into the house.

- Draperies: if they're going with you, have them dry cleaned before the move. They'll be returned with plastic bags protecting them, on hangers which can be hung in wardrobe boxes.

- Items which can be damaged by heat include cassette and video tapes, vinyl records, CDs, DVDs, computer disks and candles. Check with your mover about how best to protect them during your move, if hot weather is a possibility.

- Arrange servicing for your appliances. See *"Servicing of Appliances"* in Chapter 10.

- "Last on/first off" supplies are things which you'll want to use until right before the truck pulls away, and/or things you'll want available as soon as the movers begin to unload the truck at your new home. Gather these things in one area and make sure everyone in the family knows these stay together and don't get packed until the very end of moving-out day. They will include pliers (for pulling picture hooks out of the wall), vacuum cleaner, dustpan, broom, paper towels, trash bags, pet food, first aid kit, and so on.

- Small zipper food storage bags are a great tool.
    - ↪ Use one to collect your picture hooks, and after all of your rooms have been emptied (and you've picked up the last of them from the floor), put the bag in your car, or in that "last loaded/first off" box. This way, you'll easily find them when you're ready to hang things in your new home.
    - ↪ Use one for the pegs which hold adjustable shelves in place. Tape the bag securely to some part of the furniture the pegs go with: the bottom of one of the shelves, inside the cabinet of the wall unit—someplace where the packing tape won't cause any visible damage. The movers can suggest a good place.
    - ↪ Use some for hardware which needs to be kept with various pieces of furniture, such as bed frames. Attach the bag to the item the hardware goes with.
    - ↪ Use others for all the little pieces of things you find, as furniture is moved, which don't fall into the category of "trash".

- Gather things you'll want for the first night, such as sheets, pillows, blankets, nightlights, flashlights, shower curtain, bath needs, and see that the outside of the box is marked appropriately, so you can find and unpack it as soon as possible.

- <u>"Name" each room</u> boxes will be going to. Be consistent so that the moving men will not be confused by boxes marked "Computer Room" which need to go into the "Office". Mark what room *in the new house* the box should be placed in. Decide on a name for each room, and when you get to the new house you'll tape a sign by each room with that name, so that it'll be clear which boxes go where. Your room labels might be: office, den, master bedroom, upstairs bath, Adam's room, and so on. If the moving company will be packing your belongings, hang signs in the old house while they're packing, so they'll know how to label the boxes.

  If two children sharing a bedroom in the old house will each have a separate bedroom in the new one, place their possessions so that it's clear which room they will be going to, and use a sign to indicate "Michael's Room" or "Emma's Room" by their things.

- <u>Record the general contents of each box</u> using a permanent marker on the box itself, and also make notes in a notebook or on a legal pad. Be sure to include specific items you might be looking for, such as "TV remote". This will help you when you're unpacking, and will also help you recall what's in a box if it gets misplaced. Label at least two sides of each box you can, because when a dozen boxes are stacked up in one area, it may take work to be able to see one particular side, much less all 4 sides.

What Not To Pack

- <u>Items to take with you or purchase before the movers arrive:</u> You'll want Scotch™ tape and a black permanent marker, for various uses; scissors, for cutting shelf paper; and sticky-notes, for labeling drawers and cabinets in the kitchen. The notes will make it easier to put things away as you unpack, and it's good to leave them on for awhile to help you and your family locate things as you're all getting used to where they're kept in the new kitchen. You will also need a utility knife, for opening boxes, and some paper for signs and to make notes.

Hint: Do NOT plan to fly with a utility knife in your carry-on bag, as it will be taken away from you at security. Place it in your checked luggage instead.

• <u>Items the movers will take care of</u>: Furniture and major appliances will be padded by your movers.

• <u>Contents of your dresser drawers:</u> Another thing you usually *won't* have to pack if you're using professional movers. Verify this with your mover, because some do require you to empty drawers. However, our experience has been that as long as they are not restricted items (flammables, like matches), sharp or very fragile items, things which might leak, or extremely valuable or precious items, drawer contents can be left intact and the movers will move them as is. Note, however, that the movers will be removing the drawers from the dressers, so place a towel or bathrobe over anything you don't want them to see, and tuck it down the sides.

• <u>Items which cannot go in the moving van</u>: These include hazardous materials such as: acid, aerosol cans, ammonia, ammunition, batteries, bleach, charcoal, charcoal lighter, cleaning fluid, cooking fuel (including Sterno®), fertilizer, fireworks, frozen or perishable foods, gasoline, kerosene, lamp oil, lighter fluid, matches, motor oil, nail polish remover, oily rags, oxygen bottles, paints, paint thinner, pesticides, poisons, pool chemicals, propane tanks, and weed killer. Of course, frozen or perishable foods cannot go, either.

Your mover should provide you with a complete list.

- <u>Items which should go with you personally (not in the moving van)</u>:

  - ↪ Your inventory of possessions.
  - ↪ Important papers, including birth certificates, passports, marriage certificates, divorce decrees, bank and investment account numbers, car registration(s), insurance policies, wills, stock certificates, school records and medical records, including inoculations and other items you'll need for registering your children in their new school. *See Chapter 11 for more about school requirements.*
  - ↪ Contents of safe deposit box.
  - ↪ Computer back-up disks.
  - ↪ Valuable and/or irreplaceable jewelry.
  - ↪ Checkbook(s).
  - ↪ Prescription medications.
  - ↪ Over-the-counter medications which you anticipate using during the move.
  - ↪ Photos you've taken of the new house, to verify special items (such as a chandelier) are still in place when you do your walk thru.
  - ↪ Map of new city and directions to new house, location of closing, and wherever you're staying until you move in.
  - ↪ Paperwork having to do with the sale of the old house and the new one, including closing documents for both and mover estimate.
  - ↪ Contact information for the moving company, real estate salespeople (for both houses), relocation specialist (if you have one), family, friends, and new employer.
  - ↪ Payment (certified or cashier's check) you'll need for closing on the new house and paying the

movers (see *Chapter 9, "Paying for the Move",* under *"Selecting a Moving Company"*), plus cash to tip the movers (see *the end of Chapter 10*).

☞ One corded telephone, if you've scheduled the phone company to come before the moving van will arrive. That way, the serviceperson can plug the phone into the phone jack to verify the service is working.

☞ Anything irreplaceable which you can safely transport yourself.

Obviously, these are all very important things, and you will want to be extremely cautious when transporting them. If you're driving, keep medications where they won't be subject to very high temperatures. Use common sense—if you stay at a motel overnight, you'll want valuable items in the room with you. If you stop at a restaurant along the way, try to have tempting items out of sight—but even so, park in a location where you can face the window and keep an eye on your vehicle while you're eating. And don't ever put valuables in the trunk of a vehicle and then walk away from it. It's a much better idea to place these items into the trunk at another location, rather than let observant crooks know which vehicle they want to break into.

If you're flying with these important things, DON'T CHECK THEM WITH YOUR BAGGAGE! Your carry-on baggage is limited, but while clothing and cosmetics are replaceable, many of these things aren't. If you think I'm exaggerating the risk, check out the Unclaimed Baggage Center in Scottsboro, Alabama, and you'll find an amazing array of possessions which their owners will never see again. We've been there, and it's an adventure. You can get the idea by going to their website www.unclaimedbaggage.com. Of course, the odds are that your baggage will arrive safely at your destination when you do, but it's a big chance to take with anything irreplaceable.

If You Have The Movers Pack Your Things

<u>Do your homework.</u> Preparation is very important here, because the movers will pack everything they find unless you make sure they know what should *not* be packed. It is not their job to be selective, or question things as they go along. It's to pack what is there. Even if you put a note on items they should not pack, or boxes you've put together that they should repack, point these out to the packers when they arrive at your home.

<u>Put a note on the broiler pan </u>which goes with your oven, and any other parts which go to appliances you're leaving, so that they don't get packed.

<u>Empty your trash cans</u>. Laugh if you want, but many a customer has unpacked a trash can to find the trash still in it. Keep a number of plastic trash bags handy, for use as the move progresses. Whatever bags are unused at the end can be placed in the last box—they won't take up much room, and you'll need them right away in the new house.

Put the <u>owner's manuals, keys</u> to the house, and other things which will stay with the house in a specific area (a kitchen drawer or cabinet shelf works well), and put a big note "Do not pack" with them.

<u>Set aside or put a big note </u>on anything which you don't want packed or will need moving day. This may include a shower curtain, shampoo, toothbrushes, clothing, contact lens solution, medical supplies, diapers, and so on. Put your personal items—suitcases, snacks for packing & moving day, a cooler, sweaters, a radio, telephone, whatever, in a corner of your dining room (or other uncluttered area), again with a big "Do not pack" note. Also, the precious

items and important papers you'll be taking with you (*see "What not to pack" above*) should be set aside, so that they're not packed away.

<u>Check to see that nothing's left behind.</u> After the packers have completed an area, use a step-stool or ladder, if necessary, to verify that they've actually gotten every item out of the kitchen cabinets and from on top of the cabinets.

<u>Tools you'll want to have available</u>:

- Scissors—for various uses

- Dark colored, permanent markers with broad tips— for labeling boxes

- Pliers—for removing picture hooks and nails from the walls

- Cellophane and masking tape—for taping notes and various other uses—and packing tape, for sealing or re-sealing boxes (if you need to get something out of one that's already been sealed)

- Spackle and putty knife—for patching holes in walls

If You're Doing The Packing Yourself

Remember, the moving company isn't liable for damage to boxes packed by the customer and can even refuse to take a box that appears to be packed improperly, until it's repacked. So if you're going to do it yourself, do the job right.

<u>Purchasing Supplies</u>
To do the job right, you'll need to purchase good materials and know how to use them. You can purchase these through moving companies, truck rental companies,

mailing/shipping stores, or storage facilities. There are also a lot of providers online—search under "moving supplies"— but make sure you're convinced that these boxes are in great condition and do not have insects hiding in them. You can compare the prices of materials at moving companies, storage facilities, or truck rental companies online or by calling, but we've found them to be fairly similar.

If you purchase the supplies from your moving company, they will deliver the boxes to you. They may even guide you as to how many of each size box you'll need. Verify whether there is a charge for delivery of these supplies. Most storage facilities or truck rental locations will require you to transport the materials yourself. Since the boxes come "broken down" (flat), they aren't as bulky as you may think—except for the wardrobe boxes, which are quite large, even when flat. It will certainly take a number of trips to transport enough boxes for a 2500-square-foot home, even in an SUV, but on the other hand you can get a bunch of the boxes packed before picking up the next supply. Your moving company will probably deliver all of the materials at once, which will take up a large amount of space, but you'll most likely have everything you need.

You'll probably need way more boxes and packing paper than you think, so buy plenty of supplies and make sure unused ones are returnable (*partial* bundles of newsprint are not).You'll be amazed at how many boxes it takes to accommodate the last few things as your house is emptied, so keep a good supply until the last of your things are packed. Instructions for using these materials are included later in this chapter.

Tools for the Task
- Rolls of packing tape—2" wide, strong, clear or brown tape, for sealing boxes. Masking or cellophane tape are not strong enough for this job.

- Tape dispenser—makes it a lot easier to use the packing tape

- Bubble wrap—for wrapping delicate items

- Utility knife—for opening boxes, and occasionally for cutting down boxes to customize their size (especially ones containing fragile items, which will then be placed into a larger box). It's easy to misplace these in the midst of a move, so I suggest getting 2 or 3.

- Scissors—for cutting tape when needed, and a multitude of other uses

- Permanent markers with broad tips—for labeling boxes

- Pliers—for removing picture hooks and nails from the walls

- Small zipper food storage bags for picture hooks and other small items. *See the beginning of this chapter for additional uses.*

- Spackle and putty knife—for patching holes in walls (You may need to touch up the paint, too, unless the spackle matches the wall color. Tiny picture hook holes may be better left alone.)

- Packing paper (unprinted newsprint paper)—for packing material. Usually comes in 10-lb. bundles. Because newspaper ink can soil and even damage some items permanently, it's well worth the price to use packing paper instead. Another bonus is that it won't make your hands and clothing turn black. (Note: if you insist on using newspaper, protect your clothing with an apron or smock and keep some waterless hand cleaner or hand soap and paper towels handy.) When you crumple this to provide padding, use several sheets together. That way it won't flatten out.

- Boxes—for packing almost everything. These come in a variety of sizes:
  - ↪ 1.5 cubic ft. –for heavy items such as books, records, CDs, canned goods, small appliances
  - ↪ 3 cubic ft. – for many things, including pots and pans, toys, small lampshades, non-perishable foods, small appliances
  - ↪ 4.5 & 6 cubic ft. – for large lightweight items, such as pillows, linens, comforters, large lampshades, larger toys
  - ↪ Wardrobe boxes—large carton with a bar for hanging clothes and draperies. There may be room in the bottom of these for shoes, purses, and belts, especially under short hanging garments such as tops and shorts.
  - ↪ Mirror cartons—telescoping cartons which come in a variety of sizes, for pictures, mirror, and glass.
  - ↪ Mattress cartons—available in crib, twin, standard, double, queen and king sizes. Use one for every box spring and one for every mattress.
  - ↪ Dishpacks—very study carton for china, dishes, crystal, glassware, lamps, light-weight appliances. Partitions are available to help protect dishes and stemware.

How to Pack

General guidelines
- Things you can pack way ahead of moving day include: out-of-season clothing, holiday items, extra towels and bedding, old records and books, photo albums, and things stored in your basement or attic.

- Before you begin packing each carton, tape it securely closed on the bottom.

- Line the bottom of the box with a 2-3" layer of crumpled/wadded packing paper.

- Try to limit the weight of each box to about 50 lbs. Try not to make any carton too heavy to lift easily.

- Wrap items individually.

- Provide plenty of cushioning.

- Make sure of a firm pack—things shouldn't move around inside the box when it's moved, and the top should close firmly but not bend in.

- Pack heavy items in smaller boxes, and don't pack lightweight things in a box with heavy items. The heavy items could shift in the box and crush the lightweight items.

- Pack similar things together and keep parts of things together.

- Use a felt-tipped permanent marker to note the contents of each box. Mark "fragile" or "≤" to indicate "this end up" when appropriate.

- Mark boxes on several sides, because when a lot of boxes are stacked up, it's not always easy to see every side of a given box.

- Mark what room *in the new house* the box should be placed in.

- Mark "Open first" on boxes which contain essentials such as bed linens and towels which you'll want to use as soon as you move in.

- Have everything packed by the night before the movers arrive, except for items you need that night or the morning of the move.

- As you stack boxes, put "Fragile" ones on the top of a stack, rather than stacking anything on top of them.

- Don't pack flammable items. *See "Items which cannot go in the moving van" under "What Not To Pack" earlier in this chapter.*

- Blankets and towels can be used for cushioning some items.

- Cassette tapes and digital media should not come into contact with magnets, such as those on stereo speakers, because the magnets may damage them.

- Identify and repack (or have movers repack) items in cartons which are torn, dirty, or can't be properly sealed. These are often boxes which contain holiday decorations or mementos.

- File cabinets will need to be emptied.

- Remember things stored in the attic, crawlspace, garage and outside your home.

- Climb up on a ladder to verify there's nothing pushed back and forgotten on high shelves.

- If you have sturdy suitcases you won't be using for the trip, you may as well pack things in them. Clothing, linens, or stuffed animals might be good for these. Just make a mental note to *unpack* them when you get to your new home. Otherwise, you'll wonder where those things could possibly be. (Been there; done that.)

- Each bed frame should be tied together using rope or tape. Tape a plastic bag containing the hardware to the frame.

- Computer monitors, printers, televisions, VCRs, DVRs and speakers should be packed in their original packaging, if you still have it. If you have the box but not the packing materials, be sure to cushion the item well so that it doesn't shift. Tape down moving parts, such as turntable arms.

- Tables should have their legs removed. Pad them well and tape the hardware to the underside of the table.

- Table leaves can be wrapped in blankets and tied. To protect the wood, don't wrap them in plastic or place tape on the surface of the wood.

- Silverware: nest utensils in groups of 3-4, wrap in packing paper, and place in silver chest or a box. Fill any extra space in the chest with packing paper, so items don't shift.

- Lamp shades: nest together where possible, using a sheet of packing paper between each one. If they don't fit together easily, don't force them. Handle the shades just by their wire frames and place in a box. The bulb should be removed from the lamp and packed as any other very fragile item, but if not in the box with the lampshade, note where bulbs are packed so lamps will be useful when you're unpacking. Harp and lamp base should be packed separately, in the same box.

- Mirrors and photos/artwork framed with glass: wrap in good cushion of packing paper and place in mirror carton. Small ones can be wrapped well and then stood on end in a small box. Be sure to pack firmly, and mark "Fragile" "↑" on the outside. If you move these yourself in a car, wrapping them in blankets can be a good way to protect them.

- Rugs can be rolled up and tied with rope or tape.

- Gas-powered lawn and yard equipment: empty gasoline (or run until fuel is gone).

- Tools: wrap sharp edges and use plenty of cushioning to prevent injury or damage. Place small ones in boxes, and tape long handled ones together in small bunches so that they can be moved more easily.

Packing china
Line the bottom of the box with a 2-3" layer of crumpled/ wadded packing paper. Wrap each item separately, then wrap up to 3 in a bundle, using 2 sheets of packing paper. Place in partitioned box, placing large, heavy items on bottom and lighter, more fragile items on top. Load plates and saucers vertically, to make the most of their structural strength, with cups and bowls placed around them.

Packing glasses
Round glasses and jars can be rolled up in 2-3 sheets of paper. Begin from a corner of the sheet and fold the sides in as you roll. Place glassware on rims for maximum protection.

Packing stemware
Wrap the stems for extra protection; then wrap each glass individually and place upside down in partitioned

box. As each layer is completed, fill in empty spaces firmly with crushed paper and add more crushed paper to make a level base for the next layer. Fill in voids and top off with wadded/crumpled paper. Tape box securely closed. Make sure arrow points ↑ and you note "Fragile" on the outside of the box.

Small, fragile items should be wrapped individually in bubble wrap. Place these in small boxes, cushioning them with crumpled packing paper or Styrofoam peanuts. Then place the small boxes in a larger box, with plenty of crumpled paper surrounding them.

Items of significant value: Remember, items worth more than $100 per pound need to be noted by the movers in order to receive proper valuation coverage, so either leave the box open so the movers can inspect those items, or— better yet—have the movers pack those items themselves.

Ways *not* to save money

- Using boxes from the grocery store.
  They may work fine for 20-somethings moving between small apartments 6 blocks apart, but are not great for a larger, longer-distance household move. You want sturdy boxes in good condition, so that they maintain their integrity when fully packed and sealed. You also want boxes which will stack well, so multiple boxes of the same size are important. And, of course, you want to make sure there are no insects hiding in the box looking for a free ride.

- Using newspaper instead of packing paper.
  See "packing paper" under "Tools for the Task" earlier in this chapter, for all the reasons why.

- Packing fragile, irreplaceable items yourself.

Professional movers know how to do it and also will only accept liability for an item when they do. So unless you're pretty great at packing, and plan to take it with you as you travel to your new home, I would leave it to the professionals.

Chapter 14

Moving Days and The Closings

"Why do we need to do a final walk-thru of the house we're buying? What goes on at a closing, and how should we prepare for it? What should we expect when the packers come? And what should we do to make the packing and moving process go more smoothly, while protecting ourselves?"

In this chapter, we'll cover the very important Final Walk-Thru and how to handle any problems it reveals, different types of closings, and what to expect during a closing. Then we'll guide you through packing days (if you have professionals do the job), moving out of your old house and moving into your new one.

Important note: keep receipts for meals you eat in restaurants, fuel for your car if you drive it to the new city, and hotel expenses, as these may be reimbursable as relocation expenses.

The Final Walk-Through

Before a closing, the Buyer—and real estate agent, if one is involved in the transaction—walks through the house to make sure that all agreed-upon repairs have been made, that everything belonging to the house as specified in the purchase contract is there, and that the property is in the same condition as it was when the contract was signed (except for the aforementioned repairs, of course). This is called the "final walk-through". It's helpful to have the real estate agent be present, because it's another set of eyes, and also another person to weigh in, in case something is not as it was at contract signing. This is an essential step in the transaction. It is especially important to be thorough if the house has been vacant for any amount of time. Sometimes, through no one's fault, things happen. You need to be as sure as you can that there are no problems not previously noted with the property before you complete the purchase of it.

Sellers should make sure utilities are on so that plumbing, appliances, and HVAC can be checked out.

Buyers should plan to spend about half an hour to an hour doing this inspection. Resist the temptation to spend this time on deciding where the furniture will go, and focus your efforts on the job at hand, because once the closing is done, you have very little recourse if there are problems. Bring your photos of the house and a copy of your Sales Contract with you, so you can consult them if there's any question regarding items which should be included with the house. Verify that chandeliers and hardware haven't been swapped for other, inferior ones, and that the draperies which were to have stayed are actually there. Be sure no problems have arisen with plumbing, appliances and HVAC. Turn on appliances (washer, dryer, and dishwasher) and run a short cycle. Turn on heating and air conditioning, if possible. Flush toilets. Run water in sinks and tubs. Be on the lookout for water leaks, including those under the sinks. Try out the garbage disposal. Turn on lights, ceiling fans and exhaust fans. Check that outlets are working by plugging a nightlight into them. Look at ceilings, walls, and floors for water damage, damage done while moving out, and any deep scratches, or damage to flooring, that may have been hidden by boxes or rugs. Open and close all windows and doors. Check attics, basements, crawlspaces, garages and sheds. Check the outside of the house for any new damage.

Be sure that unwanted things haven't been left in the house. Look outside the house at the landscaping and verify that bushes or other plants have not been removed from the ground without being included in the contract. (If there's nothing in the landscaping that strikes you as obvious, there is probably not a problem.) If there is a pile of refuse at the foot of the driveway, verify that the Seller has scheduled a special pick-up and has been billed for it. It would be helpful to take a photo of anything in question. This is not the time to play "Let's Make a Deal" about small stuff, but it *is* the time to protect yourself if expensive problems have been revealed, or problems occurred, and to make sure the Sellers have lived up to their part of the bargain by keeping up the house, and not leaving you the burden of removing their unwanted possessions.

If agreed-upon repairs or inspections haven't been completed, it is still possible for the closing to take place if all parties agree to have an adequate amount of the Seller's funds placed into an escrow account until the obligations have been fulfilled. Typically, either the Listing Agent or the Seller's attorney holds the money, and all parties must sign a release before any of it is dispersed to anyone. Just go through the items in question, one by one, and make a decision as to who is responsible for each item and how it can be handled. Don't get emotional—just deal with it as a business detail and be sure to deal with it *before* completing the closing. A short addendum to the contract can be drafted, which will include these items and the terms to which both parties have agreed.

There are great reasons for not delaying the closing, if a satisfactory agreement can be reached:

1. The Buyer's goods are probably on a moving van, en route to the new house. If the closing is delayed, either there will be a hefty per-day charge for keeping

them on the van temporarily, or everything will have to go into storage, incurring both a storage fee and an additional fee for moving them from storage facility to the new house.

2. If the Buyer is taking out a mortgage for the house, the interest rate and approval may be locked in only until the date of closing or very shortly afterwards; if the loan isn't closed in time, he may have to go through the whole process again, possibly paying a higher interest rate and additional charges, and perhaps losing the opportunity to purchase the house at all.

3. If the Seller accepted the contract with a 3-day Release Clause, there may be another contract waiting in the wings, if this contract doesn't close according to the agreed-upon terms. Delaying the closing past the date specified in the contract might allow the other potential Buyer to step forward and purchase the property.

4. If the Seller is counting on the proceeds of the sale to close on another house, delaying this transaction may affect the other transaction. The ramifications continue, so if an agreement can be made, that is by far the best solution.

But what if...? Obviously, if something new and significant is uncovered during the walk-thru which makes the Buyer feel he shouldn't be purchasing the property, then the situation may need to be resolved in a different way. The Buyer should consult with the attorney who reviewed the Purchase Offer if there is any question as to how to proceed. If the Buyer didn't use an attorney to review the Purchase Offer, then if he needs advice he'll want to get recommendations for a good real estate attorney who can talk with him right away.

Assuming nothing alarming is discovered during the walk-through—and usually nothing is—if the Sellers are present, they can explain any quirks of the house, and answer any questions the Buyers may have. This also might be a good time for them to show the Buyers how the Security System works, if one is installed and hooked up.

Hint: It's a good idea for Buyers to get contact information for the Sellers, in case mail is delivered in error (sometimes after the one-year forwarding order expires, important mail still arrives) or in case of questions. When we added a screened-porch to our home in Alpharetta, Georgia, and our contractor couldn't find matching siding at any of his normal suppliers, I was able to contact the original owner and get the brand name of the siding. I then located a supplier on the internet and was able to tell the contractor where he could buy it locally. Two days later, we had matching siding on our porch.

The Closing (a.k.a. Settlement or Passing Papers)

Escrow vs. closing or settlement

In some states, particularly in the Western U.S., closings are usually done by escrow. In this case, a disinterested third party, such as an attorney, title company or escrow company, assumes the role of "Escrow Agent" and coordinates the signing of closing documents and any activities related to the transfer of the property. The Sellers sign their paperwork ahead of time, and are not present when the Buyers finalize their mortgage and sign papers to purchase the home. Escrow is considered "closed" when all details have been settled, papers signed, and monies dispersed to the appropriate parties. When closings are not done by escrow, Buyers and Sellers usually come together for this process. Much of the information in this section applies to these joint transactions, which are called closings or settlements.

Do both of us need to attend the closing?

If there are 2 of you who are buying (or selling) the home, you don't both *need* to be at each closing. You may want to be, and arrange it accordingly. However, there have been times when I was sitting in the old house with the movers loading the truck, while my husband was several states away at the closing on our new home. The way you can do this is by executing a Power of Attorney which is solely for the purpose of this particular transaction. If any questions come up, there's nothing stopping one spouse from phoning the other to ask what they think about this or that.

Where will the closing be held, and who will protect my interests?

The closing is often held in the office of the attorney who represents the loan company, assuming the Buyer is taking out a mortgage on the new house. When it is not held in the office of an attorney, it is usually held at the office of an escrow company or title company. The closing attorney or closing officer coordinates the closing but does not provide legal advice to the Buyer or the Seller. Your real estate agent should be there and can help. If you want legal protection, you should hire a real estate attorney to come to the closing with you. The attorney will be most effective if you include a contingency contract in your offer, so that the attorney has had an opportunity to review the contract during negotiations.

What happens at the closing?

The "closing" is both for the loan and for the purchase of the house. At the closing, there are many documents to sign and the Buyer pays the balance of the down payment with a certified or cashier's check made out to himself. The Buyer will endorse that check at the closing. The closing agent should explain each document that the parties need to sign, and should be patient while they read every word on those documents. (Yes, we really read them all, but I have to tell you not everyone does.) She should also explain how figures were calculated. The closing agent may have a lot of closings that day, and tend to go through the documents quickly because they are all very familiar to her. Don't let yourself be rushed. Be sure you understand what you're signing. If you have questions, ask them, but do it in a non-confrontational way.

After everything is agreed upon and documents signed, all parties receive a copy of the appropriate documents. Real estate commissions are paid, the Seller's mortgage is paid off, closing costs are paid, and the Seller receives a check for the appropriate amount. The Seller has signed a deed transferring ownership and now provides the Buyer with keys to the house. After the closing, the attorney makes sure that the deed is recorded. The Buyer will receive a new deed in the mail.

This is a very important business transaction.
Make arrangements for pets and small children to be cared for, if possible, so that you can focus on the transaction. You may want to bring a sitter with you to the closing, or have children stay with a trusted friend. Older children should bring things to amuse themselves. Often, closing locations are prepared for children with toys, videos, and people willing to keep an eye on the kids. You can ask about this ahead of time.

Get a good night's sleep prior to closing. This can be a stressful time, but you need to be able to concentrate. Usually, closings are completed in about an hour, but be prepared in case it takes longer than expected. Try to remain calm and work out any issues. Don't let others take advantage of you, but be willing to compromise if the other person has a valid point. Ideally, both parties will leave the closing feeling good about the transaction and about the fact that the sale has been completed.

What do I need to bring to closing?

If you're the Buyer, remember to take any necessary paperwork, including your driver's license or other photo identification, proof of your one-year pre-paid homeowner's insurance policy beginning on the date of closing, and a certified or cashier's check for the amount due. You'll be advised of that amount a day or two prior to closing. But do take a personal check, in the event that a small additional fee is required. If the estimate you were given is too much, you'll receive a check for the excess.

If you're the Seller, bring the house keys, homeowner's association or condo by-laws, and anything else you're instructed to provide.

Hint: Some of the closing costs, such as prepaid mortgage interest and property taxes, may be taken as deductions on the Buyer's tax return. Sellers may be exempt from capital gains if the home was their primary residence and they fulfill other requirements. Consult an accountant for more details.

Moving Out

Try to anticipate, as much as possible, what possessions you'll need to have or use during the moving days. Even after all the relocations I've done, I still forgot, a couple of moves ago, to get my coat out of the coat closet, so that I'd be able to wear it on the trip to my new house. Considering November weather in Chicago, I was glad that I remembered it before the wardrobe carton was sealed and loaded onto the moving van.

If you requested that the movers pack your things, the packers will come either the morning of your scheduled loading day, or a day or two before, depending on how long they anticipate it will take them to pack. The moving company should be able to tell you this when they give you your moving estimate. The time will be firmed up shortly before your move. Depending on the company you use, the packers may be (a)local employees of the moving company, (b)contract employees, whose specialty is packing, or (c)a team of two people who pack, load, drive the moving van, and deliver your belongings.

If you pack your household yourself, be sure that everything is packed and ready-to-go (except, perhaps, one last box) *before* the movers arrive.

Hint: You'll start the relationship with the movers off nicely, if you have water, Gatorade or soda on hand to offer them (from a cooler, if your refrigerator is unplugged). Doughnuts and coffee first thing in the morning may also be appreciated. If you really want to be nice, offer to order a pizza delivery for lunch, or have a friend make a run to a local sub shop or fast food eatery. I do not suggest that you yourself leave the house, because it's important for you to be there, noting contents of boxes, as things are being packed and on moving day noting what's happening as things are being loaded onto the moving van.

Before the packers or movers arrive

- Be sure to have your cell phone charged up, and keep your charger where it won't be packed.

- Leave your U.S. Postal Service Forwarding Order in your mailbox, if you haven't already taken care of this.

- Leave the job of disassembling goods, such as beds and wall units, for the movers to do, so that they can put them back together at your destination.

- Gather items you'll want immediately upon arrival, such as: toilet paper, facial tissues, hand soap, paper towels, cleaner (for kitchen cabinets or the bathroom), scissors (for cutting shelf paper to line cabinets and drawers), tape, paper for notes, paper plates &

cups, plastic silverware, snacks, coffee (and coffee pot), flashlight, radio, box cutter, screwdriver, pliers, can opener, and telephone (if you'll be getting a land line in the new home). Some of these items you may choose to take with you or purchase when you arrive at your new city, so that you can line kitchen shelves and use the bathroom before the moving van arrives, for instance. The others can be packed toward the end of your move out. Let your mover know you'd like these items to be packed in a box to be loaded last and unloaded first. You'll probably want your vacuum cleaner to be loaded last, too. (I know, I know....only one thing can be "last"...but you get the idea.)

• If your car is getting moved, remember to take the garage door opener out of it before the car leaves.

• Pick an area of the house, such as a corner of your dining room, to put things which will not go on the moving van. Make sure to mark the area "Do not pack" and be clear about what things are not to be packed. For packing and moving days, set aside water bottles and/or other drinks, snacks, a sweatshirt or whatever in case you get cold, etc. Expect to get grungy on moving day, so it would be good to have a change of clothes, if possible. You'll feel a whole lot better once the moving van leaves, if you know you can freshen up a bit—even if that means using the paper towels and soap you've set aside for washing up. Of course, you'll also include medications, clothing and other things you're packing for the trip, as well as items in the Survival Kit. *See Chapter 10.* Don't forget your young one's blanket and an extra pacifier, or other small items that family members will find comforting.

- Remove linens from beds and put aside any damp towels. They'll get pretty musty if they're packed while damp, so either find a "safe" place for towels to dry before they get packed, or wash and dry them, if you can. Pillows, clean towels, a few nightlights, and the linens you want to put on your beds when you get to your new house should be placed together, and be sure the box has a notation to "Open first", and a location, such as "Master Bedroom".

- Put those things you're leaving for the new owners— Owner's Manuals and warrantees, keys and garage door openers—altogether, perhaps in a plastic zip bag, and mark it clearly "DO NOT PACK". You may also want to put a phone book with these items.

- Keep a stepstool or ladder aside, so you can use it to check high closet shelves and kitchen cabinets after their contents have been packed.

- Tape signs with room names in the doorway or on the door of rooms, such as "Adam's Bedroom" or "Office". Boxes should be marked with the room name and a general description of the contents. Then when you put signs with the same room names on appropriate doors of the new house, the movers will know where these items go. If an item—such as a sewing machine—will be going to a different area in the new house, tape a note with the appropriate room name on the item, and point it out to the packers when you show them around the house.

- Walk around the outside of your house, to collect personal items that may be there, including garden hoses (drained), flower pots, metal decorations stuck in the ground, and any portable decorations. (If you have a question as to whether any item can legitimately be removed, ask your real estate sales-person.) Plants which are in the ground may only be removed if this was stated in the sales contract. If you have a mezuzah on your doorframe (Jewish readers know what this is) which you want to keep, remove it and seal it in a small plastic bag along with the nails with which it was attached. Remember "welcome" signs near your door and doormats. Place these items with other items which will be packed, perhaps in the garage.

When the Packers Arrive

- <u>Be there</u> while the packing is being done.

- <u>Take the packers on a tour</u> of your house. Point out the area where you've placed things you don't want them to pack, and show them anything else which is not going with you (you should have notes taped to these, saying Do Not Move). Show the packers any items which need special attention, including espe-cially fragile or valuable items and anything for which crating has been requested. You can also show them where you've placed the items you'd like packed in the first carton(s) to come off the truck at your des-tination, and any boxes which you know should be repacked. In one move, we wrote on several boxes "Needs to be repacked" but neglected to point them out, and they arrived at our new home just as they were when we wrote that note. I guess the packers didn't read what we wrote (or maybe, that particular packer couldn't understand English).

- <u>Label the boxes</u>. There will probably be 2-3 pack-ers, but you can go back and forth between them, marking significant contents on the outside of each box with a marker. While the packers may label a box "Kitchen" and "utensils" or "Bathroom" and

"Misc", you may want to add, with your own marker "Toaster" or "shower curtain", so that you can quickly locate that something essential for a first breakfast or shower. Also, some rooms in the new house may not have a ceiling light, so you'll want to be able to find and unpack lamps to use in those rooms, at least temporarily.

- <u>Gather the little things.</u> Use a pliers and small plastic bag to collect picture hooks as pictures and other decorative things are taken off the wall, and a separate bag to collect other small items (such as buttons or Lego pieces) which you will inevitably find, as furniture is moved.

If you have your home packed by professionals, you'll be amazed at how it's done. It's very entertaining to watch. They really know how to protect things, and I've learned a lot from them. There are various sizes of cartons, to accomodate mirrors, books, mattresses, and bulky articles. There are dishpacks for china, glassware, and other fragile items. And there are wardrobe cartons, which have a bar near the top of the box, so clothes on hangers can be hung inside the box. Special cartons will be cut and taped to be the perfect size for your framed artwork, and crates will be constructed for items which are especially large or fragile. Any crates needed should have been ordered by the representative who gave you your moving estimate.

When the Movers Arrive to Move You "Out"

It's impressive what good movers do prior to moving anything out of your home. They'll pad corners and railings and will protect floor coverings and the stairways in your house. They know how to protect your furniture while it's being moved so that it doesn't get scratched (although accidents do happen occasionally).

- <u>Give them a tour of the house</u>. Show them how you've noted anything which shouldn't be moved.

- <u>Inventory stickers & sheets:</u> Before they move anything out of the house, the lead mover will place a small, removable colored inventory number sticker on every piece of furniture, broom, box, bicycle, and other item which will be moving. The numbers correspond to an inventory sheet, which has multiple copies. One of these copies will be given to you before the moving van leaves your house. There is room on the inventory sheet to note the description of the item or some of the contents of the box. This can be helpful, especially if an item is missing or temporarily misplaced during the move. When the movers unload the van at your destination, you will be checking off each item on the inventory sheet, to verify that you received every piece of your shipment.

  Notations are made on the inventory sheets, such as PBO (Packed By Owner) or CP (carrier packed). There is a legend on the Inventory sheet which explains abbreviations used to describe furniture which is moved. Some examples are SC (scratched) or C (chipped). This is done so that all parties are aware of damage which exists prior to the shipment, to avoid claims being placed for pre-existing dents and scratches. It's easy to overlook damage when your furniture has been in the same spot for a long time and you're not used to scrutinizing it or seeing it from a different angle. If any items are damaged during the move, you should make a notation in the appropriate column of the Inventory Sheet and notify the driver.

- <u>Last on, first off:</u> One of the last things loaded onto the truck should be your vacuum cleaner (so that you can leave the house looking clean for the new owners and perhaps do a quick vacuuming in the new home before the furniture is moved in) and perhaps your broom and mop. There will also be a box or two which fall into this category.

- <u>Folklore about moving brooms:</u> There's a superstition or custom about brooms, which you may or may not want to follow. I've heard it worded in two different ways, but don't know the origin of either one: "Never take a broom along when you move. Throw it out and buy a new one." and "When you move to a new house, always enter first with a loaf of bread and a new broom. Never bring an old broom into the house." A broom is something I wouldn't worry about leaving in a house I moved out of—just leave it in the garage, and the new homeowners may appreciate it.

- <u>As the house is emptied:</u> Go through the house when it's almost empty, looking in every drawer, cabinet, closet (even way up on the shelves), and storage locker (if you're in an apartment or condominium building). *It's your responsibility to make sure nothing is left behind* which should be going.

- <u>Contact numbers are important.</u> Make sure the movers know how to reach you at your destination. If they can't reach you to arrange delivery of your belongings, they may have to put your things in temporary storage to avoid delaying other peoples' moves. That will mean additional charges for storage, handling and redelivery, which you'll want to avoid.

- <u>Before they leave, get the paperwork.</u> Before the moving van leaves with your belongings, the mover is required to give you a Bill of Lading. This is a receipt for your things and the contract with your mover for their transportation. You need to read and understand the information on the Bill of Lading before you sign it. Among other things, it specifies the services the mover will perform, terms and conditions for payment, the pick-up and delivery dates, the maximum amount to be paid if you are moving with a non-binding estimate, and information regarding the valuation of your shipment and the amount the mover will be liable for in case of loss or damage. It is important to keep this document until you are certain there are no damages or losses, or until any claims have been settled. To be prudent, keep all the moving paperwork for at least a year, because sometimes things are discovered awhile after moving in.

Also be sure you have your copy of the Inventory sheets. It should list everything which has been loaded onto the moving van, and include details of any damage noted prior to the move.

- <u>Leave the house neat and clean.</u> Once the movers have left, take the time to tidy and clean as necessary, so that the Buyers will find a nice, clean, fresh house to move into. Remember to leave those things for them that you've collected—garage door opener, owner's manuals, etc. You can leave them in the kitchen on the counter, or in a kitchen cabinet or drawer they're likely to look in soon after their arrival.

- <u>Before you leave:</u> Make sure doors and windows are locked, heat or air conditioning is turned off or set appropriately, and light switches are turned off. If you haven't already done so, read the meters for your electricity, water and gas, so that you can compare the readings with your final bill when it comes.

Moving In

Before the moving van arrives

- <u>Where will we eat?</u> Food is always an important issue with me. When you have time, look around the area, to see where you'll get your breakfast the morning the movers will arrive (assuming they'll arrive in the morning), and look for a convenient place near your new home to pick up, or order delivery for, lunch and dinner. Also, you don't have to feel obligated, but it's nice if you can manage to have beverages to offer the movers. If there are enough of you, perhaps someone can offer to go out for a meal—or you could include the movers when you call in your pizza order.

- Go shopping for any of these items you don't have with you, but may need before unpacking: shelf paper, toilet paper, facial tissue, paper towels, a broom, hand soap, cleaning supplies, cups, paper plates, and refreshments, including drinks for the crew and possibly ice.

- <u>Got the money?</u> Remember to have payment for the move as directed by the moving company. Personal checks are usually not accepted. Also be sure to have some cash to tip the movers, providing they have done a good job. *Tips are covered in detail at the end of Chapter 10.*

- <u>Set up the 'facilities'.</u> One of the first things you'll want to do is put toilet paper, soap, and towels in the bathrooms so that they can be used right away. Paper towels are fine until you've unpacked the cloth towels. We bring these things into the house as soon as we arrive, so that at least one bathroom is functional. We also clean the fixtures before using them, because then we *know* that they're clean.

- <u>Check the utilities.</u> As soon as you arrive, check the house to make sure that electricity, gas and water are on and working. Make sure the pilot light, if any, is on for the hot water heater and the stove. If any of the utilities scheduled to be working are not, this would be a good time to call the companies and try to rectify the situation.

  Take a few minutes and read the meters for gas, electric, and water. You'll want to compare them to your first bill, to make sure you're only paying for what you've used.

- <u>Label the rooms</u>. Tape a sign on each of the rooms (above the door or on the door itself) to label them, using the terms you used when marking boxes & items in your old home. (boy's room or Adam's room, family room, library, etc.). This will make it easier for the movers to know where to put things.

- <u>Label where furniture will go</u>. Consulting the drawings you've made showing furniture placement, write "Piano" or whatever on masking tape and attach it to the wall or floor, showing where items are to be placed.

- <u>Line shelves, cabinets and drawers.</u> This can be done anytime before things are put away, but if you haven't already done it and you're waiting around for the movers to arrive, this would be a helpful thing to get done.

- <u>Call your old phone number:</u> Either now, or sometime in the next day or so, call your old phone number to see what happens. If it just rings, it may not be disconnected. If you don't get what you requested, either a recording saying just that the number's been disconnected, or one giving your correct new phone number, call your old phone company to get the situation corrected.

When the Movers Arrive to Move You "In"

- <u>Give them a tour of the house</u>, showing them the signs where you've labeled each room. Also, show them how you've indicated where specific pieces of furniture will go. They'll have a lot of boxes to stack in each room, so this way they'll also know to put the boxes where furniture *won't* go. If you've managed to assemble cold drinks for the crew, let them know where they are and that they can help themselves.

- <u>Quickly vacuum?</u> If the floors need it, ask to get the vacuum cleaner off the van (remember, it was loaded last so should be easy to retrieve) and do a quick floor cleaning, so that things aren't placed on top of the dirty floor.

Your jobs during unloading

- <u>Verify that everything is delivered</u>. Receiving your household goods is at least a two-person job—one person to check off each item and the other to guide where things are being placed. As each box or item is carried into the house, you or someone you trust should be there checking off the item on the inventory list. The movers will usually call out the inventory numbers for you.They will probably be moving quickly, so you need to not be afraid to slow them down so that you can do this check off properly and accurately.

- <u>Be alert for damage.</u> Pay attention to each item as it's brought into the house, noting any boxes or other items which appear to have sustained damage. If something does wind up getting lost or damaged in the move, tell the driver about it before he leaves, if possible, and note it on the inventory sheet before you sign that document. If the driver has left before you notice a problem, you should have information on who to contact. You'll also want to notify your moving coordinator or other contact at the moving company, even if the driver does know about the problem.

- <u>The claims process:</u> When you were selecting the mover, you asked about the claims process, and you understand what kind of coverage you purchased. You should also have paperwork from the mover handy, so you can use that as a reference. Now you'll get to put this knowledge to work. Remember: if you talk nicely (even if you're feeling tired, stressed and angry), you are much more likely to get your issues resolved amicably. And don't underestimate the miracles their trouble-shooters can do; we've had small pieces chip off of wood furniture, and when the repairman came out and was finished with it, the furniture looked better than it had in years.

  Under current laws, you have 9 months in which to file a claim, but it's best to do it as soon as possible. Your mover must acknowledge receipt of the claim within 30 days, and respond to it within 120 days. For more information on this, consult the information your mover gave you about their dispute settlement program for resolution of the claim. If you are unhappy with how your claim is being handled, you can also file a complaint with the Better Business Bureau by calling their local number or visiting www.BBB.com, and/or the Federal Motor Carrier Safety Administration (FMSCA) by calling 1-888-368-7238 or visiting www.ProtectYourMove.gov. For more information on this process, go to <u>www.Moving.org</u>. Hopefully, you won't have to deal with any claims, but it's good to know how the process works, in case you need to.

- <u>Are your planned furniture placements working?</u> Remember to be flexible—look at furniture as it's placed in the rooms. It is not unusual at all to find that some of the pieces don't work where you thought they would. Maybe the chest of drawers that you thought would be perfect against a bedroom wall, actually sticks out in front of the window by a few inches. Moving the bed down a bit, and placing the chest against the wall on the other side of the bed might be much more pleasing to the eye.

  As we discussed in Chapter 10, make sure to allow enough room between your dining room table and other furniture, to allow people to sit at the table and others to pass behind them. Approximately 3-4 feet between the edge of the table and the other piece of furniture, or wall, should do it. Also make sure your traffic paths are wide enough to look spacious, as well as to walk through comfortably.

  If something doesn't look right, talk it over with your friends/family who are there, and see if you can come up with a solution. The movers are not obligated to, but usually will (maybe even cheerfully!) move things around until you're satisfied. Obviously, it's best if you don't have them do this excessively, but it's a whole lot better to have them move a few things than to hurt your back later while trying to do it yourself. You'll probably want to tip them a bit more if they do much rearrangement and if they do any of it cheerfully.

- <u>Supervise reassembly:</u> The movers will generally reassemble items they've broken down in the packing process, such as beds, and can certainly place heavy objects, such as television sets, where they belong.

Also, you'll want to get TV, stereo components, and other plugs through the hole in the back of any wall units, and plug them in, while the movers are there to reposition the furniture afterwards. This is especially important if the furniture is very heavy or you don't have people with strong backs to help you after the movers leave.

- <u>Discarding boxes (but not all of them):</u> You won't get much unpacked while your things are being brought into the house, but whatever boxes you do get un-packed (especially when the movers are taking their breaks, and you aren't otherwise distracted) will be helpful. Ask the movers if they would be kind enough to take the boxes away with them when they leave. That will free up some space in your house or garage, and reduce the amount of refuse you need to dis-pose of later. Whatever they don't take away, "break down" using your box cutter, so the boxes lie flat. They take up much less room that way.

  If you have room to keep them, you'll want to hold on to some of the empty boxes, especially the smaller ones. They come in very handy for storing out-of-season clothing on closet shelves, for instance, or mailing holiday presents out of town. Just be careful not to store them where insects may be around. You wouldn't want to send gifts along with a June bug or 3.

  You may also want to hang onto some of the very large boxes, if you have small children. Our young son and daughter set them up in our basement after one move, and using markers and scissors, made a "house" which they played with for more than a year. One box was the stove, another a dresser, and so on. They had a great time with them.

A greener idea: If you have room to temporarily stash the broken-down boxes, you'll be able to place an ad on craigslist, in order to sell or give away the boxes to someone else who can use them. That's a lot of cardboard to send to recycling after just one use, and you'll probably get responses within hours. Usually, the people who respond are able to bring a truck and haul them all away at once.

- <u>Packing paper:</u> As you unpack, it's wise to flatten **every piece** of packing paper. There may be a very small trinket or piece of something inside, and you can't tell by just holding the paper. If you have small children, save some of that the paper which is un-wrinkled. It will be great for informal art paper, using paint or markers or chalk.

Congratulations! You have now closed on the sale and/or purchase of a home, and moved into your new abode. The hardest parts are over, and now you get to put everything where you want it, get settled in your nice, new home and discover your new world.

Chapter 15

After The Movers Leave

There's so much to do! Where do I start? What should go where in the kitchen? What can I do to make the house livable as soon as possible?

In this chapter, we'll guide you through organizing your kitchen, getting your house ready to live in quickly, and keeping your family and your possessions as safe as possible right away.

First Things First: Bathroom, Beds, Kitchen

Bathrooms: You've already put soap, toilet tissue and a towel in at least one bathroom. Before you stay in the house overnight, you'll want to have your bath towels, shower curtain, shower gel or bar soap, and hair products in place. If you've pulled these items together before the move and noted something on the outside of the appropriate box, such as "Bathroom—open first", you'll be able to find your supplies easily without going through 6 boxes and a lot of frustration.

Beds: The movers will set up the bed frame, mattress and box spring, so all you need to do is locate your mattress covers, bed linens, blankets and pillows to get your beds ready for use. Of course, you may be more comfortable if you have a lamp (if there's no ceiling light) and clock radio, but those are optional. Make sure you have a clear path from the bed to the door, so that no one gets hurt going to the bathroom during the night. Use those nightlights you packed along with your linens, so that you can dimly light the hallways and bathrooms, especially for the first few nights. The rest of the unpacking in the bedroom can wait.

Kitchen: One of the most difficult rooms to organize, as well as one of the most vital to do ASAP, is the kitchen. More than a few otherwise organized, logical people have been reduced to paralysis while trying to figure out how to fit everything they had in the old kitchen into the new one. Whether there is more space than you had in your last home, or less, it's still a real headache trying to figure out where it makes sense to place things. I'll try to help.

My friend Jan taught me a great process to use, when we downsized our home in Illinois. I had always arranged our kitchens myself with very little help, but in this case, with much less storage space in the kitchen than I was used to, I just couldn't even get started. Through this process, we were able to figure it out. The trick is to look at each item as you unpack it, and consider how often you tend to use it. Is this something you use 1-3 times a year? If so, maybe it makes sense to store it in the basement, attic, that hard-to-reach cabinet over the refrigerator, or other storage area, at least for now, to make room for the things you use daily and weekly. Once you've eliminated these items from the competition, it will make the rest a bit easier. And the best thing is that after a month or 3, if you decide you don't like where you've put things, you can always move them around. It's not a big deal to move the silverware from one drawer to another, or put the dishes where the cereals have been kept. Once you live with the kitchen for awhile, and without the added stress of having the rest of the house to organize, it will become clearer to you. So do the best you can for now, and move on.

Another thing which can help you store items in the kitchen is the use of storage tools. During another move, I actually had much *more* storage room than in my previous home, but was still stumped on how to arrange things. My long-time friend Colleen evaluated my challenges and showed up the next day with some solutions. She brought small tiered plastic shelves, which were perfect for storing spices, allowing the labels to be read on all of them since they were at varying heights. She brought larger plastic shelves to do the same thing with canned goods. For the inside of cabinet doors, she brought a plastic holder to accommodate plastic container lids, and removable adhesive hooks, so we could hang cutting boards and my colander in easy-to-reach places. She also brought sturdy, clear liner for the wire shelves in the pantry, so that small items would stand upright, instead of tilting between the wires. And, of course, roll-arounds help to make the most of deep shelves. For the cabinet over your double-oven or stove, you might find it helpful to use a divider storage rack, which will enable you to store cookie sheets, casserole dishes and trays on end. You'll find a wealth of possibilities in stores which specialize in containers, closets or kitchens.

General guidelines:

- Store plates in the upper cabinets near the sink or dishwasher.

- Store glasses and cups/mugs near the sink or refrigerator.

- Store pots and pans near the oven or stovetop, and microwave-safe cookware near the microwave.

- The cabinet above the oven and/or the drawer under it are good places for baking pans, pots and pans, and Pyrex® cookware.

- Spices you use frequently should be stored close to where you use them, but not where they will be subject to heat or sunlight. If you have a large number of spices you use infrequently, you might want to put them in the pantry, rather than take up precious space near your prep area.

- Food items, and items which may melt, should be stored away from heat sources, such as the oven or dishwasher.

- Store cleaning supplies, plastic trash bags, trash can and recycle bin under the kitchen sink, if possible. Of course, if you have small children you'll need to either store harmful items up higher, and/or install child locks on the doors.

- Consider storing items used very infrequently or for holidays either up high in cabinets you need a ladder to reach, or outside the precious kitchen space. They could be stored in your dining room armoire or a closet, or in another room or the basement.

Hint: Place sticky notes on the outside of cabinets and drawers indicating what goes there—silverware, dishes, glasses, etc. It will help you put things where you've decided they should go, and will help you and your family to find things more easily over the next few days, as you all get used to the new kitchen.

Continuing the Unpacking

Keep going...box by box. Get the family room set up so that you have a comfortable place to gather and relax, and the children's rooms set up so they feel more settled as soon as possible. Televisions and computers can help with the transition, for amusement when you or the family need a break from unpacking, and also to keep in touch with the world and your loved ones.

Sometimes, the sheer number of boxes makes it difficult to move around and deal with the things you're unpacking from boxes. In that case, move some into a nearby area temporarily, or stack up against a wall.

When we moved into a bungalow in southern California, there were so many boxes in the Master Bedroom, we couldn't walk from one side of the room to the other. Since no rain was expected, and the temperature was moderate, we decided to move some of the boxes onto the adjacent patio overnight, until we could unpack them the next day. What we didn't know was that there were—are you ready to be grossed out?—roaches in the back yard....a LOT of them. When we brought the boxes back into the house the next day, we had no idea we were introducing roaches into our newly-renovated, lovely home. It took awhile for the exterminators to get rid of them all, and was a lesson we will never forget. Please don't make the same mistake we did.

Try to "find a home" for everything you're unpacking, a logical place where it should be kept. Sometimes, you'll look at an object and realize you have no need for it anymore. Keep a box or large plastic bag of these things, so that you can dispose of them after you get mostly unpacked. After you see what you've put aside, you can decide whether to donate the things to charity or try to sell them or give them away.

As you unpack, break down the boxes so that they're flat. They take up a lot less room that way. Try to keep things as tidy as possible because it will help you attack the job more logically and stay on task. It's a big job and while you may think it will only take a day or two, in reality it will take quite a bit longer. Just keep on going and eventually you will be unpacked.

Stumbling Blocks

There will undoubtedly be things which you find don't work for you in the new house, but don't get upset about it. With a little resourcefulness and time, you'll figure out how to make it work.

- If there's not enough room to hang damp clothing in the laundry room, put an over-the-door hanger, which accommodates 8-10 hangers, on the door. Over the other side of the door, hang a multi-tiered coated-wire rack, which is perfect for drying underwear.

- You may need to add towel racks in the bathroom, or hooks on the back of bedroom, bathroom, or closet doors.

- Closet organizing companies are in business for a reason. If you can't seem to make your stuff "work" with the existing closet space, bring in one of these companies and let *them* solve the problem. It's amazing how some double-hung rods and some shelving can make your things fit so well and look so good.

With some things, you need to bring in experts to help. With other things, you need to live in the house for awhile to see a solution. Just keep working at it, and you'll figure out what will make things work for you.

Fire and Carbon Monoxide Safety

Before you spend a night in your new home:

- Try to identify at least 2 exits from every room.

- Develop a family fire-escape plan.

- Pick a place outside of your home where you can all gather if you need to evacuate the house, and make sure everyone understands where that location is.

- Make sure smoke alarms are installed on every level of the house and that they have working batteries. Alarms should be listed by Underwriters Laboratories (UL) and should be replaced when they're 10 years old.

- Carbon monoxide monitors should also be in the house—at least one near the furnace and one near the sleeping area.

As soon as possible:

- Fire extinguishers should be located at least in your kitchen and garage. We feel safer having one on each level of the house.
  - Select the ABC type (which work on all types of fires) or you can research which would be best for your needs.
  - Learn how to use it *before* there's an emergency.

- Have the fireplace inspected before you use it the first time, and periodically afterwards, depending on how often you use it. And remember to open the flue each time you're ready to light a fire.

Security

- Change the locks
  Even if the Sellers gave you multiple copies of the house key, you never know if there are additional keys out there. Perhaps they left one with a neighbor or friend or relative and just forgot to retrieve it. I definitely suggest you get a good locksmith to come

promptly to re-key the locks, or add additional locks if appropriate. You'll probably want a deadbolt of some kind on all exterior doors.

- Activate the security system
  If a security system exists in the house, change the code to make it your own. If you want it monitored, you'll need to contact a security company to do that. They'll want to come out and examine the system before entering into a contract with you. If the house doesn't have a security system but you want one, be sure to interview several companies before signing on the dotted line. An important thing to remember when you're talking with them is not to divulge infor-mation which makes you feel vulnerable if you don't select that company or another right away.

The first time I ever interviewed a security company representa-tive, I answered his questions thoroughly. When he had com-pleted presenting his recommendation, he knew so much—that I had 2 small children and that my husband was often away on business—that I wasn't comfortable not having a system right away. That led me to purchase a system from him, rather than interviewing other companies over the next week or two, and that system was probably not the best choice I could have made.

Barbecue Grill

When setting up your grill, make sure to place it outside, and at least 3 feet away from other things, including the house, shrubs, and patio furniture. Purchase a replacement propane tank, if your grill uses one. We like to have two tanks, actually, so when the first runs out—inevitably when we have company over—we have a spare to finish cooking dinner with that night.

Schools/Child Care

If you haven't already done so, register your children in school. *See Chapter 11.*

Bank Accounts & Safe Deposit Boxes

If you haven't already opened a bank account, take a break and get that accomplished. It will take a week or more to get permanent checks, so it's good to get the process started. Also, you'll want to open a Safe Deposit Box to store your important papers or valuables, rather than leaving them around the house any longer than necessary. If you use an online bank or your current bank has branches in your new town, simply notify them of your address change as soon as possible and order checks with your new address on them.

Emergency Phone Numbers

Create a list of emergency contacts, and keep a copy in your wallet and post a copy on the refrigerator, so family members can consult it or grab it on their way out the door. It should include:

- <u>Your address and phone number.</u> Your children, houseguests, babysitter, or even you, in an emergency, might not remember this vital information. Be sure to include immediate family members' cell phone numbers.

- <u>Police and fire phone numbers</u>. Some locations do not have '911' service so find out if yours does. It's often helpful to have the non-emergency numbers listed as well.

- <u>Poison control hotline.</u> Locate your local poison control center by looking in the first pages of your phone directory or by searching on the internet for "poison control" and your state.

- <u>Neighbor phone numbers and addresses.</u> This may need to be added later on, after you've gotten to know which neighbors you're comfortable calling on in an emergency.

- <u>Nearby relatives' phone numbers, a few local people who can help, and your closest relatives (even if they live far away, but can be reached by phone).</u>

- <u>Physician phone numbers,</u> especially pediatricians and specialists, if a family member has a significant condition.

- <u>Schools and child care</u> contact information.

- <u>Security Monitoring Facility</u> phone number, in case the alarm goes off by mistake. A password should be known by family members but not posted.

Emergency Medical Information

Ideally, a sheet should be created for each family member, with the following information: medical insurance (including employer address and phone, if company health coverage), health conditions and a brief history, current medications, known allergies, and contact information for their physicians. These sheets should be placed in an envelope with the person's name on it, and taped to the side of the refrigerator, or in an obvious location in the freezer. I realize this is probably an overwhelming chore to attempt right now, but tuck it away in your mind and take a break from unpacking to do it before long. If you get an emergency call from someone at school or work, it will be *very* useful to grab these on your way out the door...or for someone else to grab as they take *you* out the door.

Wine

Connoisseurs usually allow a bottle of wine to rest for 7 days after a move, before they open it. Since wine shakes within the bottle when it's moved, resting allows the sediment to settle and the wine to taste better. That said, I'm sure we've opened bottles right away after moving without noticing a problem.

Ideally, wine should be stored in a dark, damp place with good ventilation, where there are no odors (such as paint or varnish) or vibrations (from local traffic or machinery), and where the temperature is approximately 50°F (or at least between 40° and 65°) and fairly consistent. Wines stored or transported at higher or much lower temperatures, or where there are big fluctuations of temperature, will deteriorate faster than they would otherwise. Bottles with corks should be stored on their sides, so that the cork stays damp, which prevents air from entering the bottle and ruining the wine. Some people keep a bowl of water near the wine, to keep up the humidity. Bottles with screw tops can be stored either standing up or laying down. Bottles of fortified wines, such as sherry and marsala, are stored standing up. However, one fortified wine—port—is an exception, and should be stored lying down.

If you're really serious about your wine, and don't have a wine cellar in your basement, you can purchase a small "wine refrigerator", also known as an electric "wine cellar". These appliances control the temperature and humidity of the wine, and can accommodate 6 to 59 bottles or more, depending on your needs and budget. Some have dual zones, where red and white wines are kept at appropriate temperatures in separate parts of the appliance. Others rely on the "hot air rises" phenomenon to keep white wines cooler in the lower racks of the unit. Some wine cellars are made to be free-standing, and others fit under your kitchen counter, perhaps replacing a trash compactor. Shop carefully, because there are a wide range of features, warranty types, and prices for these popular items.

Adjusting to the New House

There will be things which are different in the new house—some better, some worse, some neither better nor worse just...different. You'll get used to them in time.

For example, if you're used to a gas stove, it will take some time to adjust to an electric cook top. You'll learn that it takes awhile for it to warm up, but once warm it does hold the heat well. The heat can't be adjusted in an instant by lowering the flame, but you'll find you can turn it off a couple of minutes before you're finished cooking because it'll take that long for the heating element to cool. Just be sure that everyone in the family understands that heating elements can be hot even when they don't *look* hot. There *are* exceptions to this, by the way. Electric induction cooktops heat much more quickly, but will not heat paper or skin.

You may find using *any* appliances in your new home to be a challenge for the first few days, as you "give in" and look at the manual to figure out how to work the microwave (every one seems to work a little differently) or the washing machine or even the electronic oven timer.

Start making a list of items you'd like to install in your new home—programmable thermostats, towel racks or rings, organizers for the kitchen or closet, and so on. When you're ready to take a break from unpacking, you can purchase these items and install them to help you and your family be more comfortable in your new surroundings.

Decorating

Don't worry about hanging pictures or arranging doodads on shelves until you're all, or at least mostly, unpacked.

Arranging things is best done when you can look at every-thing you have to select from. You may decide it's worth bringing in a professional interior designer to help figure out if you should modify your furniture arrangement a bit, and then where to hang things and how best to group your col-lectibles. It's normal to want to get everything in its place right away, but first focus on getting the essentials for living in their place, so that you can all function. You may need to live in the house for a few weeks in order to decide how you really want to use the spaces, and there's no sense in hang-ing pictures until you have the big stuff in the right place. Then, if you need help, you can find someone whose style you like to work with you.

Homestead Exemption

Apply for a Homestead Exemption, if appropriate. This varies state to state, and in some cases the protection is automatic. In other states, homeowners must file a claim for this. You can only claim a Homestead Exemption for your primary residence, and the law offers protec-tions such as preventing the forced sale of your home to meet the demands of creditors (with some excep-tions), and providing the surviving spouse with shelter. Check with your state for more details about Homestead Exemptions.

Moving Announcements

Mail or e-mail moving announcements to friends and fam-ily, if you haven't already done so.

Send Photos

Take photos of your new home to share with your fam-ily and friends who are far away. Even your kids will enjoy e-mailing photos of the new house, especially their room after they make it "theirs". You'll be making new friends, but it's important to keep in touch with those you love who are elsewhere.

Home Owner's Warranty

If you have an HOW for the first year, you will undoubtedly receive renewal notices to extend the warranty. Be aware that many or all of these policies only cover certain problems, such as foundation wall cracks, basement leaks, bad wiring or faulty plumbing fixtures, during the first year. Make sure you know exactly what the renewal policy would cover before you consider spending your money in this way.

Update Your Household Inventory

Once you're settled in, take additional photos of the house, including any unusual features. Add these to your household inventory, for use in the unlikely event that fire or extreme weather damages your house in the future. Be sure to keep these records in your safe deposit box or somewhere else away from your house. You could even copy it to disk, and send it to a family member out-of-state for safekeeping.

Once you've got things mostly unpacked, and your house is starting to feel like your home, it's time to spread your wings in the community.

Chapter 16

Making The New Town Your Home

The excitement of the move is winding down, and the real-ization sets in that you're in an unfamiliar place and your friends and family are no longer close at hand. Here, in no particular order, are some things you can do to get to know your new area, and become a part of it.

Family Ritual

Do something as a family to officially recognize that this is your new home. Plant a tree or bush in the yard, place some rocks painted by the children near the front or rear door, or pick out an amusing lawn ornament or warm welcome sign to place near the front door. Try to make it an adventure and something that everyone can participate in. Take a picture of the process or the placement of the object(s), and get family members in the photo. It will remind you later of one of the first of the good memories you made in your new home.

Explore the Area

Familiarize yourself with your new neighborhood and community by exploring on foot, by bicycle and/or by car. There will be times when you get a little lost, and have to turn around or ask for directions. Just keep reminding yourself that this is a learning experience and this is how you'll learn your way around.

Tourist Spots

Many people live in one city all of their lives and never take advantage of much that their city has to offer. When you go to visit a city as a tourist, you look in guidebooks or on the internet to find what's worth seeing and doing in the area. Do the same for your new town. Make the effort to go visit some of the tourist spots and take advantage of the cultural opportunities. It will make you like the area more, it will help you know where your out-of-town visitors might enjoy going when they come to visit, and if you ever move away—Stop that groaning!—you will know you have really gotten to know this city.

Order Local Publications

In some cases, community publications are delivered free of charge to residents. In others, you'll need to order them. If you haven't received one during your first week in the house, ask your neighbors. These publications will keep you "in the loop" on local issues, events, and opportunities in your suburb or small town.

You may also want to order one of the city's newspapers (unless you prefer to read your local news online). It will be helpful for you to get integrated into the community, and that will be much easier when you know what's going on. You may also see ads which will be helpful as you develop the need to visit certain types of stores or use various services.

Sports

Enroll yourself and/or your children in local sports leagues.

Schools

You've already enrolled your children in school; now it's time for you to get involved in the school, if you haven't already done so. Join the PTA or PTO and attend the meetings. Volunteer in the school, if your schedule permits. If you're working full time, you can still provide baked goods for the teachers on special days, or help with some weekend or evening activities. Working on activities with other parents is a great way to get to know people.

Driver's License and Vehicle Registration

Regulations vary by state, but at some point soon after your move, you'll need to register your car and/or RV, and apply for a driver's license, if you've moved out-of-state. Depending on what state you're living in, you may have anywhere from 5 to 90 days in which to do this without being subject to a penalty, so find out where and when, and try not to put it off. If you're online, you can search for "driver's license" and your state, and when you get to the official site, look for "New to (state name)" to get the details. The locations are also listed in your phone book, but in order to avoid having to make more than one trip, check first to find out what you need to bring with you.

Join a Church or Synagogue

This is a great way to meet people, and I urge you to select at least one committee to participate in. Especially if the congregation is large, you will find it much easier to get to know people in a small group.

Library

Find your nearest library, and have every family member who's old enough to sign their name apply for a library card. Adults usually need to provide a photo ID and proof of residence (such as a utility bill which shows your name and local address). Your children do not usually need proof, if they're with you, but you can check this out before you go, just to be sure.

Register to Vote

Some libraries and driver's license facilities are able to accept your voter registration. Wherever you do register, be sure you are registering for both federal and local elections. There have been cases where certain facilities were not able to do both, and some voters didn't realize until Election Day that they weren't fully registered.

Establish a Support System

As you get to know your neighbors and make new friends, consider who among them you'd be comfortable asking for help. You may want to have a neighbor you can call if an emergency arises and you can't get home in time to meet the school bus one day. Or you may need someone to stay with your toddler if you go into labor at night. Or you might just want to borrow a cup of sugar. Whatever needs arise, it always feels more comfortable if you have someone you know you can ask. It can make you feel very lonely if you don't have a give-and-take relationship with someone nearby. Remember, the best way to encourage someone to be your friend is for you to be a friend to *them*.

Welcoming Organizations

They may eventually find you anyway, but it never hurts to contact welcoming organizations directly when you move into an area. There's Welcome Wagon, Newcomers, New Beginnings, New Neighbors League and others. Look in the phone book under "Welcoming Services", or search for "welcoming services" and your city online. Some of these organizations, such as Welcome Wagon, will send a representative to your house. She'll bring materials on many local businesses. Usually these include coupons, a few free items, and sometimes a map and community guide. It's a good way to learn about groceries, restaurants, stores,

and services in your new area, and the coupc
those for grocery stores) are a nice gift. The re
may also be able to answer some of your que
the area. It usually takes about 20 minutes to
the materials, unless you care to chat longer. . ɪıke to set
up visits with any of the organizations which want to come,
because they often have different sponsors.

Another type of organization for new residents, such as
New Neighbors League and Newcomers, is more of a club.
They have meetings and other activities so that you can
get to know other recent arrivals in your area. You can learn
a lot about your new town from those who have recently
learned it themselves. Often, membership is limited to
those who have moved to the area within the last 2 years.
Some of these organizations charge a nominal fee and
some are pricier. Check out the fees while you're exploring
them.

Health Professionals

As mentioned in Chapter 10, we like to schedule appointments with physicians and dentists soon after the move,
because then we get to know each other while there are
no big problems. If we're comfortable with the professional,
then when a problem does arise, we know who to call and
they know what we're like when we're feeling good. Plus,
it's always easier to get an appointment at a doctor's or
dentist's office if you're an established patient. If we're not
comfortable with the medical professional, we can continue to ask around for references, and hopefully have
someone good lined up for when we need them.

Co-workers and neighbors can be helpful in locating
good medical professionals, and you can verify they're in-
network providers by checking with your insurance company or by calling their office to ask.

Some of the things we consider when looking for a new doctor or dentist are:

- Age
  You might not want to get started with someone about to retire, or you may feel better knowing they have many years of experience. Of course, being a new physician has the benefit of being trained with the most updated information. Ask when they got their degree, because some physicians get trained later in life. You'll have to decide what's important to you.

- Where they got their medical degree
  If it's a school with a great reputation that's a big plus; an obscure school or one out of the U.S. is not so positive, in my opinion.

- What is the doctor's specialty?
  Often internists specialize in something like allergies, sports injuries, or whatever. They can certainly treat other things, but if they specialize in something which applies to you, that might sway you in their direction. Your primary care physician can be an internist or family practice physician; your children will need a pediatrician or family practice physician.

- Gender and language
  (a)Gender: Some people have a strong preference for going to a male or female physician. You may as well look for someone you'll be the most comfortable with.
  (b)Foreign language: If English isn't your first language, you may want to seek out a doctor who can speak your native language.
  (c)English: Even though this may not be politically correct to say, if you have trouble understanding those who speak with a strong accent, you could

wind up with a doctor who can't effectively communicate with you. This is an important factor in your care, so don't ignore it, but please be tactful as you consider this. Many foreign-born doctors are excellent physicians, who can effectively communicate in English.

- Convenience
  Is their office near your home or work? What days are they in that office, and during what hours? Do they have walk-in hours? Do they have weekend and evening hours?

- Compatibility
  It's important to us whether a physician will explain things to us, so that we understand what we're being tested or treated for and what we need to do. It's important that the physician stay in the exam room with us long enough to answer our questions and also how patient-friendly their office staff and procedures are. If we can't seem to reach a person to talk to when we call the office, and it takes hours for them to respond to a voicemail, we usually try looking elsewhere for care providers.

Remember, if you make an appointment with a doctor, it doesn't mean you have to stick with him if you wind up not liking him for one reason or another. Just try someone else next time.

Attorney

Since laws vary state by state, it's important to review your will with a reputable local attorney, to ensure that all of the terms are valid in your new state. You may also want to discuss inheritance laws and trusts, if appropriate, as they may differ also.

Certified Public Accountant (CPA)

State tax laws may be different in your new state, but even if they aren't, you may want to use a CPA to do your taxes, at least for the year in which you relocated. Tax returns can be complex when a move is involved, and you'll want to be sure you get all the deductions and refunds to which you're entitled.

It may be helpful to gather your moving financials prior to meeting with a CPA. You'll find info about moving deductions at the IRS website: www.irs.gov. Select "Individuals", "Forms and Publications", then under "Download Forms and Publications by" select "Topical Index". Click on "m" and scroll down to "Moving Expenses".

Embrace the Local Culture

Resist the temptation to fuss when things aren't done the way you're used to them being done. One of the great things we've learned from our travels and our moves is that there can be many ways to live one's life and, amazingly, people can survive very nicely even when they do things differently than we do. People tend to get irritable when you tell them they're not doing it right. As the late great Southern humorist Lewis Grizzard used to say, "We don't care how y'all did it in Cleveland. If you don't like it here, Delta is ready when you are."

Take Advantage of Cultural Opportunities

Look in local newspapers for one-time lectures or classes at hospitals, schools, museums, botanical gardens, or zoos. These are often free or require only a minimal fee.

Re-invent Yourself

Now is the time to re-invent yourself. You probably gave up certain responsibilities when you left your old community;

now you can start with a clean slate and participate in whatever things interest you now.

The More You Give, the More You Get

This is where you're living now, and you may as well make the decision to like it and enjoy it. As in so many areas in life, if you make the effort to get involved in your new community, you will feel more alive and know more people, and feel that you are a part of the community and that you *belong* here. Make that effort, push yourself out of your comfort zone, and go for it. You'll feel better about yourself, and both you and your world will be better for it.

Chapter 17
Helpful Websites

Helpful websites are mentioned throughout this book, but we thought it would be good to list most of them here in one place. Websites are redesigned periodically, so layouts change and some topics are eliminated altogether. Be creative as you look for the topics. If the website, or information on it, has disappeared, just do a search and you're likely to find several more. To be on the safe side, use sites at well-known companies with good reputations, such as real estate firms, newspapers, national moving companies, professional organizations, etc.

This chapter is organized in alphabetical order, by category, followed by the larger category of "General Buying/Selling/Moving Information". There is often additional helpful information on the websites, besides the specifics we've mentioned here.

Address Change

USPS.com – Website for U.S. Postal Service. You can submit your Change of Address online if you have a valid e-mail address and use a debit or credit card to pay the tiny (currently $1) fee. Otherwise, you can print the form and mail or deliver it to your local post office.

Assigning a Value to Things You're Donating

www.SalvationArmySouth.org/valueguide.htm - Salvation Army tool helps you determine what your donations are worth.

charity.lovetoknow.com/Goodwill_Donations_Value - Scroll down to Donating Household Items.

Credit Score & Credit Reports

www.AnnualCreditReport.com - View your credit report from each of the 3 credit reporting agencies. *See "Review Your Credit Report" in Chapter 1.* You can also request your FICO score, for a price, when you request your credit report.
www.MyFico.com – Another site where you can access your Fair Isaac FICO credit score, which determines which loans you can get and on what terms. There is a charge for this.

Note: You are entitled to view your credit report once a year from each credit reporting agency, free of charge. You do not have to purchase credit monitoring in order to see your credit reports or FICO score.

Decorating

www.Behr.com – Select "Explore Color". You can preview paint colors using photos of your own rooms under the Paint Your Place™ feature.
www.BenjaminMoore.com – Select "Explore Color". Choose a room or building which looks similar to yours, and see how it looks painted in different color schemes.
www.FurniturePlanning.com – Offers a magnetic furniture planning kit, for a price.
www.Glidden.com – Select "Color", then "Room Painter" to see how a room looks, painted in different color schemes.
www.HealthyHome.com – Check out their paint and many other products, including paint with no or low VOC emissions. All products meet standards for sustainability, safety, efficiency, low carbon footprint, and economy.

Evaluating Cities

www.City-data.com – Maps, statistics about residents, cost of living, weather, and much more, organized by city, county or zip code.

www.Moving.com – Select "Learn and Explore" and "City Profiles". Provides demographics, climate, crime statistics, and more, organized by zip code. Select "Compare to Another City" to see information side-by-side. *Be aware that the information is just for the zip code you select, usually is not a whole city.*

Profiles.NationalRelocation.com - Demographics, statistics, hospitals, colleges, universities and more. It is not clear how current this information is.

Flood Risk

www.Fema.gov/hazard/flood/index.shtm - FEMA's website alerts you to flood risks in a given area, but you'll probably have to contact them for help in understanding the maps on their site, because they're not user-friendly for the novice. The website also provides information about protecting yourself from a flood, including what to do before, during and after a flood.

For Sale By Owner (FSBO) assistance companies

These are some of the companies you might consider when selling your home, if you choose not to use a traditional Real Estate Broker. *For more information, see Chapter 3.*

These websites can also be used to look for homes to buy, although you may need to register with them before you're allowed to search.

www.Assist2sell.com
www.BrokerDirectmls.com

www.BuyOwner.com
www.ByOwner.com
www.ForSaleByOwner.com
www.HelpuSell.com
www.HomesByOwner.com
www.Resultsmls.com
www.SaleByOwnerRealty.com
www.ZipRealty.com

Home Inspectors

www.ASHI.org - American Society of Home Inspectors

Insurance

www.III.org/individuals/homei - The Insurance Information Institute (I.I.I.) provides information about insurance: what it does and how it works. Includes information on home-owner's insurance and information about taking a home inventory.

Mortgages

www.NAMB.org - National Association of Mortgage Brokers. Select "Home Buyers" for information on mortgage brokers, types of mortgages, and more.
www.HomeLoanLearningCenter.com – Information about home loans, including a quick tool to suggest what size mortgage you may qualify for. Website provided by the Mortgage Banker's Association.
www.HUD.gov - A great resource. Select "Buy a Home", and scroll down to "Looking for the Best Mortgage". You'll be able to view a brochure which contains a lot of helpful information, as well as a Mortgage Shopping Worksheet.

Movers

www.ProtectYourMove.gov - a website provided by the Federal Motor Carrier Safety Administration (FMCSA), whose mission is to "decrease moving fraud by providing consumers with the knowledge and resources to plan a successful move". There's a lot of helpful information, including specifics on what constitutes an interstate move. (It's not as simple as you might think.)

www.ProtectYourMove.gov/consumer/awareness/rights/rights.htm - Booklet on the above site, entitled *Your Rights and Responsibilities When You Move*. Your interstate mover is required give this to you. It includes what to do if you have claims, complaints, or questions.

www.Moving.org - The American Moving and Storage Association (AMSA) website. Helpful information about movers and moving, including a Mover Referral Service and a list of ProMovers, to help you avoid hiring a con artist.

Moving Pets

www.USAHA.org/StateAnimalHealthOfficials.pdf - Contact information for U.S. state health authorities to consult for regulations, when relocating your animals to their state.

www.OfficialPetHotels.com – Provides pet-friendly hotels and travel tips.

www.PetsWelcome.com – Lodgings, travel tips, day care locations, emergency veterinarians, pet sitters, and fun locations to take pets.

Moving Plants

www.AtlasWorldGroup.com/howto/plants - Atlas World Group (including Atlas Van Lines) makes suggestions.

Real Estate Companies and Listings

Realtor.com – Website for homebuyers, by the National Association of Realtors. Information and searches.

NOTE: If we tried to list all the major real estate companies and their websites, we know we'd probably omit some. So please consider all the real estate companies in your area, and try the companyname.com. If that doesn't work, search for the company name. Some real estate agents have their own websites as well. Many of these websites have helpful information for home buyers and sellers, as well as listings to review.

Selling Things You Don't Want to Keep

CraigsList.org – Local classified ads placed online, usually free.
eBay.com – Worldwide online classified ads, for a fee.
877isoldit.com – You drop off your things, they sell them online and ship them, and you get a percentage of the sale. These are franchises, only available in some areas.
www.SnappyAuctions.com – You drop off your items, they'll sell them on eBay and ship them; then they'll send you a check for your portion of the sale. These are also franchises.

There are a number of other businesses springing up, which sell things for you online, as isoldit and Snappy Auctions do. Just look around in your neighborhood or search the Yellow Pages or online. We suggest you check with the Better Business Bureau before using any of the companies which sell things for you.

General Buying/Selling/Moving Information

www.AHSwarranty.com – American Home Shield, one of the companies which offers home warrantees.

www.HomeDepotMoving.com - Information on Preparing for Sale, House Hunting, Organizing the Move, Moving Day, Settling In, Decorating, and more.

www.HUD.gov - Great information on buying a home.

www.IRS.gov - Internal Revenue Service information: Select "Individuals", "Forms and Publications", then under "Download Forms and Publications by" select Topical Index". Click on "m" and scroll down to "Moving Expenses" to find out which expenses are deductible. Or select "H" and scroll down to "Tax Information for First-time Homeowners" and "Home Mortgage Interest Deduction".

www.Lowes.com – Search for "Moving" for tips, and see "Mover's Toolbox" for tasks associated with moving, and the tools and materials you'll need to perform them.

www.Zillow.com – Shows the price that homes have recently sold for, and an approximation of their current value. Also shows homes currently for sale. However, information is not necessarily current or complete. *See Chapter 3 under "What Price Should You Ask For Your House?" for more information.*

Many of the large real estate firms and some newspapers also have a wealth of information about buying and selling homes on their websites.

Appendix
House Hunting Form

ADDRESS _____ MY RATING_____

SUBDIVISION? ____W/POOL?_____ W/TENNIS? ____ ASSOCIATION DUES $____

MANY CHILDREN IN NEIGHBORHOOD? _____ LENGTH OF COMMUTE_____ STORES

NEARBY?___

EXTERIOR: _____ CONDITION: _____

DRIVEWAY FLAT? _____ GARAGE: Y/N____ 2-CAR? ____ 3-CAR?

BACKYARD: FLAT AREA FOR PLAY? _____PRIVATE?_____

LANDSCAPING: _____

INTERIOR: HEATING METHOD: _____ WATER HEATER HOLDS _____ GALLONS

KITCHEN: STOVE- GAS?_____ ELEC?_____ ROOM FOR DINETTE SET?_____

PANTRY?___

WINDOWS: PULL OUT TO CLEAN?_____ STORM WINDOWS OR DOUBLE-PANE?_____

LAUNDRY ROOM: LOCATION _____ SINK?_____

       GAS HOOK-UP FOR DRYER? _____ AREA TO HANG CLOTHES?_____

DINING ROOM: LARGE ENOUGH FOR CURRENT FURNITURE?_____ FOR LARGE

GATHERINGS?_____

MASTER BEDRM:_____WALK-IN CLOSET?_____

       BATH: 2 SINKS? _____ WHIRLPOOL TUB? ___PRIVATE TOILET AREA?____

ATTIC: ACCESS LOCATION_____

       PULL-DOWN LADDER?_____ SUB-FLOORING?_____

BASEMENT?_____ CRAWLSPACE? _____

DECORATING:

       THINGS THAT NEED TO BE CHANGED IMMEDIATELY: _____

       _____

       THINGS THAT WE'D LIKE TO CHANGE BEFORE LONG: _____

       _____

ADDITIONAL WORK NEEDED: _____

HOW TO USE HOUSEHUNTING FORM

This is a form which we have used in the past because there were things important to us which usually weren't obvious from the listings or individual house brochures. Personalize the form, depending on what is important to YOU. Make notes freely as you go along, of things which you care about. This will get you started but you need to make it yours in order to get the most out of it.

RATING: This is your own personal scale. You may choose to use a 1-10 scale, or descriptive terms like "possibility", "OK but small", "very nice", "too dark inside", "small backyard but otherwise great" or "best yet". It will help you sort out which ones are worth considering at the end of the day.

SUBDIVISION: Yes or no; you may choose to add "large" or "small".

EXTERIOR: Brick; stucco; or cedar, vinyl, or aluminum siding. Many houses have brick front and 2 or 3 sides with siding. Brick is generally more expensive than other materials but is a great insulator and also basically maintenance-free. Also: have window trim & soffits (the horizontal underside of the eaves) been vinyl-clad? Part of the reason for wanting to know this info is so you have an idea of how much maintenance (mostly painting) will be required for upkeep. CONDITION: Does the house need painting? Are shutters or siding in need of repair? Anything you see outside which you feel you would spend money on to get the house/yard in good condition should be noted here.

DRIVEWAY FLAT? You might care if you have children who play basketball, hockey, etc, and/or if you're in a climate which gets snow which needs to be removed or driven through.

BACKYARD: How you want to use your backyard will determine what you'll be looking for here. We always wanted a large, flat area where the family could play badminton; sometimes we had to compromise, but that was always a factor in the equation. You may want to note if there's room for a screened-in porch or if the deck has a great view or steps you'd be nervous to have small children around.

LANDSCAPING: Is it OK for now, or would you want to spend a fair amount right away to remove overgrown bushes and replace with a fresh look?

HEATING: Forced air or baseboard or steam (radiators).

WATER HEATER: Many older homes have a 20- or 30-gallon water heater, but newer ones for larger families have 40- or even 50-gallon ones. This translates to how much hot water will be available for showers, dishwashing, and washing clothes before waiting for the water to reheat. If you look at the year a water heater was made and how many years it's "rated" for, you'll have an idea of how soon you'll need to invest in replacing it. There are several types of water heaters available now, including tankless water heaters, so if you decide you'd like to replace it sooner, do your homework.

KITCHEN: Is the stove gas or electric? Is the kitchen spacious enough? Note anything special, positive or negative.

WINDOWS: Who ever thinks to look closely at the windows when you're house shopping? I usually don't...there's too much else to consider. But it sure is great when the windows are newer, energy-saving, easy to operate and they tilt inside the house to clean. If the windows are difficult or impossible to open, you may find yourself making an investment before long. It would be wise to consider that before deciding how much to offer.

LAUNDRY: Besides where it's located, does the laundry room have a sink? This isn't as important if there's a kitchen sink nearby. Where will you hang your clothes when they come out of the dryer? Do you have a gas dryer you want to use? If there's only electric available, you'll need to get a new dryer (or contract for the Sellers to leave theirs in the house).

The other items are self-explanatory.

Acknowledgements

There were many times through the years it took to write this book, when I needed to check out how specific real estate matters are dealt with in different parts of the country. I am indebted to Leslie McDonnell of ReMax Suburban in Libertyville, Illinois, and Will Brown of Bonino & Brown Realtors, Prudential CA Realty, for reviewing some specific material in the book, and especially for answering my numerous questions so patiently. I also appreciate the time Dave Areen and Marc Savitt took to clarify some points about financing real estate purchases. And many thanks to those who read parts of the book, or the entire manuscript, and made significant helpful suggestions: Sue Burnley, Gary Fradkin, Michelle Fradkin, Sheri Malman, Gail Maurer, Hope Miller and Valerie Harms. Your caring input helped the book to be better, and helped to motivate me to complete this project.

LaVergne, TN USA
06 April 2011
223150LV00014B/55/P